the art of teaching writing

LUCY McCORMICK CALKINS

Teachers College, Columbia University

HEINEMANN

Portsmouth, New Hampshire

HEINEMANN EDUCATIONAL BOOKS, INC.
70 Court Street, Portsmouth, New Hampshire 03801
Offices and agents throughout the world

10   9   8   7

The following have generously given permission to use material in this book: From *The Poetry of Robert Frost* edited by Edward Connery Lathem. Copyright © 1947, 1969 by Holt, Rinehart and Winston. Copyright © 1975 by Lesley Frost Ballentine. Reprinted by permission of Holt, Rinehart and Winston, Publishers, and Jonathan Cape Ltd. The poem ''Oldfields'' reprinted by permission of Georgia Heard. The poem ''The Red Wheelbarrow'' from William Carlos Williams, *Collected Earlier Poems*. Copyright © 1938 by New Directions Publishing Corp. Reprinted by permission of New Directions Publishing Corp. ''We Real Cool. The Pool Players. Seven at the Golden Shovel.'' From *The World of Gwendolyn Brooks*. Copyright © 1959 by Gwendolyn Brooks Blakely. Reprinted by permission of Harper & Row, Publishers.

Library of Congress Cataloging-in-Publication Data

Calkins, Lucy McCormick.
  The art of teaching writing.

  Bibliography: p.
  Includes index.
    1. English language—Composition and exercises—
Study and teaching. I. Title.
PE1404.C29   1986   808'.042'0712   85-21922
ISBN 0-435-08246-9

Designed by Wladislaw Finne.
Cover photo by Mark Mittleman.
Photo on back cover by Paul Korker.
Photos on pp. 1, 29, 115, 161, 217, and 259 by Peter Michaels.
Printed in the United States of America.

To John, with love

contents

acknowledgments

Alan Purves has said, "It takes two to read a book," and for me it is true that the books I remember are those I have talked about. But the truth is bigger than this. The truth is that I learn best when I am part of a community. Although I can see for myself that the forsythia bushes are in bloom and feel the new energy for writing which comes from them, it is only when I tell this to my colleagues that I begin to see the implications for classrooms. As we weave together related ideas, a chapter emerges. My writing process, then, does not begin with jotted notes or rough drafts but rather with relationships within a community of learners.

Communities have always been part of the fabric of my life. There were nine children in my family, and on weekends when we pitched in to build sheep houses or stone walls, we found that because the projects were shared, there was a thin line between work and play. We talked and laughed as we worked, and each of us developed faith that when a person works wisely and well, anything is possible in life. I am grateful to my parents, Evan and Virginia Calkins, for the sense of optimism they gave us. It has led each of us to live our lives as if one person can make a difference, and to believe in the old-fashioned value of having a mission.

Freud has said that a healthy person needs two things, work and love, but for me it is when the two come together that I learn best. If I were to make a time line of my own professional development, each of the growth stages would be marked by important relationships.

My first teaching experience was at Weaver High School in the North End of Hartford. In retrospect, I am glad that the nice literature lessons which had worked for my suburban teachers did not work in this setting, for I was forced to rethink my assumptions about teaching and to recognize how much I did not know. Because I taught alongside a lifelong friend, Peggy Walker Stevens, I was able to see my mistakes and disillusionments as a beginning rather than an end, and to view the year as an introduction to a profession which was vastly more challenging than I had anticipated.

In search of a vision, I traveled to Oxfordshire, England, to spend a year working in the famed British primary schools. Often on weekends, I participated in in-service courses which were held in castles. They began Friday nights with sherry and poetry readings; and the weekends, like the schools themselves, were filled with collaboration, craftsmanship, and reflection. That year I formed a vision of what schools can be for children and also of what schools can be for teachers. I agree with Seymour Sarason who writes, "The assumption that teachers can create and maintain those conditions which make school living and school learning stimulating for children without those same conditions existing for teachers, has no warrant in the history of mankind." (1971).

Back in America, I found a community of educators who shared some of my ideas, and we established an alternative public school in Middlefield, Connecticut. It was a place where teachers learned as well as taught. We attended courses together, exchanged books, studied trees and flowers, and taught each other what we knew. Many of my values today can be traced back to the vision which Bud Church, Joy Mermin, Sue Devokaitis, and I shared.

It was while teaching at Center School that many of my ideas about children's writing began to emerge. Those ideas became rooted in a larger world of scholarship when I left Center School to become a research associate at the University of New Hampshire. Donald Graves, Susan Sowers, Mary Ellen Giacobbe, and I observed children for several years at Atkinson Elementary School in order to understand the day-to-day changes in their writing. I learned a great deal during those years, and the lessons came not only from the children but also from my colleagues. I learned from Don Graves' gift for working with people and from his ability to see the significance in little things. I learned from Mary Ellen Giacobbe's easy delight and knack for knowing what is essential. During those years, I also worked closely with Don Murray, and I am immensely grateful to him for teaching me to write. His ideas on teaching writing form the bedrock upon which this book is written.

It has now been eight years since I began my research on children's writing development. The research has continued, but now we are learning from children in New York City's schools, and the research community is larger. I am grateful to Nancie Atwell, Peter Elbow, Jerry Harste, Howard Gardner, Tom Newkirk, and Frank Smith; their contributions are evident throughout the book.

But the people who have given the most to *The Art of Teaching Writing* are my colleagues in the Teachers College Writing Project. Every day when I make the long drive from Connecticut into the city, my heart sings with gratitude for this learning community that now circles my life. There are sixteen of us in the Writing Project, a team comprised of researchers and teacher-trainers. Our two goals—improving the teaching of writing in the New York City public schools and learning important ideas on staff development—are big ones, and our success thus far is due largely to support from the Spencer Foundation, Morgan Guaranty Trust Company, and from Jack Isaacs and Steve Tribus of the New York City Board of Education.

But it is the team itself which most deserves my thanks. I am grateful to Shelley Harwayne, the Assistant Director of the Project, whose brilliant insights are woven into every page of the book. Hindy List is, in many ways, the heart and soul of our Project. She has transformed the largest, most complex school system in the world into a warm and human place. Georgia Heard has taught me a tremendous amount about poetry; Kathryn Schwertman, about fiction; Rob Cohen and Eileen Jones, about adolescents; Marilyn Boutwell, about the reading workshop. Martha Horn and JoAnn Curtis have helped sustain my own belief in the Project. Their delight in teachers and children is infectious, and my friendship with each of them makes all the difference. Two years ago, Halima Touré came to the Teachers College Writing Project as a secretary. Now she is our Project Manager, and is perhaps the only member of the team who is indispensable.

Although I am lucky enough to be part of a wonderful network of professionals, the community which means the most to me is the one I return to when the work is done. Although it is traditional to end the Acknowledgments with a paragraph giving special thanks to one's spouse for not protesting over the long hours of deskwork, I want, instead, to thank my husband, John Skorpen, for calling me away from the desk. I'm grateful for the days of hiking in the Wind River Range and of exploring Caribbean islands, and I am grateful for the quiet adventures with our cat, dog, home, and family.

I

the essentials in teaching writing

1

tap the energy to write

Human beings have a deep need to represent their experience through writing. We need to make our truths beautiful. With crude pictographs, cave men inscribed their stories onto stony cave walls. With magic markers, pens, lipstick, and pencils, little children leave their marks on bathroom walls, on the backs of old envelopes, on their big sister's homework. In slow, wobbly letters, the old and the sick in our nursing homes and hospitals put their lives into print. There is no plot line in the bewildering complexity of our lives but that which we make and find for ourselves. By articulating experience, we reclaim it for ourselves. Writing allows us to turn the chaos into something beautiful, to frame selected moments in our lives, to uncover and to celebrate the organizing patterns of our existence. This is why Anne Morrow Lindbergh says, "I must write, I must write at all costs. For writing is more than living, it is being conscious of living."

We write because we want to understand our lives. This is why my closets are filled with boxes and boxes of musty old journals. It is why I found pages of poetry under my stepdaughter Kira's mattress when she went off to camp. It is why my father tells me he will soon begin his memoirs. As John Cheever explains, "When I began to write, I found this was the best way to make sense out of my life."

But in our schools, our students tell us they don't want to write. They need not bother to tell us: we can feel their apathy as they crank out stories that are barely adequate; we can hear their question, "How long

3

does it have to be?" We forget that we, too, would yawn and roll our eyes if we were asked to write about our summer vacation or our favorite food. We do not consider how we would feel if the only response to our hard-earned stories were red-penned "Awks" and "Run-ons." We forget how vulnerable we are as learners and as people, and how easy it is to protect ourselves with layers of bored resignation. Instead of thinking honestly and deeply about why students have learned to dislike writing, we rush about, pushing, luring, encouraging, motivating, stimulating, bribing, requiring. . . .

The bitter irony is that we, in schools, set up roadblocks to stifle the natural and enduring reasons for writing, and then we complain that our students don't want to write. The cycle continues. After detouring around the authentic, human reasons for writing, we bury the students' urge to write all the more with boxes, kits, and manuals full of synthetic writing-stimulants. At best, they produce artificial and short-lived sputters of enthusiasm for writing, which then fade away, leaving passivity. Worst of all, we accept this passivity as the inevitable context of our teaching.

Within this cycle of failure, it is absurd to talk about students drafting and revising their writing, or the importance of peer conferences, or new methods for teaching poetry and fiction. The teacher will, quite rightly, not want to hear about ways to encourage a child beyond an early draft, or about the importance of classroom-based research. None of this will sound feasible to a teacher straining against the giant boulder of student resistance. Such a teacher will only want a way to cajole students into checking for periods and capitals, or better yet, relief altogether from the burden of teaching writing. When students resist writing, teachers resist teaching writing.

I have finally begun to realize why, when six years ago I moved from New Hampshire to New York City and began telling the teachers here about Jennifer's five drafts of her report on deer, and Andrew's early forays into fiction writing, they shook their heads and sighed deeply. At the time, I thought the problem was that Andrew and Jennifer were suburban children, that Atkinson Elementary School was a white clapboard schoolhouse in a little New England village, and that all of this was worlds away from the huge cement school buildings in New York City, where chain link fences covered windows, and six stories of dimly lit hallways were lined with crowded classrooms of thirty-five children each, most of them second-language learners. And indeed, the communication gap was partly the result of classroom contexts that were worlds apart. But the difference that mattered most was not the family backgrounds of the children, or the physical layout of the classrooms, but the fact that during the two years in which Donald Graves, Susan Sowers, and I were live-in researchers at Atkinson Elementary School, the teachers there had learned to tap children's natural desire to write—and that makes everything else in the teaching of writing seem possible.

Don't get me wrong: in New York City, many teachers had struggled valiantly for years to motivate students to write. But "motivating writing" is very different from helping young people become deeply and personally involved in their writing. Throughout the country, we are more apt to do the former than the latter. Let me clarify. At Teachers College, where I am a professor of English Education, I often ask my preservice students to present model lessons to the group as a whole. Although their lessons vary, there is something similar about them. In a typical lesson, for example, the person role playing teacher divides the class into pairs, asking one person from each pair to draw a complex geometric design (secretly) and to write directions that will guide his or her partner to reproduce the original drawing accurately. The exercise is great fun, we all fail miserably, and for fifteen minutes we are very involved in writing.

So what? When the fifteen minutes are over, we are left with nothing. Teacher-led activities such as these may "stimulate writing," but they do not help students become deeply and personally involved in writing.

Yet we continue to search for the motivating activities, the bag of tricks that will somehow cajole students into writing. When I taught elementary school, I went so far as to bring a hornet's nest to school, and displaying it proudly, I told all the children they could write about it. Only now, in retrospect, do I realize I was being patronizing. I was assuming my students didn't have their own trophies to share, their own stories to tell. Only now do I realize that what is true for me, for my father, and for Kira, is also true for most people: we will care about writing when it is personal and interpersonal. Beneath layers of resistance, we have a primal need to write. We need to make our truths beautiful, and we need to say to others, "This is me. This is my story, my life, my truth." We need to be heard.

Now, whether I work with children or with adults, I know that teaching writing begins with the recognition that each individual comes to the writing workshop with concerns, ideas, memories, and feelings. Our job as teachers is to listen and to help them listen. "What are the things you know and care about?" I ask writers, and I ask this whether the writers are five years old or fifty.

Each summer, Teachers College holds a two-week institute on teaching writing. Participants write about love and fear and growing old. They write about what they know well, and what they don't know about what they know. They write about emigrating from Russia, about moving from a house to an apartment, and about raising a learning disabled child. They do not write stories called "My Life as a Waterfall" or "The Day I was a Pencil." They do not write fake Peace Corps letters, make-believe book jackets, or plot outlines of the books they are reading. They do not choose to write alternate endings for a book or to send letters from one character to another. We, as adults, want to write literature far more than we want to write about literature.

Our children are no different. They, too, have rich lives. In our classrooms, we can tap the human urge to write if we help students realize that their lives are worth writing about, and if we help them choose their topics, their genre and their audience. Haniff writes about how, from his kitchen window, he could see the fireworks during the Brooklyn Bridge's one hundredth birthday celebration. Maria writes about missing her grandma's farm in Puerto Rico. Roberto, the son of a migrant farmer from Florida, writes stories, poems, and personal narratives—all of them about his dog. "I move so much that my dog's the only friend I have for always," Roberto explained.

Gwen is only six, but already she uses writing as a way to deal with the hardest issues in life. Figure 1-1 is her story.

These children will not always find topics that matter so much to them, and they will not always write so well. They will have their ups and downs as writers, but these will occur within the context of personal involvement in writing. Something happened in their classrooms to produce this involvement, something essential to the teaching of writing. Topic choice is part of it, but the larger issue is that, when we invite children to choose their form, voice, and audience as well as their subject, we give them ownership and responsibility for their writing. This transforms writing from an assigned task into a personal project. Nine-year-old Debbie puts it this way: "Sometimes when I've had a really tough day and nothing seems to be going right, I think, 'nothing is *mine*.' Well, my writing is. I can write it any way I want to. You know how your mother can tell you, 'Go up to bed right now.' Nobody can tell you how to write your piece. You're the mother of your story."

When writing becomes a personal project for children, teachers are freed from cajoling, pushing, pulling, and motivating. The teaching act changes. With a light touch we can guide and extend children's growth in writing. Also, our teaching becomes more personal, and this makes all the difference in the world.

Through his study of the norms which exist in thousands of American classrooms, John Goodlad has helped me understand why the teaching of writing has become so important to teachers and children throughout the country. The writing workshop provides a place for teaching to become deeply personal. Both teachers and children focus on topics which matter to children. Yet in most American classrooms, the teacher's focus is not on the child, but on a unit of study, the textbook, the prepackaged curriculum. Children, meanwhile, have their own concerns: a newborn brother, their grandmother's farm in Puerto Rico, a letter to one's father. The two agendas—the teacher's and the child's—are miles apart. In *A Place Called School*, Goodlad writes, "Data . . . suggest to me a picture of rather well-intentioned teachers going about their business somewhat detached from and not quite connecting with the 'other lives' of their students. What their students see as primary concerns in their daily lives, teachers view as dissonance in conducting school and classroom business" (Goodlad 1984, 80). The image Goodlad conveys is of two cogs in a wheel, spinning separately but not touching. Teachers teach, and children watch, glassy-eyed and detached.

There are, of course, those wonderful moments when "something clicks" and the curriculum no longer looms between teacher and children. We reach the end of *Where the Red Fern Grows*, and for a moment the class is

---

Figure 1 – 1

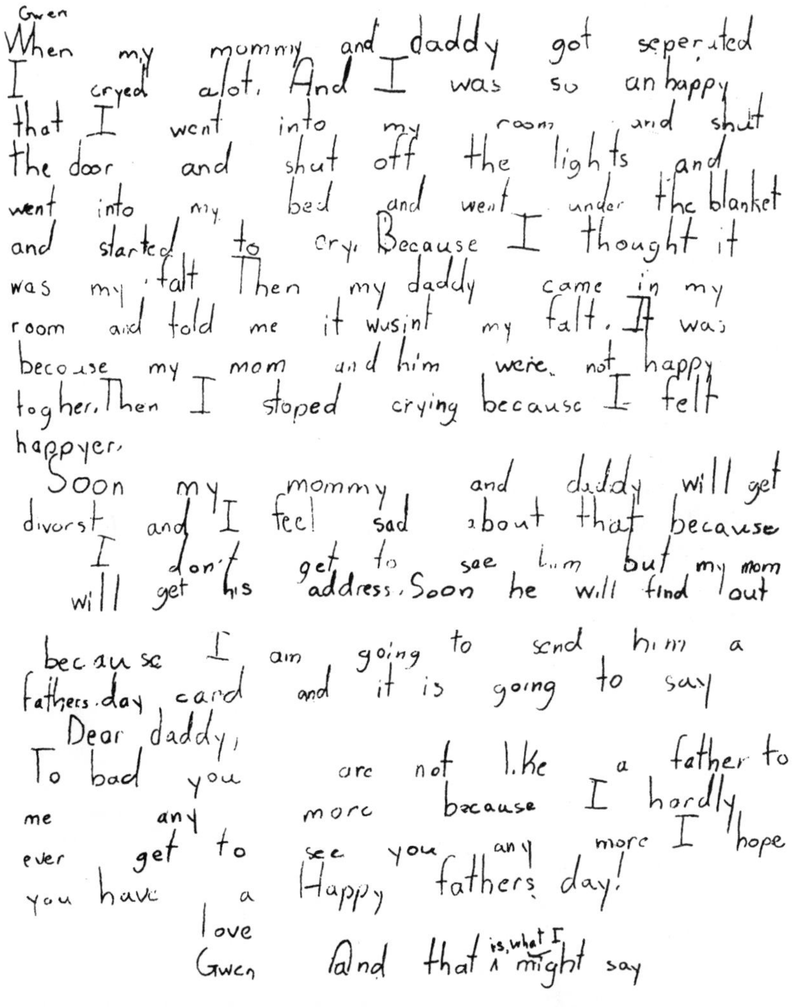

Gwen

When my mommy and daddy got seperated I cryed alot. And I was so unhappy that I went into my room and shut the door and shut off the lights and went into my bed and went under the blanket and started to cry. Because I thought it was my falt. Then my daddy came in my room and told me it wusint my falt. It was becouse my mom and him were not happy togher. Then I stoped crying because I felt happyer.

Soon my mommy and daddy will get divorst and I feel sad about that because I don't get to sae him but my mom will get his address. Soon he will find out because I am going to send him a fathers day card and it is going to say

Dear daddy,

To bad you are not like a father to me any more because I hardly ever get to see you any more I hope you have a Happy fathers day!

love
Gwen   And that is what I might say

silent, tears glistening in everyone's eyes. Or a cluster of children come in tearfully from recess, holding the limp body of a dead chipmunk. They ask if they can have a funeral for the poor chipmunk and we nod, putting aside the spelling test and math dittos. Or one child reenacts a scene from *James and the Giant Peach* and others join in until the whole class is intently focused on reliving their favorite story. These moments are the reason we chose teaching; yet we generally arm ourselves against them. We focus so intently on the curriculum that when a child finds a moth fluttering inside his desk, we view the ripples of energy it produces in the classroom as interference. We continue with our curriculum, and the room settles back to emotional neutrality. "Classes at all levels," Goodlad observes, "tend not to be marked with exuberance, joy, laughter, abrasiveness, praise . . . but by emotional neutrality" (Goodlad 1984, 112).

Goodlad's study has helped me understand that although the purpose of the writing workshop is ostensibly to help children grow as writers, the workshop can have an even farther-reaching impact. Around the country, we are finding that the writing workshop can provide a new image for what classrooms can look and sound and feel like, new expectations for what it means to teach wisely and well, and a new sense of personal connectedness. In the writing workshop, moments of personal connection are the matrix out of which everything else develops. Children write about what is alive and vital and real for them—and their writing becomes the curriculum. Their teachers listen, extend, and guide; we also laugh, cry, and marvel. The workshop has none of the emotional flatness that characterizes most of the school day. The content of the writing workshop is the content of real life, for the workshop begins with what each student thinks, feels, and experiences, and with the human urge to articulate and understand experience. The structure of the workshop is kept simple so that teachers and children are free from choreography and able to respond to the human surprises, to the small discoveries, to the moth as it pokes its antennae over the top of the desk.

2

respond to writing: give readers to writers

As teachers, we are called upon to be artists. We must remember that artistry does not come from the quantity of red, green, and yellow paint, or from the amount of clay or marble, but from the organizing vision that shapes the use of these materials. It comes from a sense of priority and design.

If our teaching is to be an art, we must remember that it is not the number of good ideas that turns our work into an art, but the selection, balance and design of those ideas. Instead of piling good teaching ideas into the classroom, we need to draw from all we know, feel, and believe in order to create something beautiful. To teach well, we do not need more techniques, activities, and strategies. We need a sense of what is essential. For this reason, I have begun this book with the question "What is essential in teaching writing?" and with my answer to this question.

For me, it is essential that children are deeply involved in writing, that they share their texts with others, and that they perceive themselves as authors. I believe these three things are interconnected. A sense of authorship comes from the struggle to put something big and vital into print, and from seeing one's own printed words reach the hearts and minds of readers.

During the first day of kindergarten this year, a little girl sat away from the other children, sniffling and crying. "I want my Mommy," she said whenever we tried to work with her. The next day Maria drew a primitive picture and wrote an assortment of letters. I was delighted, and at the end of the writing workshop I asked if she would sit in the place of honor, the author's chair, and share her story. Maria held up her picture and told her story:

The girl is sad.
She has no friends.

Several children raised their hands. "I like your picture," one said.
"I like your writing," another said.
Then a tiny boy with big solemn eyes looked up at Maria and said, "I'll be your friend."
This incident captures something essential about the teaching and learning of writing. We need to write, but we also need to be heard. As François Mauriac says, "Each of us is like a desert, and a literary work is like a cry from the desert, or like a pigeon let loose with a message in its claws, or like a bottle thrown into the sea. The point is: to be heard—even if by one single person."
Listening to children—taking lessons from them—is essential to the teaching of writing. Archibald MacLeish points out that the "whole situation in a writing course is a reversal of the usual academic pattern. Not only is there no subject, there is no content either. Or, more precisely, the content is the work produced by the students. And the relation of the teacher to his [her] students is thus the opposite of the relationship one would expect to find. Ordinarily it is the teacher who knows, the student who learns. Here it is the student who knows, or should, and the teacher who learns, or tries to" (MacLeish 1959). MacLeish is right: the teacher of writing must be a listener, a coach. But it oversimplifies things to suggest that the classroom teacher is the only one to play the role of the listening teacher. The writing classroom as a whole must become a learning community, and everyone in it must be both a teacher and a student.
Two classmates listened as six-year-old Greg read the beginning of his story aloud:

We got on a big bus. It took us to the game. The Patriots and the
Jets played. The score was 55 to 21. We saw two men in long underwear
at the game.

Then the story shifted back to the bus:

There was a bathroom on the bus. There was a lot of people on the
bus.

Once again, the story shifted:

The policeman at the game made us throw our Coke in the garbage.

At this point, Sharon interrupted. "Greg," she said, "it isn't about one thing. It goes hippety-hop from one thing to the next. It's like you had a crazy dream. It's all mixed up." Seeing Greg's worried look, Sharon hurried to reassure him that with Jaws, the class staple remover, he could take his book apart and put the pages back together in a more logical order.

Meanwhile, in a sixth grade classroom, Mario told his buddy, Chai Fai, that he might write a poem about break dancing. "I was thinkin' about break dancing. There are a lot of mysteries going on in it. In the olden days, the only dances were the classics, but now everybody likes to break and pop. It is a new day and there should be new poems."

Chai Fai agreed. "But is the *topic* the only thing in your poem that will be new," he wondered, "or will *the way* you write it be new?" Soon the boys were looking through an anthology of contemporary poetry and plotting out ways to make the form match the content. "The outside of the poem should match the inside, the subject," they explained.

In each of these instances, writing teachers have carefully structured their classrooms so that students learn from each other as well as from their teacher. The pace, sound, tone, and texture of life in these classrooms did not happen by accident; it happened because teachers provided a structure that allowed for and encouraged a free-floating hum.

Janet Emig tells the story of an elementary school principal who went into a writing workshop to observe the teacher. For a moment, he stood in the doorway, glancing around the room. There was no sign of the teacher. Two youngsters worked at the chalkboard, one of them drawing a crude diagram depicting the sections of his volcano report. Nearby, three children clustered closely together on the floor, listening to Act 2 of Jorge's play, "The Missing Egyptian Pearl." Other children worked at their desks, some scrawling furiously—or doodling idly—on pads of legal paper, and some carefully copying their work onto white paper. Occasionally a child would turn around in his or her chair to read a line or discuss a point with a classmate. On the edges of the classroom, children met in twos, listening to each other's pieces. In the far corner, three or four children worked at a table full of dictionaries and editing checklists. The principal finally spotted the teacher, who was sitting alongside one student in the midst of the workshop; the principal made his way across the room to where she sat and, leaning down, said in a stage whisper, "I'll come back when you are teaching."

How little he knows! How little he knows about the amount of forethought, wisdom, and skill that went into establishing in the workshop that elusive background hum. How little he knows about the challenge of teaching writing well. Instead of asking, "What should I say and do tomorrow?" the teacher of writing must ask, "How can I establish a classroom environment that supports growth in writing?" The *content* of any one writing lesson matters far less than the *context* of it.

I used to think that in order to teach creative writing I needed to have a creative management system. I thought creative environments, by definition, were ever-changing, complex, and stimulating. Every day my classroom was different: one day we wrote for ten minutes; another day, not at all; sometimes students exchanged papers, and other days they turned them in; sometimes they published their writing, sometimes they didn't. The classroom was a whirlwind, a kaleidoscope, and I felt very creative. Rightly so. My days were full of planning, scheming, experimenting, replanning. Meanwhile, my children waited on my changing agendas. They could not develop their own rhythms and strategies because they were controlled by mine. They could not plan because they never knew what tomorrow would hold. They could only wait.

I have finally realized that the most creative environments in our society are not the kaleidoscopic environments in which everything is always changing and complex. They are, instead, the predictable and consistent ones: the scholar's library, the researcher's laboratory, the artist's studio. Each of these environments is deliberately kept *predictable* and *simple* because the work at hand and the changing interactions around that work are so unpredictable and complex (Calkins 1983, 32).

Teachers often ask me, "How do I start the writing workshop?" They want to know what to say on day one and day two. Although I try to answer the question, I also emphasize that the content of a writing lesson matters far less than the context of it. If day one, two, and three are to go well, we need to structure the workshop carefully, thinking about time, schedules, rules, expectations, and materials. There is no one right way to structure the workshop, but there are principles that can guide us. These principles will be the subject of chapter 4, but let us turn first to a discussion of current research on teaching writing. Decisions about the structure of a writing workshop should be grounded in an understanding of the research that informs our practices.

3

---

when research informs our practice

Things are changing in the field of writing. Over the past fifteen years, interest in the teaching of writing has soared: throughout the country there are summer institutes, workshops and in-service courses. Thankfully, the rising interest in writing is accompanied by a growing knowledge base. During these last fifteen years we have had, for the first time, major studies on how children develop as writers. Unlike most educational research, these studies are having a direct and powerful effect on classroom teaching. In this chapter, I hope to convey the spirit and message of current research on writing and to show how this research can connect with classroom practice.

A paradigm shift: from products to process

When I went to school, writing was rarely taught; rather, it was assigned and then corrected. If there was any teaching, the focus was on categorizing written products. My teachers listed the traits of science fiction, fantasy, tall tales, haiku and sonnets and showed me examples of each. In high school, they taught me the characteristics of expository, persuasive, descriptive, and narrative writing. Their emphasis was on final products, not on the processes that produced them. I do not think a single teacher ever watched me as I wrote, heard my ideas about good writing, or spoke with me about my composing strategies. They never knew how I spent my evenings before a paper was due.

I remember them well. I would solemnly close my bedroom door, draw my chair alongside the desk . . . and sit there. Staring at the blank page, I felt hollow and frantic. I'd clean the room, eat, and sharpen my pencils until they were stubs. Finally I'd return to the desk, only to delay some more. Usually it was long after my brothers and sisters had all gone to bed and the house had grown quiet that I would finally put something on paper. My writing always seemed pathetic. Looking at it, I had the same hopeless feeling I now have when I draw: my pictures look sick. But it is one thing to produce lousy drawings and another thing altogether to produce stupid words, stupid ideas. I saw myself in the strained platitudes and clichéd ideas on my page. My writing was a reflection of me, and I didn't like what I saw. It was far from the ideal text I had in mind, and it was far from the models my teachers had shown me, but I didn't know how to bridge the gap.

My experiences were not unusual. The dominant method of composition instruction since the late nineteenth century has been to describe and differentiate the modes of discourse, and to show models of each mode. But recently the field has undergone a paradigm shift. Now, instead of asking only, "What are the forms of good writing?" many teachers and researchers ask, "What processes do writers use?"; "What do children do when they write and how do these behaviors change as they grow older?"; and "How do the behaviors of skilled and unskilled writers differ?" The focus has shifted from products to processes.

We now realize it was misleading to have elevated form over content. Writers do not begin a piece, as many curricula suggest, saying "I want to write a three-paragraph persuasive essay." They begin, instead, with something to say: "I need to convince people to take care of the salt marshes," or "I want to explore the relationship between critical reading skills and revision." Then, too, in real life there are no clear distinctions between modes. The writer may begin with the idea of writing a descriptive journal entry and end up writing a poem, an essay, or a newspaper article. Descriptive writing is often woven into a narrative; persuasive writing is often built out of stories; and so on.

We also realize now that, although much of the language arts curriculum is based on the primitive notion that by naming something, we master it (Moffett 1968), many researchers argue that knowing the characteristics of ideal finished products has little to do with developing the skills to produce those products. Students may be able to recite the characteristics of a tall tale, but this does not mean that they can write one. English composition is a skill that can be learned rather than a content that must be covered. Teaching English, and certainly, teaching writing, must become more like coaching a sport and less like presenting information.

Many of our students know their pieces of writing are far from ideal, but they may not know how to make their actual texts more like their ideal ones. In the same way, I already know my tennis game is far from ideal. If my tennis coach simply watched where my ball went, calling, "Against the net!" or, "Out!" this would not be helpful. If I am going to improve my game, I need help with the process rather than simply evaluations of the products. So my coach watches *how* I play the game, noticing what works and what does not work for me. "You are stepping away from the ball," he says. "Try stepping into it." If we, as writing teachers, watch how our students go about writing, then we can help them develop more effective strategies for writing. In doing this, we can draw on two major areas of research:

Studies of how students   Reports on how professional
go about writing.   writers go about writing.
(Perl, Sommers,   (Murray, *Writers at Work*
Emig, Graves,   interviews, Elbow,
Calkins, etc.)   Macrorie etc.)

Teachers as researchers: the first area of research

From the first strand of research, we learn that each of us, and each of our students, has a composing process. We each have our own strategies for composing and our own rhythms of work that we draw on whenever we write. But some of these are dysfunctional. I named my first book *Lessons from a Child* (1983) when I realized that the most important thing I could say to teachers was that we must become researchers, observing how our students go about writing and learning from them how we can help:

My hope is that through closely observing one child's growth in writing, we'll learn to watch for and to respect each child's growth in writing. . . . In the end, we always teach unique children: all our students are case-studies.

Or is the reverse true? Is it the children who teach, and we who learn? The irony of this book is that when we regard our students as unique and fascinating, when they become case-study subjects even while they are students, then the children become our teachers, showing us how they learn (Calkins 1983, 7–8).

There is a thin line between research and teaching. We can assist writers best if we observe what works and what does not work for them as writers.

By the time many unskilled writers have written three words, for example, they already believe they have made an error (Perl 1979). They continually interrupt themselves to worry about spelling, to reread, and to fret. This "stuttering in writing" leads to tangled syntax and destroys fluency. It is a dysfunctional strategy, one that impedes effective writing, and the teacher who understands this can help students develop more effective methods.

Many upper elementary school children have problematic strategies for writing fiction. Perhaps because they believe a story will be interesting only if it contains two murders, a robbery, and a suicide, many young authors string together all the traumatic events they can recall from television shows. They begin writing with a burst of energy, but soon *they* want the story to end, and *we* want it to end; yet they keep writing and writing, hoping to come upon an end somewhere in their narrative yarn. If we, as teachers, understand what these students are doing and why, then we can begin to help.

Many high school students actually believe the way to write an essay is to sit down at the desk, pick up a pen, and then put down a main idea followed by three supporting paragraphs! No wonder these students produce limp, bland writing. They are using a dysfunctional strategy for writing. They do not realize that it is only through musing, drafting, revising, talking, and musing some more that most writers know what they want to say.

Administrators have also earned a reputation for having dysfunctional writing strategies. When building principals, for example, write letters home to parents, they often believe that they are writing for a large and critical audience. They often write in a murky, impersonal style, full of passive sentences in which no one is doing anything so that no one can be blamed. Their prose is purposely vague. Zinsser's book is full of examples of this style, perhaps the best of which was written by the president of a major university during the campus unrest of the late 1960's. "You are probably aware," he wrote to alumni, "that we have been experiencing very considerable potentially explosive expressions of dissatisfaction on issues only partially related" (Zinsser 1980, 8). Administrators would do well to write for a single, friendly reader and, if necessary, to rewrite for their less friendly readers.

Teaching the writing process: the second area of research

The first strand of research, then, offers us an invitation to become researchers, observing how our students go about writing and helping them see what works and what does not work. The second strand of research offers a different sort of invitation. From the work of scholars such as Murray, Macrorie, Elbow and from what writers report about their composing processes, we have begun to recognize that many writers follow a process of craft when they work, much as researchers follow a scientific method. When we understand the writing process, we can help each of our students invent, use, and adapt effective writing strategies. Theorists describe the writing process in different ways: as prewriting, writing, and rewriting; as circling out and circling back; as collecting and connecting. I prefer Donald Murray's terms: rehearsal, drafting, revision, and editing.

Rehearsal is, above all, a way of living. People who write regularly live with a sense of, "I am one who writes," and this consciousness engenders an extra-susceptibility, an extra-awareness. "Stories happen to those who tell them," Thucydides said. Just as photographers are always seeing potential pictures, so too, writers see potential stories everywhere. This is rehearsal. A draft may begin as an image, a sentence which lingers in the mind, a memory. Faulkner began *The Sound and the Fury* with the image of a little girl in knickers, sitting in a tree. My rehearsal for this book began twelve years ago when I first spoke to teachers about the teaching of writing. Rehearsal, for me, did not occur within the weeks preceding my first sentence. Instead, the seeds of this book were planted long ago. For many writers, rehearsal also includes gathering raw materials: noticing shades of sunlight or the lilt of a voice, finding connections between ideas. Just as sculptors are fond of saying that they discover their subject in the block of marble (Barzun 1957), so too, writers begin to sense the shape of their subject as they explore and gather their raw materials. Perhaps a controlling vision emerges, or a way to begin, or a sense of audience. Sometimes during rehearsal, writers map possible lines of development for their pieces, or sketch out the patterns in their ideas. Often they rehearse by talking, observing, or reading. During all of this, they experience a growing readiness to put themselves on the line.

I like the word "drafting" better than "writing" for the next stage in the composing process because it implies the tentativeness of our early efforts. Like an artist at a sketch pad, we begin to find the contours of our subject. We make light, quick lines; nothing is permanent. Each writer has his or her own style. Some bolt quickly down the page, their momentum building, their pencil leading in unexpected directions. Others work in smaller units, toying with their beginnings, trying a line one way and then another, drawing in to write, then pushing away to see what they have said. "Get it down," Faulkner writes. "Take chances. It may be bad, but it is the only way you can do anything really good."

Drafting soon becomes revision. Revision means just that: re-vision, seeing again. The words become like a lens (Murray), helping us see our emerging subjects and our developing meanings. I begin a piece for example, by working to capture the respect I feel for my mother. Halfway down the page, I realize that a puzzling contradiction has emerged. I reread what I have written, re-seeing what I have said; the writing becomes a lens. I revise, and by moving the words on the page and looking through them at my unfolding subject, I explore, and discover what I have to say. Murray describes the process this way:

The writing stands apart from the writer, and the writer interacts

*with it, first to find out what the writing has to say and then to help
the writing say it clearly and gracefully (Murray 1980, 5).*

Writers become readers, then writers again. They cross out a section, insert a line, move a detail, turn a personal narrative into an essay.

Editing has negative connotations. The term calls to mind corrected pages branded CARELESS and margins filled with AWKs. But for me, editing is one of the best parts of writing. The major decisions are behind me, at least for the time being, and I bring out my thin-tipped pen. With quick, precise strokes, I trim and carve and link my sentences, working with the feel of my material. I see the shape of my words on the page. I listen to their sound. "Walked quietly" becomes "crept," "quite angry" becomes "peeved." I replace a list of examples by a single, more vivid detail. My text begins to look stronger, to sound better. I type it, leaving triple spaces. New challenges surface. Again I take my pen in hand and set to work: tightening, linking, clarifying. Now, ready for the last touches, I pull back from the page and make believe I am someone else. I read it objectively, with a critical eye. I change a word, delete a line, and it is ready for final copy.

Whether we write a poem about shadows or an article about a geological expedition, we all move through these stages. Some of us spend longer on rehearsal, others on revision. Some revisions fit between the lines of a draft, others require a sequence of drafts. We may edit a great deal when working on an expository essay and not at all when writing a letter. Or the opposite may be true. In their own way and at their own pace, most writers follow a cycle in their writing: rehearsal, drafting, revision, and editing. Several years ago, Susan Sowers, Donald Graves and I found that even young children go through these processes.

Often when I speak with teachers, I ask them, "If youngsters begin a piece on Monday and end it on Friday, what part of the writing process do you estimate would occupy them on Monday? Tuesday? Wednesday? and so forth?" As I move about the room, I hear teachers speculating whether rehearsal will take one day or two, and whether it is feasible to expect children to revise. Usually the consensus goes: Monday, rehearsal; Tuesday, drafting; Wednesday and Thursday, drafting and revision; and Friday, editing.

Of course, my question is a set-up; it is not like that at all. The shifts between rehearsal, drafting, revision, and editing occur minute by minute, second by second, throughout the writing process. The writer thinks of a topic, jots down a few lines, rereads them. Dissatisfied, the writer may cross out a line and recopy the remaining text, making small changes. The piece still looks feeble. Trying again, the writer asks, "What do I want to say?" and this time, jots down some notes. They are messy, so the writer recopies them. Already the writer has shifted from rehearsal to drafting, to revision, to editing, to rehearsal, to editing.

Meanwhile, if a classroom is filled with thirty young authors, they are all working at very different stages in their writing. On any given day, one or two children may edit and recopy a piece, while others will begin a new one. Still others will be immersed in drafting. Some will need a peer-conference; many will not. Some will toy with alternative titles, and some will tinker with their lead sentences. Some will stall.

The writing process does not fit into teacher-led, whole-class methods of instruction. Unfortunately, that is the only kind of teaching approach many teachers know.

It is tempting, therefore, to interpret the stages of the writing process as discrete, linear steps. Then a teacher can feel justified in keeping the entire class synchronized, working through them in unison. On Mondays, everyone lists possible topics, circles the best choice, and free writes for twelve minutes. Then, all the children reread what they have written and select their best sentence as a lead. If a brave youngster raises a hand to say, "I already know what I want to write. Can I start a draft?" the child is reminded that Tuesdays are for drafting. Wednesdays are for revision: all must write a second draft, whether or not they need it. So it goes in many "research-based" writing programs across the country.

Researchers, aghast at what they have created, have hastened to correct themselves. "The writing process does not contain discrete, linear steps but recursive, overlapping ones," they say. Many suggest that the terms rehearsal, drafting, revision, and editing are no longer helpful, and recommend new metaphors.

For me, it is helpful to think of writing as a process of dialogue between the writer and the emerging text. We focus in to write, then pull back to ask questions of our text. We ask the same questions over and over, and we ask them whether we are writing a poem or an expository essay:

- What have I said so far? What am I trying to say?
- How do I like it? What's good here that I can build on? What's not so good that I can fix?
- How does it sound? How does it look?
- How else could I have done this?
- What will my reader think as he or she reads this? What questions will they ask? What will they notice? Feel? Think?
- What am I going to do next?

In his important article, "Teaching the Other Self: The Writer's First Reader," Murray (1982) likens writing to a conversation between two workmen muttering to each other at the bench. "The self speaks, the other self listens and considers. The self proposes, the other self considers. The self makes, the other self evaluates. The two selves collaborate" (165). Closeness and distance, pushing forward and pulling back, creation and criticism: it is this combination of forces which makes writing such a powerful tool for learning. Whereas spoken words fade away, with print we can fasten our thoughts onto paper. We can hold our ideas in our hands. We can carry them in our pockets. We can think about our thinking. Through writing, we can "re-see," reshape, and refine our thoughts. Frank Smith explains, "Writing separates our ideas from ourselves in a way that is easiest for us to examine, explore and develop them" (Smith 1982, 15).

I have always believed that revision is essential to the writing process; that writing helps us develop our thinking precisely because it allows us to revisit our first thoughts. But recently I've begun to realize that our drafts are not the cutting edge—the growing edge—of writing, but the results of it. Instead, the cutting edge of writing is the interaction between writer and developing text. The writer keeps asking "What am I trying to say?", "How does this sound?", "Where is this leading me?"

In my research, I have found that when teachers ask these questions of children in conferences, children internalize them and ask them of each other in peer-conferences. Eventually, they ask them of themselves during writing. "I can conference with myself," nine-year-old Becky said to me one morning. "I just read my writing over to myself and it's like there is another person there. I think thoughts to myself. I say things others might ask me." The brown-eyed youngster paused. "I talk it over with myself. I ask myself questions."

Scott is six, and he, too, engages in dialogue with his emerging text. I watch him scowl as he rereads his homemade book. "This story should go in the trash can," he mutters. "See, the kids will have so many questions."

I SAW MY FATHER'S COLLECTIONS. THEN WE LEFT.

"I go through it wicked fast. The kids will say, 'What were the collections? What'd ya see?'" Scott's voice trails off as he begins to wind words up the margin of his page. He reads the insert to me.

WE SAW BUTTONS, COINS, STAMPS AND OTHER STUFF.

"The kids will have questions still," Scott says, "but at least I got rid of some of them."

During the writing workshop, Maria sits in the author's chair. It is not yet time for the children to gather for a sharing session and so there is no one on the rug in front of her. Maria's teacher, Aida Montero, sees the youngster and asks, "What are you doing in the share area now?"

"I'm pretend-sharing," Maria answers.

Puzzled, Ms. Montero asks, "What do you mean?"

"I'm thinking; if I get to share this piece with the kids, what will they ask me?" Maria reads the story to her teacher:

I HAV FUN WIF MY UBWALA.
I GO EVRY SATRDA.

(*Abvela* is Spanish for grandmother)

Then Maria says, "I think they'll ask me, 'What ya' do with her?' so now I'm going to make a page two." Soon Maria has gone back to her desk and written:

WE WACH TOM AN	*(We watch Tom and*
JERRY AN EAT	*Jerry and eat*
FETOS AN PLA	*Fritos and play*
TRABL.	*Trouble.)*

Scott, Becky, Maria and their classmates have learned to interact with their texts by asking questions because their teachers and classmates have conferred with them about their work-in-progress. For this reason, the writing process approach to teaching writing is also called the conference approach to writing. Teacher-student conferences are at the heart of teaching writing; it is through them that students learn to interact with their own writing.

4

create classroom settings which allow us to listen

The writing process approach requires a radically different pace and classroom structure than we are used to in our schools. If students are going to become deeply invested in their writing, and if they are going to draft and revise, sharing their texts with each other as they write, they need the luxury of time. If they are going to have the chance to do their best, and then to make their best better, they need long blocks of time. Sustained effort and craftsmanship are essential in writing well, yet they run contrary to the modern American way. We live in a one-draft-only society, a land of instant diets, frozen waffles, and throw-away razors. We choose ephemeral, 'quick' and easy solutions in the United States. Our society allows little time for sustained effort, for knowing what it is to do one's best and then make one's best better. At times, I wonder if my stepdaughter Kira and her friends have ever known what it is to do their best. They vacuum by standing in the middle of the room and pushing the vacuum as they turn around in a circle. They scrub the bathtub by turning on the shower. Sometimes it seems that the only area in which young adolescents really know the meaning of revision is their hairstyles, which quickly move through draft one, draft two, draft three.

Like our society, our schools have adopted a one-draft-only mentality. Their motto seems to be "get it done" and "move along." It is a sign of the times that "silent, sustained reading" lasts for only twelve minutes. The entire school day is fragmented: ten minutes on spelling, six minutes on a ditto, fifteen minutes for a class discussion, three minutes to copy off the board. Graves describes this as the cha-cha-cha curriculum. Many researchers emphasize that, because the school day is so segmented, teachers spend an average of 40 percent of their time on choreography. We move the class from one thing to another: "sit there," "come here," "open this book," "close that one," "get such and such out," "put it away," "line up," "sit down," "do this," "do that. . . ."

Interruptions shatter the school day, making absorption in a project almost impossible. Children are shuttled in and out of classrooms for music instruction, remedial reading, testing, and computer classes. Then, too, there is the PA system: "Mrs. Jones, you have a package in the office. It's nothing important." "Buses 16 and 9 will be late." "The game at Frontier has been cancelled." Added to this, there is the problem of "specials." Although I am not against policemen, grandparents, trees, or international relations, "specials" such as "Love Your Grandparents" days, "Honor the Police" ceremonies, and "Draw a Tree" contests are becoming commonplace. Where, in the helter-skelter pace of the school day, is there time for the probing, experimentation, dialogue, and reflection that contribute to genuine learning? It seems to me we have added enough to the school day. We now have courses in philosophy, critical thinking, health, housing, decision-making, career education, and law. We have layers and layers of pullout programs. When is someone going to be an activist and speak out against the rampant inflation of the curriculum? When is someone going to take a radical stand?

In addition, the myth of "coverage" contributes to the frenzied pace of the school day. "Have I covered the sixteen causes of the Civil War?" "Have I covered the thirteen uses of the comma?" We worry about covering the curriculum as if we believe that covering a topic means children will have learned it. We don't stop to realize that we are rushing to "cover" the thirteen uses of commas in third grade, and again in fourth, fifth, sixth, seventh, eighth, ninth . . . and still students don't use commas correctly.

The writing process approach requires a radically different pace than we are used to in our schools. But time is our scarcest resource. Teachers often ask me, "How do I squeeze writing in on top of everything else?" My suggestion is simple: don't. Instead of squeezing one more thing into the crowded curriculum, I suggest that we each take a good hard look at our school day to determine what is no longer needed there. My husband and I recently moved from one Connecticut town to another, and the thing that surprised me most about the move was the amount of junk we had accumulated. We took fifteen *car loads* of trash to the dump. Sometimes I think that if we, as teachers, want to move on, we too need to take car loads to the dump. Most of our curricula still include things we no longer need or no longer feel strongly about. It is only by cleaning out some old things that we can give time and space to new ones.

I urge teachers to set aside an hour a day, every day, for the writing workshop. Once the year is underway, some of this workshop time will be used for researching content-area reports. Always, the writing workshop will encompass all of the language arts. It is very easy, then, to see why writing deserves an hour a day.

Sometimes this isn't possible. Secondary school English lasts for only forty minutes a day, and this time must be divided among literature, writing, and language. (In chapter 11, I will suggest more extensive ways of working within these unfortunate constraints.) Kindergarten teachers often have their children for only a half-day. Teachers in other grade levels may not be ready yet to give writing the same amount of time as reading.

Let me warn you, however, that it is almost impossible to create an effective writing workshop if students write only once or twice a week. If on Monday, Emmanuel begins a piece about how he stayed overnight with a friend who lives in a private house, and he doesn't see that piece again until Friday, he will find it hard to sustain an interest in it, and harder still to remember the questions his friends asked during a conference. It is like any sport. If we jog only once a week, it is hard to break the inertia brought on by six days of not jogging. But if we jog every day, it becomes easier and easier; we get into a rhythm, we find our stride. The same is true of writing.

My suggestion, therefore, to those teachers who hesitate to give an hour a day to writing is to take whatever time there is and clump it together. Instead of writing one day a week for a year, they can try writing three days a week for half a year. I also recommend that writing time be scheduled regularly so that children can anticipate it. If children know that every morning will begin with an hour for writing, or that Tuesday, Wednesday and Friday afternoons will be for writing, then they come to school ready to write. "Last night in bed, I was thinking of a story," they tell us, or they say, "I decided on a different way to start my piece." Children, like the rest of us, will "write" when they are not writing if writing becomes a regular and frequent part of their lives (Graves).

Setting aside predictable time for writing is important for another reason: it allows children to take control of their own writing processes. When children know the parameters within which they are working, they can develop strategies and plan their writing. If they know there will be writing tomorrow, they can say to themselves, "I'll just write a sketchy draft for now, and tomorrow, I'll redo the sections that seem weak." They can also make plans to confer with a friend, or put aside a piece until later. But if the writing workshop schedule is always changing, always haphazard, children remain pawns waiting for their teacher's agenda.

For this reason and others, I think it is important for each day's workshop to have a clear, simple structure. Children should know what to expect. This allows them to carry on; it frees the teacher from choreographing activities and allows time for listening. *How* we structure the workshop is less important than *that* we structure it, but most of the K–6 teachers with whom I have worked tend to begin their workshops with a four or five minute mini-lesson (chapters 18 and 19). After talking to the children or giving them tips about good writing, the teacher sends them off to draft, revise, and confer with each other. The teacher moves around the room, talking with individuals about their writing, quietly managing the flow of the room, and meeting with informal clusters of children. The workshop ends with either a whole-class sharing session or small response groups.

Few teachers have theoretical problems with any of this. It is hard to disagree *in theory* with the importance of moving about the room or talking with individuals about their writing. The problems are not theoretical, but practical. While we talk with one child, what are the other twenty-nine children doing?

Only when most children are personally interested in their writing and when there is a clear, consistent workshop structure can teachers have the chance to move about and talk with individual writers. Simple, clear rules and expectations are essential, and each teacher needs to choose his or her own rules and routines.

For example, I find it helpful to begin the workshop on a quiet, calm note rather than with a flurry of disorganized energy. Therefore, I spend time early in the year helping children know my expectations about how they come and go from mini-lessons. If we meet together for our mini-lessons on the floor, I caution them against running and shoving for their favorite spot in the meeting area, and I ask them to push in their chairs before leaving their desks. If students remain at their desks for mini-lessons, I ask them to clear their desks beforehand. I also try to find ways to smooth the transition between the mini-lesson and writing time. I might suggest that we work silently for the first few minutes of writing so that everyone can center on what he or she will be doing that day. There are other, small ways to streamline classroom operations. I might color-code the writing folders so that only five youngsters have blue tabs and five have red; then children would not have to search through thirty folders in order to find their own.

Simple, clear rules also help during the writing workshop. In New York City, the classrooms are so crowded it sometimes becomes disruptive if children confer with each other while sitting at their desks. In these classrooms students know that peer-conferences should take place at the edges of the room. Usually "the edges" consist only of a narrow border of floor, but the children have named this "conference alley," and it serves the purpose. We also ask youngsters not to bring pencils or pens to a peer-conference. This may sound trivial, but if children bring pencils, they either write on each other's drafts, or else the writer spends conference time making small revisions in his or her text. This means that conferences last forever, problems are not only raised but also resolved during a conference, and children often leave a conference with nothing else to do.

In most of these classrooms, the writing time ends with a sharing session during which the entire class gathers together to respond to two or three students' work-in-progress. Again, there are routines and rules for the sharing sessions. Generally, the author sits in a special chair, the author's chair (Graves and Hansen 1983), and the class gathers at the author's feet. The author begins explaining why he or she has come for help. Then the author reads and asks the listeners for their questions and responses.

"Doesn't it get boring when every day is the same?" teachers ask. I don't think so. We do not worry that the artist at work in a studio will grow bored. We do not worry that the writer at home at the desk will grow bored. Many teachers do make some changes over the course of the year, and later, I will discuss some of their strategies. Some upper elementary and secondary teachers phase out whole-class sharing meetings in favor of small response groups. Some primary school teachers devise other ways to share writing, such as asking children to find partners and listen to each other's pieces. Especially for five- and six-year-olds, these pairs sometimes work better than whole-class share meetings.

Teachers also find that, because writing materials significantly influence what and how children write, simply changing the shape and size of available paper can pose new challenges for children. In the primary grades, teachers generally begin the year by providing single sheets of unlined white paper and experience chart paper, on which there is space for a drawing and writing. Within a few days, children and their teachers will be stapling two or three sheets together to make simple books, or taping one paper onto the bottom of another to produce long scrolls. For a while, the stapling and taping are exhilarating, a physical and concrete celebration of the child's growing prowess. Later, when these activities become time-consuming chores, teachers will want to provide ready-made books. If energy begins to wane, teachers may want to try introducing new kinds of paper. Connie Norgren, a kindergarten teacher in Brooklyn District 15, convinced a paper company to give her huge square sheets of paper. In her class, children often wrote on the floor, with their writing spread before them like a rug. Carol Seltzer, another kindergarten teacher in that district, gives her youngsters sheets of computer paper; she also gives them tiny three-inch-square books, long strips of adding machine paper, and long sheets of yellow legal-pad paper. Because the paper in kindergarten and first-grade classrooms is often very large, we find that children need writing folders equally large. In some classrooms, teachers hang paper bags below the chalkboard for work-in-progress. In others, teachers make giant-sized manila folders or give children "mailboxes" for their writing. Of course, writing implements are as important as paper. In kindergarten and first grade, many teachers provide thin marker pens and crayons as well as regular-sized pencils.

The upper-grade teachers I know best pay less attention to materials. Usually they provide yellow paper for rough drafts and white paper for final drafts, and leave it at that. I wonder, though, if this hasn't been a mistake. Why have we assumed that fourth graders are too grown-up to enjoy writing in a miniature-sized book? I buy new spiral notebooks for myself as a way to ensure that I will keep a journal, yet I act as if young people "outgrow" the pleasure of new materials and tools. Recently, I have begun to encourage teachers of every grade to provide a wide variety of paper. My only caution is that if children write rough drafts on pristine white paper they may not see drafting as tentative, messy, and experimental. The materials should encourage exploration. This also means that spiral notebooks or bound books are probably less than ideal for rough drafts, since children will find it difficult to shuttle between one draft and another or to paste and cut if the pages are bound together.

Folders are as important for the upper grades as they are for young children, and generally teachers maintain two folders for each child: a daily folder for work-in-progress, the editing checklist, and perhaps notes on potential topics; and a cumulative writing folder for finished work, containing rough drafts carefully numbered and stapled together with the final draft clipped onto them. In some classrooms, large mailing envelopes are used as cumulative writing folders, and the face of the envelope becomes a place for a Table of Contents.

TITLE	DATE FINISHED
1.	....
2.	....
3.	....

I could continue. The writing teacher also needs to provide tools for revision: scissors, tape, staplers and staple removers. Materials and procedures for publishing are important, as are the checklists, dictionaries, red pens, and rules for editing. All of this will be woven into the chapters which follow. My point for now is that, behind the seemingly effortless hum of a successful writing workshop, there must be a tremendous amount of wise planning. As teachers of writing, we need to structure classroom environments carefully, so we can listen to young writers, and so we can help them listen to each other and respond to their texts. These interactions are at the heart of the writing workshop, and they will be the subject of chapters 12 through 16. Now we will turn our attention to an even more fundamental topic, children's development as writers.

how children change as writers

5

introduction

When children write, we are often overwhelmed by what they reveal to us: so many different voices, errors, choices, experiments, hopes. What does this child need next? What about that one? Why does this youngster reread so often? Why does that one reread so rarely? What does it all mean?

Renee is only four. When I first met her, she was drawing a picture of Santa Claus.

"Do you want to write some words?" I asked her, but she didn't seem to understand. I tried again. "Can you say Santa slowly, listening to the sounds?" Soon we were sounding out Saaaaaaannnta. "What sounds do you hear?" I asked.

Renee looked up at me, listening intently to "Saannta."

"Ho-Ho-Ho," she said.

Liliana is five. When she hears Tashena's story, she is confused by it. The sentences blur together. Pulling the page from her friend, Liliana says, "You are reading it wrong." Liliana rereads the story with pen in hand, this time adding stop signs to Tashena's story, telling Tashena where to pause.

Brad is also five. When he brings me his story about rabbits, I can't resist commenting, "I notice that you put an S for two rabbits!" "Yup," Brad replies, "One S for two rabbits, two S-es for three rabbits."

Carlos is nine. His story is half a page long, and it has thirteen exclamation marks, a whole hierarchy of them: fat ones for important sentences and six in a row when the hero dies.

31

What does it all mean? What are these children showing us and how can we help them grow? In that whole maze of writing development, where is Carlos with his exclamation marks, and where might he be going? And what about Liliana, Brad, and Renee? The question, of course, is larger than Carlos or Liliana or Brad or Renee. The question is two-pronged: how do children change as writers and how can we extend that growth?

When these questions guide our teaching, then the two gears—the teachers' teaching and the students' learning—mesh. The point of contact comes when we allow students to teach us how they learn. This transforms our teaching into a course of study, and our students' learning into the curriculum for that course. When we, as teachers, pull our chairs alongside young writers and try to understand their ways of understanding, when we search for the logic in their errors and the patterns in their growth, then we no longer spin our wheels.

I recently asked my students at Teachers College to form an image in their minds of themselves performing as superbly successful teachers. "Write down what comes to mind," I said. Most students described themselves gesturing strongly from the lectern while a roomful of students leaned forward in their seats to catch their teacher's every word. Good teaching is just the opposite: *we* are the ones who must lean forward in our seats.

Researchers have suggested that the communication patterns between newborn infants and mothers provide a powerful example of a natural, effective teaching-learning interaction. The two respond to each other in such a way that only with the help of slow motion films is it possible to tell who is initiating and who is following. The films reveal that in fact, the infants smile first and the mothers follow, their responses fitting so closely with the infants' smiles that the action and response seems all of a piece. Roger Brown calls this responsive teaching "tracking," and it has much in common with Bruner's scaffolding (1982), Erikson's mutuality of generations (1964), Friere's dialogue (1982), and Holdaway's role-playing (1979) the mentor's activities. Each of these theorists is part of an emerging paradigm of literacy-learning. Basic to this paradigm is the notion that teachers must *extend* rather than simply *teach*.

Most of what happens in schools supports a very different sort of teaching. Teachers are asked to deliver a ready-made curriculum, devised by reading specialists, publishing companies, or language arts coordinators. Perhaps because pressure to improve the teaching of writing is so great, people everywhere are hurrying to write a district-wide writing curriculum. "What are some neat ideas for teaching writing," they think, and then they put these ideas into manuals and guides. I don't think we can hope to have a child-centered approach toward teaching writing until we begin to watch how children grow as writers in classrooms conducive to that growth.

For this reason, much of my current research focuses on teachers becoming researchers in their own classrooms. Thirty teachers from our writing project have received grants to conduct small-scale research projects in their own classrooms, and they meet weekly to develop ways of learning from young writers. What I have found from working with these practitioner-researchers is that, just as the meaning a reader finds in a text is influenced by that reader's prior knowledge, so too, when teachers have a prior knowledge of writing development, it is easier for them to pay attention to what children show them. In the chapters that follow, then, I share some of what I believe about writing development in the hope that these tentative observations will invite readers to pull their chairs alongside children and ask, "Am I finding what she found?"

My kid-watching experiences began eight years ago, when the National Institute of Education funded Susan Sowers, Donald Graves, Mary Ellen Giacobbe, and me to spend two years observing day-to-day changes in sixteen children. Throughout the study, we continually asked, "In among all the wonderful diversity, are there characteristics common to many first graders—or to fifth graders?" I think this is an important question, for unless we have some sort of road map of how children change as writers, it is hard for us to understand, participate in, and celebrate that growth.

Although I did, for example, find ways of characterizing the third graders I knew best, it was unclear whether I was documenting the results of development or of instruction. The two are so intertwined that, in their recent book, *Language Stories and Literacy Lessons,* (1984), Harste *et al.* go so far as to claim that there are no developmental stages in literacy learning, "only experience, and with it fine-tuning and continued orchestration." It is important to remember that what children do as writers depends largely on the context in which they write and on their backgrounds as writers. This is why scope and sequence charts on writing are inadequate and perhaps harmful. Furthermore, even within any one writer, development does not consist of forward-moving progress. One day the writing is good, one day it is lousy, and often what seem at first to be regressions turn out to be the moments of imbalance through which new levels are reached.

By studying the ups and downs of what individual children do in effective writing classrooms, and by reveling in the tremendous diversity within these classrooms, I have begun to form tentative notions about the range of writing-behaviors one might find in first-grade, in fifth-grade, or in eighth-grade rooms. It is, of course, a vast oversimplification to speak of writing development in terms of grade levels, but I hope this tentative road map helps teachers become observers, and inspires them to pull their chairs alongside children like Liliana, Brad, Renee, and Carlos.

6

---

kindergarten and first grade: early forays into writing

"Teaching writing in kindergarten? I don't believe in it," a friend recently announced, punctuating her remark with loud sighs and the shake of her head. "Children need time to be children; to grow through play and song, dance and art."

I agree. Children need time to be children, to grow through natural childhood activities. It is not children—but adults—who have separated writing from art, song, and play; it is adults who have turned writing into an exercise on dotted-line paper, into a matter of rules, lessons, and cautious behavior. Children view writing quite differently. For them, it is exploration with marker and pen. Long before they come to school, youngsters leave their mark on foggy car windows and wet beaches (Graves, 1983). We, as adults, may not believe in writing for kindergarten children—but the children believe in it.

The young child's writing is an outgrowth of the infant's gestures. As Vygotsky points out, "Gestures are writing in air, and written signs frequently are simply gestures that have been fixed" (Vygotsky 1962). The urge to write begins when a baby, lying in her crib, moves her arms, and we draw close to the crib, our faces lighting into smiles. "She's waving to us," we say. Because we attach meaning to what could be called meaningless gestures, the gestures assume meaning. Babies learn the power of their gestures by our response to them.

Similarly, the infant propped up in his high chair says "mo mo." Although he may well be making sounds for the pure pleasure of it, we, the proud

35

parents and friends, want to believe our wonderful baby is saying something significant. "He's asking for more," we say and rush to the chair with a dish of mashed bananas. Our response leads babies to know the power of their early sounds. Children have nearly invariable success in learning the complex and subtle skills of talking. "By the age of four to six, the child . . . controls the phonetic system of his language; he handles the grammatical core; he knows and uses the basic vocabulary of his language." Philip Morrison writes (Morrison 1964, 63–70).

If we are to help young children break into the code of written language, we need to take our cue from how babies learn to talk. As Courtney Cazden emphasizes, this language development "takes place on a non-sequenced, whole-task basis" (Cazden 1972, 138). We wouldn't think of dissecting oral language into component parts, of ranking phonemes from simplest to most complex and then teaching them, one at a time, to children. The sounds coming from such a household would be very strange indeed, with the little toddler going about saying /p/ /p/ /p/ /p/ (Holdaway 1979, 21). We laugh at the idea of drilling children on the components of oral language before allowing them to try whole words, and yet this is what so many people do when introducing children to the code of written language.

If we take our cue from how children learn oral language, then we will allow children to learn written language by using it, as best they can, for real purposes, and by having adults see through their errors to what they want to say. The baby says "ady" and yet we wouldn't think of responding, "Oh, no! He is saying Daddy incorrectly. He is clearly not ready for whole words yet, he needs to drill on the *d* sound." We do not for a moment consider whether "ady" is right or wrong—error is not even an issue when children are learning to talk. Instead, we look at children's efforts as closer and closer approximations of adult language, and we marvel at what they can do, fully trusting that in time their speech will encompass the complexities of our language. When the infant says "ady," we phone the relatives from across the country and, holding the receiver close to the youngster in hopes of a repeat performance, we celebrate what the child can do.

In classrooms throughout the country, teachers have begun responding to children's early writing just as parents respond to their children's early speech. On the first day of school, we give children paper and pens saying, "You can draw and write." We know their early efforts will be a testimony to what the children can do, and we know that although few children begin school with a mastery of every sound-symbol relationship, most begin knowing the names and shapes of at least a handful of letters. This knowledge provides them with tools enough to write phone messages, shopping lists, labels, and stories. Most of the articles my colleagues and I have written stress that when children have a rudimentary knowledge of print they can perceive themselves as writers; within this gestalt they quickly learn more conventions of written language. Sometimes teachers say to me, "*Our* children don't come to school knowing a handful of letters—what then?" Often, when the teacher and I work together in these classrooms, we discover that the children know more than we suspected. I have also been in kindergartens where the children know *less* than I suspected. Usually these children come from homes without books and from families who do not read, from families where parents may not have time to talk with and listen to their children. For these children, even more than for the others, it is important that we turn classrooms into literate cultures, enfranchising students as readers and writers. And we can begin on the first day of school.

Long before youngsters know a handful of letters they can begin writing "as best they can." I do not say this lightly. I know some children cannot hold a pencil and that many still desperately need oral language enrichment work. But in schools throughout New York City we are finding that when we give children the time, materials, and encouragement to write, they use whatever they *do* know in amazing ways. David does not know any sound/symbol correspondences, yet he knows how to write his name, and he uses what he knows to write the story shown in Figure 6-1. When David read the story aloud to me, he carefully matched each word of the story with a letter:

I took the A train to Botanical Gardens.

Other children will not have David's understanding of the correspondence between words and print. When I asked Tiziana to read her piece to me,

Figure 6 – 1

she ignored her "letters" altogether and, looking in the sky, told me what she hoped she had written (Figure 6-2).

Figure 6 – 2

I drew Tiziana's attention to her letters. "Wait, let's read it," I said. By working together, we began to match meaning to the marks, as David had done on his own. Tiziana's ten marks represent a very long story, but in time this will change. Like David, she will probably go through a stage in which each mark represents one syllable or one word. Eventually, the length of her text will correspond to the length of her story.

In the meantime, our job is to respond to children's products in such a way that youngsters learn that marks on the paper have the power to convey meaning. Just as infants learn the power of their gestures through our response to those gestures, language learners discover the power of their print and pictures through our response.

If Estella brings the piece shown in Figure 6-3 to me, I would probably

Figure 6 – 3

respond by saying something like, "Oh, Estella! Will you read it to me?"

Even though Estella's writing does not utilize the conventions of adult writing, she can sit in the author's chair and "read" her piece to the class. The listeners can ask her questions, and then Estella may decide to add to her story, either by stapling on another page or by squeezing more marks on the existing page. Of course, in some classrooms children have not had much experience asking questions to clarify meaning, so this will become an important part of the experience. Although her story is nothing more than wavy lines across the page, because we treat it with tremendous respect she will learn the power of print.

Recently I was in a kindergarten classroom in Upper Manhattan. Two children were fooling around with the water fountain. Seeing this, five-year-old Latrice ran to her writing folder and pulled out her writing. The piece looked like nothing more than rows of circles to me, but to Latrice, it was a list of class rules. "Look at this!" she said sternly, waving her page in front of the misbehaving boys. "Can't you read? It says 'No fooling around in the water fountain!' "

The wonderful thing is that within this kind of context, growth happens very quickly. Recognizing that writing involves particular kinds of marks, children may move from wiggly lines to rows of lollipops and triangles, from these to the alphabet letters in their own names, and then to the letters they find in environmental print and in their early reading experiences. Figures 6-4 through 6-6 show several examples of children's early writing, each with an oral transcript written alongside it.

Eventually young authors realize that the choice of letter depends on the sound it represents, and they develop a growing repertoire of sight vocabulary words. The spellings which result will be discussed later in this chapter and in the next one.

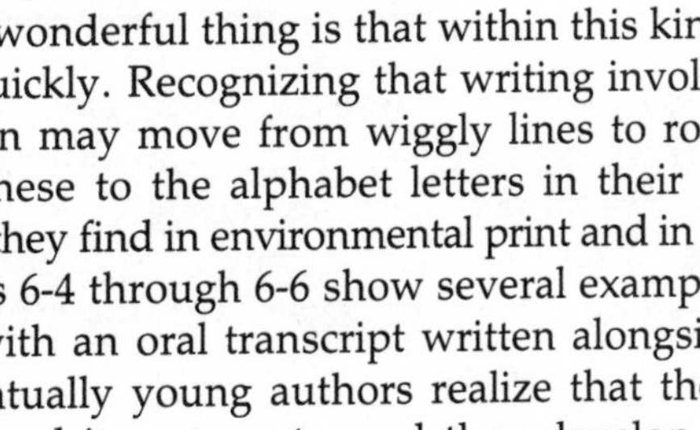

Figure 6 – 4

Translation:
Talyah Shapiro
I came from Israel.
I is [am] five.

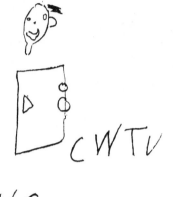

Figure 6 – 5

Translation:
Victor's watching television.

Meanwhile, some children will be more interested in developing their story line than in using the written code. These children may, for a time, bypass print altogether and convey their meaning through pictures. In our eagerness to see evidence of writing on the children's papers, it is easy to dismiss these picture-stories. It is, however, very helpful if we

Figure 6 – 6

Translation:
Today is
Johnny's
birthday.

can focus on what children are doing rather than on what we wish they would do. Usually more is happening in their drawings than meets the eye. Recently, a kindergarten teacher told me in despair that she had given up on one youngster. "It's not that he doesn't write," the teacher said. "I'd settle for drawings. But all he does is draw the same thing over and over." When I looked at the child's most recent book, I found that the teacher was right. On each page, the boy had drawn a little square person standing in midair—and that was all. Only the final page was different. On it there was a funny looking shape that could have been a flower. Because I wondered about the drawing (and because I had no encouraging words to say to the teacher), I asked the boy to tell me about the book, and to my astonishment, he responded by opening to page one and then reading the entire book to me, turning the pages as he went along.

"Once upon a time Mr. Toastman wanted to make a flower," he said, "so he got a seed." The boy showed me page one, with Mr. Toastman and the seed. "You can't see the seed," he explained. Then, on page two, Mr. Toastman got some dirt (and sure enough, there was a smudge on his hand), and on page three, he got some more dirt (a bigger smudge). The book ends with the seed growing into a flower.

When we attend to children's first books, we create a mood of appreciation in the classroom. It is a beautiful sight to enter these rooms and see clusters of children sharing their writing. Some may be lying together on the floor; perhaps two children will be sitting, arms linked, on a single chair. Everywhere youngsters are writing and reading writing. In the library corner, homemade stapled-together books are propped up on the shelves between the hardbound books, and there is a mood of celebration. Recently Hindy List, the Director of Curriculum in our model district, Brooklyn District 15, went into one such classroom to select several bits of early writing to duplicate. As she was leaving the room, a small boy came running after her, waving his piece and calling "Here, take mine, I'm an author too."

What a wonderful teacher that boy must have! His drawings were wobbly and sparse, and he seemed unsure whether lollipops or letters were preferable for the writing, but that youngster knew he belonged to the world of authors. What a gift!

Sometimes people ask me what I think is the most important message I could convey to teachers of young children. My answer is simple: I want teachers to delight in what youngsters do. There is nothing I want more than for those teachers to carry some of their children's writing into the staff room to share with each other, or for them to bring pieces home to share with their own families. I want teachers to have a wonderful time watching and admiring and working with young writers.

It is easy to enjoy teaching writing because the children do such terrific and funny things. I think of Ariel who came to me with a big wad of paper and said, "Would you staple my story together? Whenever I staple it, I do it the Jewish way (Hebrew books are read back to front). Would you staple it the regular way?"

Another time a child brought me a story about a peanut butter factory. He'd divided his page into four frames and on each one he'd drawn a picture of the factory. Solemnly the boy told me about how they slop the peanut butter about and then add nuts. After a while he paused. "It isn't real, you know," he whispered. "But don't tell her," and he motioned to the teacher, "She thinks it is."

I think also of Michelle. Shelley Harwayne, the Assistant Director of our Writing Project and a teacher-of-teachers throughout New York City, met Michelle in the hallway of P.S. 230 in Brooklyn. Michelle was looking at a ragged bit of paper and saying something as she walked.

"What do you have there?" Shelley asked her, crouching down so she was at her eye level.

"The Bible," she said. "My Mama gave it to me. She said it'll make me strong; it'll make me strong if I say the words, if I read it."

Michelle was right—she did have a little piece of the Bible in her hand. "Would you read it to me?" Shelley asked.

Holding the torn page upside down, Michelle looked at it and read, "Spinach, rice, beans . . . " then she looked at Shelley and said, "They make you strong, right?"

But my favorite story of all is the book, "Baby," written by five-year-old Marisol (see Figure 6-7).

There was not a single bit of print in Marisol's "Baby" story. Marisol "read" the story to a teacher-trainer in the Writing Project, JoAnn Curtis, which is how I know the oral version. Had Marisol read it to me, after listening to and enjoying it with her, I might have asked the youngster if we could work together on putting down some writing. Choosing a page to start on, I would ask her, "What should we write?" and if the child rattled off a long narrative, I would say, "What is the *one* thing we should put down first?" If she chose to label her drawing with a word, I would coax the child to say that word slowly with me, listening to the sounds in it. "*B-a-b-y*" we would say, "B-a-b-y." Then I would ask, "What sounds do you hear?"

Often the children can isolate a sound; in this instance it would probably be the /b/. The child might say, "/b/ /b/"and if she couldn't guess the letter, we might look at the alphabet to see if she could point to a letter which made the /b/ sound. If she had no idea, other children at the table might volunteer their ideas. Sometimes, of course, the children suggest the wrong letter—perhaps a *p*—but it is important to realize that, although the final product may be wrong, the children will have gone through an important process. I wonder what message I would give them if, at the end of all their sounding and searching, I dismissed their chosen letter and substituted a "correct" one?

Figure 6 – 7

"*The lady is going to have a baby.*"

"*They drove to the hospital.*"

"*And she had the baby. They were so happy and they loved the baby so much...*"

"*. . . they decided to get married!*"

If we are not afraid of children's errors, if we give them plenty of opportunity for writing, and if their classrooms provide rich literate environments, the children will learn quickly. By the end of kindergarten, many children are writing long stories such as the one shown in Figure 6-8.

The teacher's role is to provide the time, materials, and structure for all of this writing/talking/reading/listening, and by responding, extend what children do. Teachers can help by providing many functional reasons for writing. We can give children index cards and marker pens and invite them to label areas of the classroom. We can give them paper and envelopes

I Have a pair of skts.
I Like my skats.
You kow wut some
but win my bruthr
he pushis re ol over the pla
haha ha ha ha ha ha ha
and I sa pies sto pit;
and I er hrt and
At na I tor etil A

Figure 6 – 8

Translation:
I have a pair of skates.
I like my skates.
You know what?
But when my brother
he pushes me all over the place
"Ha ha ha ha ha ha ha,"
and I said, "Please stop it!"
And I felt hurt.
And I am telling.

and encourage them to write letters. Figures 6-9 and 6-10 depict several examples of letters written by kindergarten children.

In the "house-corner," we can leave a notepad beside the telephone so that children can take down pretend messages; in the make-believe kitchen, there can be paper for shopping lists. Children can make miniature books

MRS SLSR
WAN YOU
DAI I WAL
ILOVE TAC
YOU LOUR
LOVE BETH PIAS

Figure 6 – 9

Translation:
Mrs. Seltzer
When you die,
I will take your place.
I love you.

Love,
Beth

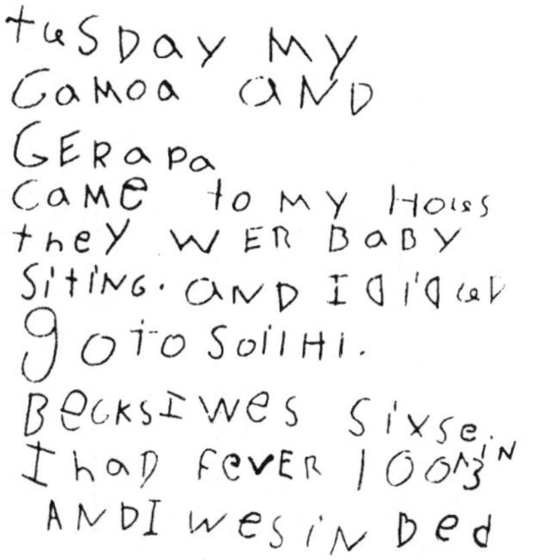

tuSDay MY
GaMoa aND
GERaPa
CaME to MY Houss
theY WER BaBY
Siting. aND I diq'ql
go to Soi'lHi.
BecksIwes Sixse.
I haD feveR 1 0ông'N
A NDI wes iN Ded

Figure 6 – 10
Tashena's absence note.

Translation:
Tuesday my grandma and
Grandpa came to my house.
They were babysitting and I
didn't go to school because I was
sick. I had a fever, 100 and 3,
and I was in bed.

for reading aloud to their dolls. In the block corner, we can give children manilla cards and marker pens, in this way encouraging them to make road signs and billboards. The calendar shown in Figure 6-11 (p. 46), which now hangs over my desk at Teachers College, was written by a five-year-old.

If the new hamster needs a name, children can register their vote on the clipboard beside his cage. Attendance can be taken by having students sign in every morning (Harste 1985). I recently found a sign on a make-believe grocery store in a kindergarten classroom (see Figure 6-12, p. 46).

Perhaps, in time, parents will learn from examples like these and begin providing more reading-writing opportunities at home. But most importantly, we hope parents will join us in celebrating and extending what young children do as language learners.

Figure 6 – 11 A Five-Year-Old's "Calander"

Figure 6 – 12

Translation:
Sorry that we have to close our store, but we are closing for the holiday. We will reopen on April 30th.

7

first grade:
an era of confidence

My first message, then, is that children can write sooner than we ever dreamed was possible. Most children come to school knowing a handful of letters, and with these they can write poems and calendars, letters, stories, labels, and songs. They will learn to write by writing, and by living with the sense of "I am one who writes." This self-perception will give children the eyes to see, and they will notice the conventions of written language everywhere. They will learn punctuation and spelling from billboards and environmental labels and books. They will ask about the letters that initial their father's briefcases, they will imitate their big sister's cursive writing, and in doing so, they will gather a knowledge of print conventions. Their growth is spectacular. All over New York City, there are five- and six-year-olds who write with voice, skill, and confidence. The examples shown in Figures 7-1 through 7-3 show some of the more advanced stages that we see in kindergarten and first-grade classrooms.

We can best help young children grow as writers when we understand some of the sequences of development that commonly occur in the early grades. In order to suggest developmental trends that may be evident in a first-grade classroom, I will oversimplify and divide writing into rehearsal, drafting, revision, and editing.

Rehearsal

Five-year-old Chris opened his book to a blank page and took hold of his pencil. Cheerfully, I asked, "What are you going to write?" The boy stared

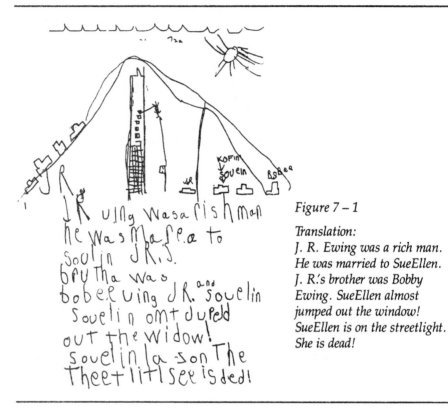

JR uing Wasa rish man
he Was Mafe.a to
Soul in J R .S.
bru Tha Wa s
bobee uing J R. and Souel in
Souel in omt duPeld
out the widow!
Souel in la son The
Theet litl see is ded!

Figure 7 – 1

Translation:
J. R. Ewing was a rich man. He was married to SueEllen. J. R.'s brother was Bobby Ewing. SueEllen almost jumped out the window! SueEllen is on the streetlight. She is dead!

I visit my Gramr
the nrsing Home
was verc nevle the
Hous. som tim's
I felt/dePrcsskd)
Becas it wus
Sickanig Bcase
taey had tow Bs op
tar nose and
otres as

and the nrseing
home wus Deypricging
be coes taye were
in weell chrse and
it smelld like ballont PU
!!! and the pashits
are Sicotic

Figure 7 – 2

Translation:
I visit my Grandmother. The nursing home was very near the house. Sometimes I felt depressed because it was sickening because they had tubes up their noses and other reasons. And the nursing home was depressing because they were in wheelchairs and it smelled like blank [because this is a swear word] P.U.!!!! And the patients are psychotic.

re 7 – 3

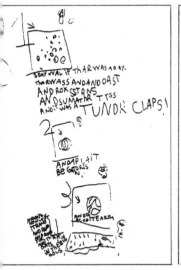

nslation:

One day, well if there was a day. There was sand and dust and rocks and stones and some other
ngs. And it was a thunderclaps! 2. And a planet began to rise. 3. And they called it Earth.
And do you know what? It rained and rained and rained for thirty days in the big holes. 5. And
we began to grow. 6. And the first animal was a little dinosaur. When the Earth turns around
sun, the sun turns around the Earth. The sun isn't really a big ball. It is really a giant star. It
really far and so it looks like a circle. Don't listen to the newspaperman, all that about the sun.
n't be afraid because the sun will last for ever. That's all there is.

at me as if astounded by the stupidity of my question. "How should I know," he said. "I haven't drawed it yet."

For a few minutes, Chris glanced around the classroom and then he began to draw. He made the standard figure of a person; his dad had taught him to draw people, so now he followed those directions with care. Partway through the drawing, Chris announced, "This is gonna be my brother. He's fighting," and he added a giant fist to the person as if to symbolize the fight. Then he drew a second person, again with an oversized hand. "We're fighting," he added and began to write.

Like many youngsters, Chris rehearses for writing by drawing. This does not mean that his drawings accomplish the purposes we, as adults, normally connect with rehearsal. As he draws, Chris does not weigh one topic against another, nor does he anticipate an audience's response to his story. He doesn't even plan the direction his writing will take. Just as when he plays in the block area, he does not begin with armchair speculation over what he will build but with piling one block on top of another until he announces, "I'm makin' a tower"; so, too, in the writing area he does not begin by thinking about his final product but by drawing the conventional person; then, in the middle of drawing, he announces, "This is gonna be my brother."

For older children, rehearsal involves considering various topics, planning a story, anticipating an audience's response and pushing beyond writer's block. Each of these functions is dependent upon a wide time-space span, and Chris, like many kindergarten and first-grade children, tends to operate in the present tense, in the here-and-now. He rarely anticipates his to-morrows. He doesn't fret about whether his writing topic is "good enough" any more than he frets about whether his block tower will be acceptable. He writes the way he plays blocks—for the sake of the activity rather than for the creation of a final product.

Drawing has an important role to play. The act of drawing and the picture itself both provide a supportive scaffolding within which the piece of writing can be constructed. When he writes, Chris is like a newborn foal; he stands on shaky legs. When he does not have a visual memory for a word, he sounds it out: "Fight-ing." He isolates a sound, /f/, then asks, "How do you spell /f/?" When no one answers, he scans the alphabet, guesses at a letter, and puts it onto paper. Meanwhile, he's forgotten what he wanted to write. What a relief it must be to return to the drawing, to darkening his brother's fist! As he carefully fills in the hand, Chris remembers what he wanted to write, and so he returns to print. Back and forth he switches, from drawing to writing, then back to drawing again, moving between the relief and stability of one media and the challenge of the other.

Alongside a crayoned picture of two cars crashing, another child writes BOOM. This child is able to convey her story through a single word, and

Figure 7 – 4

Translation:
When you get
to be a big person . . .
cemetery.

she can do this only because the word is lodged within the context of the picture. Most of the child's meaning is carried by the picture. Not only the act of drawing but also the picture itself can provide a supportive framework for young writers. In time, children learn to create autonomous, explicit texts, but during their early forays into writing, they often embed much of their meaning in the picture rather than in the text. Figure 7-4 shows another example. In nine words and a picture, this youngster has made a powerful statement about the meaning of life.

I imagine drawings also help youngsters with the problem of selection. The world involves such a rapid flux of activities and ideas, and writing is so slow, so limited, that selection is a problem even for skilled writers. How much more true this must be for beginning writers! In their drawings, children take one bit of the world and hold it still for a moment; then, with the picture lying in front of them, they begin work on the accompanying words.

Kindergarten children's drawings often hold the world totally still. Their pictures tend to be a collection of objects placed here and there across their page: a boy, a dog, a house. It is a great day when a thin line appears on the bottom of the paper. With common ground comes the possibility of relationship: the boy and dog are beside the house. Will they enter it?

Do they live there? For a while, the action is only implicit: the drawings show only a static frontal line-up. But soon, through spaghetti arms, or through lines, dots, and arrows, as in the pictures in Figures 7-5 through 7-7, action enters into the drawing.

Figure 7 – 5

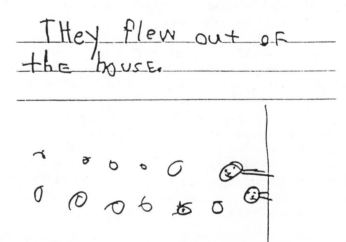

Figure 7 – 6

Susan Sowers found that when action enters children's writing, their texts tend to change from "all-about" or attribute books into narratives. In November, only 16 percent of Mrs. Giacobbe's children's published books were narratives; by May, the percentage had reached 78 percent (Sowers 1979). Sowers classified a book as a narrative if it was chronologically ordered. The examples shown in Figure 7-8 illustrate the differences between narratives and "all-about" books.

At Atkinson Elementary School, it was when children began drawing their figures in profile that the biggest breakthrough into narrative seemed to occur. Now horses could be led on a rope, people could kiss and dance together, dogs could drink out of their bowls. Characters could interact with each other and with their settings.

Because of the many ways in which drawing contributes to early writing, I encourage kindergarten and first-grade teachers to provide their children with marker pens and with either unlined or experience-chart paper, preferably stapled into small, informal books. Our provision of materials affects children's choice of activities: with young children, the medium is often the message.

A word of caution. I recently visited several primary classrooms where the drawings were no longer helping the writing. In several instances, a child's choice of writing topics was limited by the youngster's pictorial repertoire. One young fellow was very skillful at drawing the Pink Panther, so, although he had nothing to say about Pink Panther, the character starred in every book he wrote. Other children were drawing after they wrote rather than before; the pictures served as final punctuation at the end of writing. "I'm done," the pictures signified. How much better it

Figure 7 – 7

Figure 7 – 8

NARRATIVE

ALL ABOUT BOOKS

YesrDaY
a old lady
Fell She did
Wont eniBu
To HelP Her
When The
Pilace Come
She STil
didt Wont
HelP When TreeBu
Come She When

Translation:
Yesterday an old lady fell. She didn't want anybody to help her. When the police came she still didn't want help. When the ambulance came she went.

1   My alive crab

Peter Fitzgerald

he lives in darty watter.

3   I Put him in matcs.

He liks shade.

5   He runs very fast.

He is a boy

7   I had him for 2 months.

He eats seaweed and fishfood.

9   He desen't nip.

nip!

I keep my crab in thes.

A house is on fyere and ol ov the shops ar coming to hlppe the people and the fagin is os a coming to and the phcdis came to the end.

Translation:
A house is on fire and all of the troops are coming to help the people and the fire engine is also coming too and the police is coming too. The End.

would have been had the children ended writing with a peer-conference. Instead of creating premature closure, conferences help children reread and learn from what they have done.

In classrooms where drawing no longer seemed an effective means for rehearsal, I asked teachers, "Why not steer them away from drawings?"

"But you told us young kids should draw first," they answered, baffled. It is important to remember that no solution works for every child and no solution works forever. We can introduce drawing as a form of rehearsal, but then we must watch for signs indicating whether drawing is extending or limiting the child's writing. If it limits the writing, then perhaps it needs to be given separate time and space, for clearly drawing is important to children's growth, if not to their writing.

Drafting

Earlier in this chapter, we saw the growth in spelling which often occurs during kindergarten and first grade. Children begin by writing with initial consonants only, but soon they are using initial and final consonants, with a sprinkling of other sounds thrown in. Before long, young writers use a letter to represent each sound in a word. Their choice of letters is not always correct, but research has shown that it is usually logical. Many children, for example, use letter names to represent sounds. *Are* is spelled *R, you* is spelled *U.* The /ch/ sound is often spelled with an *H* (hai*ch*) and the /w/ sound with a *Y* (*why*). For a fuller discussion of the logic in children's early spelling, I recommend *The Beginnings of Writing* by Temple, Nathan and Burris.

Children's growth in spelling is so spectacular that it is easy to overlook other aspects of their growth in writing, including changes in conventions, voicing behaviors, and story content. When children write before they read, they often don't know how written words are laid out on a page. Five-year-old Mark Goulet wrote his name like this:

TELUO

MARKG

Mark was troubled by the layout of his name. Adding an arrow, he said, "Now they'll know where to put their eye."

TELUO

MARKG

In Elizabeth's early writing, there were no spaces at all between words. Her stories looked like the example in Figure 7-9.

Figure 7 – 9

Translation:
Spring is nice to me. It is wonderful
weather. I like it very much. I like it and I
like it very much. The End.

Once children begin to realize that words need to be separated, they often go to the other extreme and write one word on each line so their stories look like the one shown in Figure 7-10, written a few weeks later by Elizabeth.

Other children insert dashes, dots, or slashes into their texts to separate words. Not uncommonly, they are not sure where one word ends and another begins. *Ham and eggs* is written HAMANAGS, *Steve Austin* is STE FSDN. *All of a sudden* is ALLUVA SDN, and *other reasons* is OTRSNS.

Figure 7 – 10

Translation:
Once I had a strawberry plant and it grew
strawberries until the bugs came to eat the
berries.

When kindergarten and first-grade children write, they often use darkened letters, oversized print, or capitals to add the sound of a voice to their print. After six-year-old Brad put the word *pull* into his story, he returned to it and carefully darkened each of the letters.

"Why'd you do that?" Don Graves wondered.

"Because I want them to know to really PULL," Brad answered. Hearing this, Brad's teacher showed the boy how to use exclamation marks and soon they were spreading from child to child throughout the classroom. "I like them," one child told me. "You use them when you yell, and when you are excited. Usually I put them at the end of every line, but if it's somebody's birthday or the guy's dying, I put them at the end of every word." Another youngster told me exclamation marks are really called "happy marks."

Quotation marks are equally popular in kindergarten and first-grade classrooms, for they, too, give voice to print. One six-year-old put comic-strip balloons around spoken sections of her stories until Mrs. Giacobbe showed her the conventional way to represent speech. Like exclamation marks, quotations spread quickly. Even very young children want their characters to talk like real people. By the end of the year, 30 percent of Mrs. Giacobbe's first graders were using quotation marks correctly in their stories.

In addition to changes in the use of conventions, observers of young children will quickly notice changes in the voicing behaviors that accompany writing. For Andrea, as for many young writers, writing is deeply embedded in oral language. Speech—like drawing—provides a scaffolding within which the text can be constructed. A tremendous amount of talk surrounds the production of even just a few written words, as this transcript shows:

TRANSCRIPT	COMMENTARY
Andrea is singing to herself as she draws. "My little caterpillar, my little caterpillar, little, little, little . . ."	*She voices as part of language play.*
"There, that's my caterpillar," she says as she finishes her drawing. "Now, let's see . . ."	*This is procedural talk. Perhaps it orients Andrea, helping her organize the task before her.*
"I've got two pages done, now, let's see."	*She gauges her progress. Talk keeps her company.*
"I-like-my-caterpillar."	*She isolates what she will write and says it slowly.*

TRANSCRIPT	COMMENTARY
"I. . ."	*She moves from whole to part. Here she isolates her first word.*
"I" she says, writing the letter.	*Procedural talk.*
"I like my caterpillar."	*She reads what she has written and adds on, through speech, what she will write next. She moves from part to whole.*
"I-like, like. . ."	*She isolates her next word and repeats it, listening to it.*
"/llll/" "L!"	*She sounds out the word, names the letter.*
"Like. /ll-i/. . ."	*She moves from part to whole, then sounds out the whole again.*

As children's writing becomes more fluent, the gap between their speech and their writing decreases, and they are more apt to write without verbal accompaniment. The running commentary that once surrounded writing becomes unnecessary. In my research, I have found that when youngsters face new challenges, however, their vocalizations often return, as if they once again need a supportive context for their writing.

As a child's confidence and skill in writing increases, the youngster is apt to produce several pieces of writing in a single session. For a while, children write *more* rather than *longer* stories. Even when a child is composing on paper stapled into books, each page is apt to hold an entirely new piece of writing. It is a step forward for children to produce longer pieces. Often they do this first by sustaining a single topic over several pages, one sentence and one picture to a page. It would seem that the picture plays the role of a conversational partner, allowing the youngster to alternate between short bursts of writing and an interval when the other person— in this case, the other activity—nudges the "conversation" onward. Perhaps part of the difficulty in creating a single page of extended text is that the child must be able and willing to carry on a written monologue.

When writing consists of only a label or a sentence alongside a picture, neither organization nor gaps in content are vital concerns. Longer pieces of writing—whether in a book or on a single page—provide new challenges. As pieces of writing become more extended, the distinction between narratives and "all-about" books (attribute books) becomes more apparent (Sowers 1979), each form posing its own possibilities and problems. In attribute books, children list what they know or feel about a topic. Jen lists information (and misinformation) about worms; Rosie tells about colors, and the feelings and images she relates to each one. These inventories of information are an extension of children's early propensity to make collections, and they are the seeds of both content area reports and expository writing. Early on, attribute books seem more prevalent than narratives, but they also become more problematic. Let me explain.

When children write attribute books there is no sequence of events which propells them to add on. Each sentence can be the last one in the text. Jen could write only this line:

I LIK WRMS

or she could sustain the text with one more sentence, with two more, with fifteen more. *The End* could be inserted at any point in this piece:

I LIK WORMS. THEY ARE KUT. THEY
HAF FET. SUM WRMS ARE FAT. SUM
WRMS ARE TIN. WRMS ARE SKIGLE.

There is no built-in propulsion to continue as there is in a narrative, nor is there a ready-made ending. In a personal narrative, the sequence is provided by the topic, by the chronology of events. Sometimes, especially early on, children bypass the linear sequence of time and tell the entire event in the first line:

WE WINT TO THE BECH AND WE KAM HOME.

When children approach personal narratives in a step-by-step fashion, their topics provide both a propulsion to continue and an organizational framework.

WE GOT UP, REDE FOR THE DAY AT THE BECH. WE HAD BEKFIST AND
WE GOT IN THE CAR. WE DOVE TO THE BECH . . .

This is less true of attribute books and perhaps this is why they often contain a hodgepodge of vaguely related categories of information. One page in a child's book tells about kinds of dogs, the next page about training dogs, the next page returns to kinds of dogs, and the next, to cats. As books become longer, they often become more chaotic. And so, especially in late first grade and in second grade, it sometimes helps if children are encouraged to divide their "all-about" books into chapters with a table of contents, as Ramon has done:

ALL ABOUT DOGS

chapter 1   kinds of dogs
chapter 2   training dogs
chapter 3   taking care of a dog
chapter 4   a dog I had once

Revision

Five-year-old Mellisa had only been in kindergarten for a few days. On a sheet of construction paper she'd written a line of letters and from them she read, "Dear Daddy, I love you. Love, Mellisa." Crouched alongside Mellisa, my arm around her, I listened to the story. "You really love him, don't you," I said, confirming what I'd heard.

"Yes, I love him because he lives with me," she solemnly answered.

I nodded, thinking to myself that having a father who lives with you *is* becoming a big thing. Turning the paper from one side to the other, I asked Mellisa, "Where did you put that, Mellisa?" as if I was surprised that such important information hadn't been included. Melissa told me there wasn't enough room, so I took her hand and we headed to the writing corner where I stapled two more pieces of construction paper onto the first. "Now you have a lot of space," I said, and the little girl returned to the patch of floor which served as her desk. From across the room, I watched as she counted the blank pages in her newly formed book, shrugged, and began filling them up. The cardinal rule in kindergarten and first grade seems to be, "Thou Shalt Fill Up the Space."

Adding on is a very natural part of young children's writing. It can be regarded as an early form of revision or as part of drafting, for there is no clear division between the two. Children write, and if given the chance to share their pieces with a responsive listener, they often realize they have more to tell and someone who hopes they will tell it. Before long, children are "making stories grow" on their own: one page becomes three, a six-inch text is extended into a giant scroll. Children enjoy stapling and taping, and they quickly learn to add on.

They are less quick to reread their own emerging texts, to shift from being writers to being readers, from pushing ahead to looking back. This is not unique to writing. In all they do, young children seem to be always moving on. They finish a drawing and stuff it into their desk without a second glance. They finish a painting and immediately their attention shifts to whatever is next on their schedule. In writing, adding-on without looking back leads to stories which are a collage of pieces held together with staples and tape. One way to support young children's growth in writing, then, is by encouraging them to read what they have written to the children working alongside them, and most of all, to themselves.

Realizing this, many primary-grade teachers encourage children to work at tables so they will interact with each other (and with their texts) throughout the workshop. Sometimes teachers also set aside areas for more extensive peer-conferences. Some primary teachers begin or end the writing workshop by asking each student to each find a conference partner and to have a brief conference.

"But are five- and six-year-olds really capable of holding effective peer conferences?" teachers ask. The question calls to mind a conference I recently observed involving two first graders. The youngsters pulled chairs close together, then each girl took hold of her story and, in unison, they read their stories to each other. Neither child listened and neither child was listened to, but both girls seemed pleased with their conference. They happily trotted back to the writing table and tackled writing with renewed vigor. In later chapters I will show how we can help young children with their peer-conferences, but it is also important to recognize that even when neither child really listens to the other, these interactions serve a purpose.

Although adding-on is probably the most common form of revision, youngsters can also learn to make their written texts more explicit. Information contained in the picture and in the surrounding oral commentary can be moved into the text. Six-year-old Dana read her recipe to Mrs. Giacobbe:

Put the macaroni in the water and stir it on and off. After ten minutes
it is done and you put the cheese in. Then you eat it all up.

Before Mrs. Giacobbe could respond, Dana added another bit of information—orally. "It'll get nice and bubbly, the tip-top will get all bubbly, and that's how you know it's done."

"Oh, I see!" Mrs. Giacobbe said, "I'll know if it's done because it gets all bubbly. Are you going to include that in the recipe, Dana, because I didn't know about that?"

"No," Dana shook her head. "People should know that. If they don't, then I'll invite them to my birthday and I'll *show* them how."

Mrs. Giacobbe tried again. "Dana," she said, "what if Chris takes this book home and his mother is going to follow your recipe. How will she know about how it gets nice and bubbly?"

"Okay, okay," Dana said and began inserting the missing information into her text.

Sometimes young children's revision involves rearranging the pages in their books. After six-year-old Sharon told Greg that his story about the football game went hippety-hop from one thing to another, for example, Greg took apart his book and, spreading the pages in front of him, reordered them. When Shanti wrote about her birthday party, she put the roller skating before the cake, but when her friends pointed out that the cake came first, she rearranged the pages accordingly.

Then, too, when first-grade children jumble several stories into one, revision may involve dividing a book into smaller pieces. One child proudly showed me her four-page-long book. Although the story was entitled "My Hamster," it was only partially about the hamster. There were large sections about the girl's father, and others about her school. After admiring the length of her masterpiece, I said, "What I'm wondering about is why the title is 'My Hamster' when parts are about your father, school, and other things." The youngster was quiet, her eyes scanning the story. Then she said "I know" and jumping up, she ran to the writing corner. I expected her to return with scissors, in recognition of the fact that there were three stories in one. When she returned, however, she had instead brought a pen. Beside the title "My Hamster" she added, in her own spelling, "And My Father and School and Other Stuff."

My favorite revision story, however, involved not the title of a story, but the ending. Six-year-old Lori had written a sad tale about a princess who was attacked by a witch, and when the princess ran away, the witch followed. The tale ended abruptly with the words *The End*.

"What happened next?" Mrs. Giacobbe asked, as if she couldn't stand the suspense. Lori answered slowly, and it seemed clear she was making up the ending as she spoke. Mrs. Giacobbe listened intently to the conclusion of the tale. Then she said, "You know, Lori, I think maybe you should change the end—because I didn't know what happened next."

Lori nodded and, pulling the book close to her, she opened it to the last page where she had penciled:

The

n

d

This time, she set to work with bright colored crayons, revising the ending until it read:

It would be easy to look at this incident and say, "The intervention didn't work." But although Lori did not change the ending of her tale, she did reread her draft, and perhaps she even saw her writing through the eyes of a reader. Revision means, quite literally, to see again and it needs to be interpreted in the broadest sense. Sometimes revision involves reseeing our subject, sometimes it involves pulling back to take a look at our emerging text, sometimes it involves changing

The
n
d

to something like

TH E
N
B

The point is to use writing as a way to experiment, to reflect, and to learn.

Editing

When I first taught young children, I encouraged them to use word banks, lists of key words, and picture dictionaries as resources during writing. If they wanted still more assistance, they could line up beside me for spelling help or they could dictate the story, and I would write it for them. I am, to this day, convinced that none of this was harmful to children. I was warm, supportive, helpful, and, above all, well-intentioned. But I do not recommend any of these things anymore, and I want to give my reasons.

First of all, I have begun to realize that concern for spelling competes with concern for content. When children continually interrupt themselves during writing to worry about or search for a correct spelling they often lose track of what they wanted to say in the first place. These interruptions produce a staccato sort of writing, and they prevent writers from finding their own pace and rhythm. Whether children get the spelling word from a dictionary, a word book, a list of key words, or from their teacher makes little difference, because in each instance they interrupt writing to worry about spelling. I would much rather they learn, from the start, to focus on content and language during a first draft. Therefore, if I wanted primary-school children to find correct spellings in dictionaries or word banks, I would ask them to do this *after* drafting and revision, when the piece was done.

"But what if the children just call out the words they need, and I write them on the chalkboard?" teachers ask. "That takes no time at all."

I have two problems with this system. First, teachers spend all their time writing words on the chalkboard, and this time could better be spent observing children, conferring with them, and enriching the classroom environment. Second, why should spelling be the teacher's responsibility— we know teachers can spell. Isn't it more important for *children* to have the chance to visualize the word, listening to its sounds and hypothesizing on a way to spell it?

"But my kids *keep* asking for spelling help," teachers tell me.

I tell them, "That's because you keep giving it." If we are clear and consistent, children stop asking for spellings and become independent writers. It is when we provide intermittent reinforcement, sometimes giving out spellings and sometimes not, that children keep on asking. I want to be very, very clear about one thing. I am not saying that spelling or punctuation does not matter. What I am saying, instead, is that it is more important for young children to be *learners* of spelling than for them (for us) to produce correctly spelled texts. Also, concern about spelling belongs in the final stages of the writing process.

I *do* believe that five- and six-year-old children should be encouraged to edit their drafts, and that a simple form of editing can be introduced during the first few days of a writing workshop. On the second or third day of a workshop in the New York City schools, we often bring in "The Big Blue Box" for final work. During the mini-lesson, we tell children that, when they receive their writing from the day before, they are to look it over and think, "Is this my very best? Am I done or do I have more to say?" If they are finished then they can put the piece into the Big Blue Box and begin a new one. (Eventually the Big Blue Box will hold writing folders, and children will insert their pieces into their folders.) Before the piece goes into the box, however, children need to edit by following directions on the sign above the box. The sign might say:

1 Author's name?
2 Page numbers?
3 Does it make sense?
4 Title?
5 Date?

Later, the editing checklist can be more complex, but for a while, the most important thing is that children form the habit of rereading their pieces to check for certain things.

Afterward, depending somewhat on class size, we can go over a child's paper and hold an editing conference with the youngster. These conferences are described in more detail in chapter 20.

Before turning our attention to second grade, I want to give a special tribute to teachers of young children. Recently my colleague Hindy List found a third grader who was writing about the "Good Old Days" of kindergarten and first grade. I think the piece provides a well-deserved compliment to teachers of young children.

THE FIRST DAY OF KINDERGARDEN

When I first came to this school, when I started kindergarden, I was very nervous. But the next day I got to know some of the children and we sang songs together. It was a lot of fun. Oh—those were the good old days. We did not have so much work then, but now I am growing big and I am jammed full with work. But I am still thinking about kindergarden and first grade and all the fun that I had. Sometimes I wish that time flies back to the kindergarden. I was so smart back then. You know what? Some day I'll be a kindergarden or first grade teacher myself.

The End.

second grade: new concerns and new competency

Six years ago I wrote an overview of the writing process approach to teaching writing for *National Elementary School Principal*. After introducing the basic concepts of the writing process, I illustrated them with descriptions of first- and third-grade writing workshops. I told myself the choice of first and third grade was arbitrary: I simply wanted to suggest a spectrum of grades. In truth, it was no accident that I bypassed second grade. I had nothing "in general" to say about seven-year-old writers.

In some second grades, children write fluently. With carefree confidence, they fill fat homemade books with incidents and feelings strung together on a chain of "and thens." In other second grades, children slowly mark their names onto their pages. If the pencil slips, causing one letter to slant against its neighbor, the youngster discards the entire page, slowly and carefully beginning yet another paper, another false start. These—and other—extremes are so common among second-grade writers that for a long time the only generalization I could make was that theirs was a land of opposites.

Six years later, second grade still impresses me as a land of opposites, but underneath the differing writing behaviors I now suspect there are general growth currents. During first and second grade, most children seem to move in these directions:

- From writing for oneself toward writing also for an internalized audience.
- From writing for the sake of the activity itself (all process) toward writing also to create a final product.

- From less to more fluency.
- From writing episodes that do not begin before or last beyond the actual penning of a text, toward broader writing episodes that encompass looking ahead and looking back, anticipating and critiquing.

The diverse writing behaviors of second graders may represent varying ways in which youngsters deal with these general growth currents. In order to look at this more closely, let us once again oversimplify, dividing writing into rehearsal, drafting, revision, and editing.

Rehearsal

"I'm broke," Greg said, pushing his chair away from the desk. "I'm clear out of stories. I'm out of space stories, I'm out of car stories. I'm broke."

Jenn, another second grader, has begun six stories in three days—and she has discarded each one. Her writing folder is a compost of false starts, of stories which trail off after a few lines. But Jenn's mother tells us that late at night, Jenn often sneaks a flashlight into bed with her and, safely hidden from the eyes of others, writes story after story, filling books with the large, carefree letters and animal drawings that were the trademark of her first grade books.

Like Greg and Jenn, Maria is also seven, but unlike them, she has no difficulty getting started writing. She had just completed "the longest book ever." On a huge collection of papers, stapled together by Maria herself, she has told about each activity and each meal throughout each day of her vacation.

Both extremes are common in second grade classrooms, but it is Greg and Jenn who are showing totally new writing behaviors. They are only a few months older and a few inches taller than they were in late first grade, but their writing habits have changed markedly. Gone is their easy confidence. "It is as if the protective cloak of egocentricity has been taken from them," Graves has said. Jenn and Greg are aware of an audience. With audience awareness comes worry. "Will the kids like my story?" "It's messy. It's stupid. It's dumb." For the first time, they suffer writer's block.

Ironically, their worries—so common in second grade-children—are a sign of growth. First graders rarely agonize over topic choice or fret about whether their stories will be good enough. As we saw in chapter 6, first graders often write as they play blocks: for the sheer fun of the activity more than for an eventual product, for themselves more than for an audience. As these children become older they are more able to distance themselves and to see their work through the eyes of another. They look back to assess what they have done and they look forward toward an eventual audience. These abilities bring new concerns.

Developmental psychologist Howard Gardner characterizes the seven- and eight-year-old child by saying that now, for the first time, the child in the middle of singing or dancing will stop and anxiously ask, "Is this right?" Gardner claims that because seven-year-old children want to use words "right," their use of figurative language declines. In their drawings, they replace expressive dynamic pictures with spiked suns and rows of tulips. In their playground games, these children argue over how to play "the right way." The seven-year-olds' concern with the right way to do things, combined with their new ability to look ahead and to look back, means that rehearsal takes on a very different meaning for them than it does for their younger counterparts (Gardner 1980, 150).

More than anything else, during rehearsal Greg and Jenn need to realize they have something worth writing about. If they do not learn this, they will probably resort to the formalized, voiceless stories which are so common in classrooms where children rarely write. Writing well requires an act of confidence. A writer implicitly claims, "I have something important to say." When an author speaks out clearly, forcefully, and honestly, the writing is strong. It is this forthright, honest quality which brings charm to many first-grade pieces. First graders often assume that their ideas are worth writing about (after all, these children are the center of their universe). Second graders, like the rest of us, tend to be less self-assured, and so rehearsal becomes a time for finding topics, for pushing beyond writer's block.

In later chapters, we will look in some detail at ways in which teachers can help youngsters find and explore topics. Some of these methods are more appropriate for second graders than others. Whereas drawing is a predominant form of rehearsal for first graders and mapping may be for fifth graders, talking is particularly effective for second graders. Let me explain.

In kindergarten and first grade, many children convey their meaning more easily through drawing than through print. Drawing, therefore, can provide a supportive scaffolding for the writing. Because more information is embedded in the pictures than in the print, drawing provides a horizon and leads the child deeper into the writing. In a sense, our goal is to help children's writing catch up with their drawing.

By second grade, writing has often surpassed drawing. Although these children may still find it easier to draw than to write, most find it easier to embed meaning into a written text than into a drawing. When second graders draw before each new page of writing, the pictures often hold back the written texts. In this example, the story line is little more than a collection of captions.

Here is my little dog. We are in the kitchen.
Now he is happy! I am happy too.
Knock, knock. "Who is there?"

Here is my father. "What do you have?"
I rip off the paper.
Now I am happier.

For most second graders, talking rather than drawing can provide a horizon and a supportive scaffolding. Just as in first grade, where the goal was to have writing catch up to drawing, in second grade, the goal is to have writing catch up to talking. The goal is fluency and voice, for the lilt of oral language to come through in a child's writing.

There will come a time when writing surpasses talking. When I write, I still aim in early drafts for fluency, for the rhythm of oral language. But in later drafts, I expect my writing to become more explicit, more layered with meaning, more structured than oral language. For me, rehearsal includes abstracting: mapping, jotting notes, and thinking analytically.

But in second grade, chatting about one's subject with an interested friend seems to be an ideal method for rehearsal. Because the focus of these discussions is on content, they draw the writer's attention away from conventions and rules. Because the discussions are interactive, writers learn not only that they have something to say and a voice with which to say it, but also that somebody values what they have to say. When I work with second graders, I often encourage them to interview each other before they write. "Find a partner," I tell the children, "and a quiet place in the classroom. Then take turns telling each other about your topics." Soon there are no quiet places in the classroom!

The first interviews are invariably happy disasters. Roger says, "I'm going to write about my grandma's new car. She is going to take me for a ride in it." Mark cuts him off to announce, "I'm going to write about a big dinosaur and he eats a lady up. In his mouth, he just chews her up." End of interview.

Sometimes I demonstrate interviewing skills by publicly interviewing one child and asking the others to note what I do during the interview, or by letting children interview me and varying the tone of voice in my answers in order to illustrate the effect of good questions. As the year goes on, I might talk to the children about the importance of listening, or about letting writers lead us to the topics they care about, the need for open-ended questions, and the importance of following a line of questioning. But I think it is easy to put too much emphasis on teaching the skills of peer conferences. Even if children simply chat with each other about their topics and their writing, these discussions are important.

This trust does not mean that I turn my back on whatever happens during peer interviews. On the contrary, I find it helpful to listen as youngsters talk together. I began doing this in order to supervise the children, but soon found my respectful interest elevated the peer conferences in children's eyes. It also became a way to learn about children's interactions with each other. For example, I found that inadvertently interviewers often led writers exclusively toward "all-about" writing. If a child begins by saying, "I'm going to write about my bike," the natural response seemed to be, "Tell me about your bike," or "What kind of bike do you have?" Both lines of questioning nudged writers toward listing attributes about their bikes. If teachers see this pattern in conferences, they may want to model a different form of question, saying for example, "Tell me about things you've done with your bike."

A second recurring problem I see in second graders' peer-conferences is that once some children have told their story to a friend, it is hard for them to cycle back to the beginning of that story in order to write it down. Instead, after telling a story they write a sequel to it or even an entirely different piece. It may help if conferences end with the listeners asking the writers how he or she might begin the story.

Second grade *is* a land of opposites. Rehearsal will mean something very different to one child than it will to another. For some children, drawing will continue to be the most helpful form of rehearsal. For others, talking will be more satisfactory. Some children, even after talking with each other, will consider their topics stupid. These are the youngsters who resort to retelling the plot of movies they've seen or to writing over and over on the same theme. But this will not characterize all second graders. Some will quickly see that their lives are full of topics, and therefore rehearsal will not involve generating topics so much as selecting among them. "I think up topics all the time," Randalio explained to me. "If we have a beautiful Christmas tree, I think that I could write about it. If I'm playing car races with my friend, I think I could write about it. Choosing is the hard part."

Second grade is not unlike adolescence. Both are times of vulnerability. Writers in both age groups sometimes feel awkward and self-conscious, and they sometimes hide behind hasty efforts and comfortable convention. But the sense of audience, the increasing abilities, and the growing self-consciousness, which make both second grade and adolescence times of vulnerability and awkwardness, can also make them times of fervor, energy, and involvement. If both second graders and adolescents are known for writing short, conventional little pieces, they are also known for writing the "longest stories ever." Perhaps our goal is to help them move from one to the other.

Drafting

When I first launch second graders in the writing process, I often find that the children spend more time on their margins and headings than on the stories. After a few blissful moments when everyone is busily working (mostly on their margins and headings), one child will jump up from his seat. "I'm done," he says, "What do I do now?"

Another jumps up. "I'm done." Then another, another, and another. Their pieces are short. Perhaps this is because a few sentences sufficed in first grade, but since then, the children's abilities have grown while their expectations have not. Or perhaps it is because in second grade there are fewer built-in nudges. A year earlier, many of these children alternated between drawing and writing, their pictures fueling the text. They wrote in books, and the sequence of pages lured them on. Now they are given single sheets of paper without space for drawings.

Then too, children may not approach writing with the intention of building a story or unfolding a line of thought. Often the child's first line conveys the entire message, as in this example: "For my birthday, I got a lot of presents and then I came home and went to bed." This youngster has set herself up for a brief story, or at least for a story that can end at any point. Within a few minutes she is done. No wonder it is like popcorn: "I'm done," "I'm done," "I'm done."

What is the teacher to do? A dozen children believe they are finished, and we are supposed to have one-to-one conferences with each one? In no other elementary grade is the problem so difficult. In first grade, children will happily occupy their time by drawing. By the middle of second grade and certainly by third grade, many children sustain work longer, and consequently the "I'm dones" are not confined to one fifteen minute time slot. But when writing is first launched in many second grades, teacher-student conferences present a mammoth challenge.

"Keep working," I have told second graders, trying to encourage the group with one hand while I conduct super-quick conferences with the other. But the line behind me grows, and if I take time to notice, I find children leaving our hasty conferences with puzzled, unhappy looks. If I miss these signals, the drafts themselves contain more warnings that something is wrong. When I urge children to keep working on a piece and they do not understand what it is I expect, the original piece becomes like a leggy plant, dangling trails of unrelated information. In this very typical example, I can almost picture the youngster trying to eke out ways to add to his already completed text.

ME AND MY CAT
by Lawrence

My cat was playing with me and I was having fun with my cat.

Then we went to the park. I had a race with my cat. Then I came home and washed up. Then my cat came in the bathroom and stood on the side of the tub and slipped and got wet. Then we went to sleep.

Then the next day we had more fun. When we got home we watched T.V. Then my father gave it away because my mother got alergec to animals.

Then I never got animals again.

*But my grandmother got a rabbit and a cat and got some more
animals. Then one day I went to my grandmother's house and played
with the animals. I stayed for two weeks.*

*Then I went home and I went to sleep and the next day I had waffles.
I love waffles.*

From pieces such as this one, I have learned that hurried conferences and vague admonitions to "tell more" confuse more than they help. Now if half the class needs me at the same time, I ask the whole class to look up from their work. "Children," I say, "many of you are coming to me saying, 'I'm done, what do I do next?' When you finish your writing or when you get stuck with it, I suggest you find a writing teacher and have a conference. BUT there is not one writing teacher in this classroom. There are thirty-two of you." And then I teach the children how to confer with each other.

Soon children move between drafting and peer-conferences. In some classrooms the conferences are informal ones, held at children's desks. In other classrooms, children regard their desks as quiet offices, and they use the edges of the classroom for peer-conferences.

When children interview each other before writing, and when they share drafts with each other during or after writing, their talking often moves their writing forward. There is always more to include, more to tell, and because they are becoming more fluent and more ambitious as writers, they are able to include more and to write with greater fluency. Soon the lilt of oral language begins to appear in their stories. Since children often anticipate that they will write long stories, they divide their pages into chapters. In the following examples, we can almost hear the author's voice coming through.

WHEN I THINK ABOUT HE-MAN

*I think a lot of he-man. I want to be He-man. When I go to bed, I
think of He-man. I wish he was real and then I fall asleep. And then
in nine hours, I am awake and the first thing I think about is He-
man. Then after some time I have to go to school. When I reach the
school I have forgot all about He-man. This may sound a little corny
about He-man and my thoughts, but it won't if you think about the
story a little more.*

MY COUSIN

*I play with my cousin. When someone rings the bell, he jumps up.
Do you know what? He is a dog. His name is Alfee. He lives in Long
Island. He is a golden color. He is tall. He is skinny. Sometimes he
knocks me down. I love my cousin. Do you know why I call him my
cousin? Because my Aunt and Uncle have no children.*

DRESS UP THE SAME

Me and my friend were going to make plans to dress up the same. It was a Thursday. We were going to make the plans. We were going to wear the same burgundy Lee pants and a black sweatshirt and we were going to be the same.

It is a step ahead when children's voices come through their writing, but we pay a price for this step. Their pieces are often filled with "and thens." They include colloquialisms. It is not uncommon for the stories to go on and on and on.

I recently asked my seven-year-old nephew about a television show he had just watched. "How was the show?" I expected a one word answer, but Geoff proceeded to give me a minute by minute rendition of each and every episode in the program. This chart represents the way he described the story line:

$$X \rightarrow X \rightarrow X \rightarrow X \rightarrow X \rightarrow X$$

As we shall see in chapter 10, a fourth or fifth grader would be more apt to summarize some sections, and to give more weight to others. But like many seven-year-olds, my nephew doesn't stand back from the sequence of events in order to manipulate, evaluate, and synthesize them. Similarly, in their writing, many second graders set out to tell everything that happened on their trip or their vacation. Because these stories often begin, "I woke up and had breakfast," and end, "I went to bed," Giacobbe, Graves, Sowers and I refer to them as bed-to-bed stories.

In our study funded by the National Institute of Education, second graders became famous for their bed-to-bed stories. These pieces didn't necessarily begin and end with bedtime: a shopping trip could be written as a bed-to-bed story if the first line was "We got on the bus to go shopping," and the last line was "We finally got home."

During that study, teachers who were hoping to move youngsters toward more focused pieces, often asked them, "What's the one particular thing, out of all this, that you want to focus on?"

I can still hear the children's response. "I want to tell the whole thing!" I suspect selection is difficult for some second graders. They tell the whole story line because they are proud of their new ability to write long stories, but also because focusing on one particular incident requires more distance and more abstract thinking.

Bed-to-bed stories are chronological narratives, but it would be a mistake to suggest that second graders only write narratives. Depending on subtle influences in their classroom or on their interests, they are equally apt to produce all-about books. These catalogs of information are usually organized according to the children's stream of consciousness during the writing episode. If teachers help children to organize their books into a sequence of chapters, the children can sort their information into categories.

Whether the second graders are working in narrative or expository modes, it is not uncommon for them to develop patterns in their writing, as this second grader has done:

One day my whole family went skating.
My father thinks he is Dorothy Hamel.
I think my father is crazy.
My mom thinks my father is crazy.
My sister thinks my father is crazy.
My dog thinks my father is crazy.
My Mom, my sister, my dog and I think my father is crazy.

I do not know why second grade is—or seems to be—a time for writing in patterns. Could it be that, as their writing begins to resemble oral language, they enjoy listening to the sounds of their texts? If they reread for sound, especially during the writing, perhaps the reading leads them to develop rhythm and cadence in their writing. Or could it be that their new ability as readers, combined with a growing awareness of their own written products and their interest in "the right way," means that they want their texts to resemble those they read?

In the second-grade classrooms I know best, there were many indications that children wanted their texts to resemble those they read, but I do not know if this accounts for the patterns in their writing. It was in second grade that many of the children at Atkinson Elementary School consistently began to use traditional story beginnings and endings.

One child wrote a book entitled "All About God." She struggled for a long while over her ending, finally deciding on this one:

God has to go now. Good-bye God. We love you God.
Good-bye.

Then for extra measure, she wrote *The End* and circled it with a giant period. "Periods mean to stop. The giant period means 'stop reading.' "

Second graders in these classrooms used many other conventions in their writing. One youngster asked me why the capital letters on the first page of her reading books had flowers and leaves growing out of them. I told her it was for decoration and soon she, too, was decorating her capital letters—every one of them!

Other youngsters notice that "real" books have dedications, pages entitled "About the Author," and lists of the author's other books. They notice other conventions, too, and adopt them: the blurbs on the back cover, the table of contents, chapters, subheadings, captions underneath pictures. In some classrooms, by late second grade it is not uncommon for children to spend more time—and to use more paper—for the trappings to books than for the stories themselves.

I have often wondered if the second-grade interest in form, pattern, convention and "real books," might not make second grade a good time for working with children on poetry specifically, and on different modes of prose in general. These youngsters might enjoy knowing the differences between friendly and business letters, and they might want to try writing fables, essays, science fiction, and plays. But I have rarely seen a second grade where the modes of writing were taught well, and so I leave the question in the hands of my reader.

Revision

Some children write short, formal pieces. Others write long, fluent bed-to-bed stories. These differences, however, are not random variations: they represent points of growth. I have described second grade as a land of opposites, but it is more accurate to speak of it as a time for growth. Revision is a force for growth in second grade.

Some students, for example, will write in short bursts. Carl Bereiter (1982) points out that this may be because in oral language, after one person speaks in a short burst, the other person says, in effect, "tell me

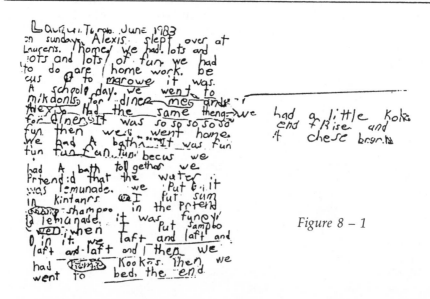

Figure 8 – 1

more." Peer-conferences play this same role for the young writer. In these conferences, the listener says, in effect, "tell me more."

With scissors and tape, or with arrows drawn in their margins, writers extend their first bursts. Some second graders call their additions "spiders" because the added information is often put onto strips of paper which dangle from the text (see Figure 8-1). Other second graders prefer to cut their paper at the point where they need to insert information. The end result looks like the example in Figure 8-2.

These adding-on revisions are easy for second graders because they are concrete. They do not involve weighing various alternatives for a text, nor do they require children to critique their original text. The *activity* of

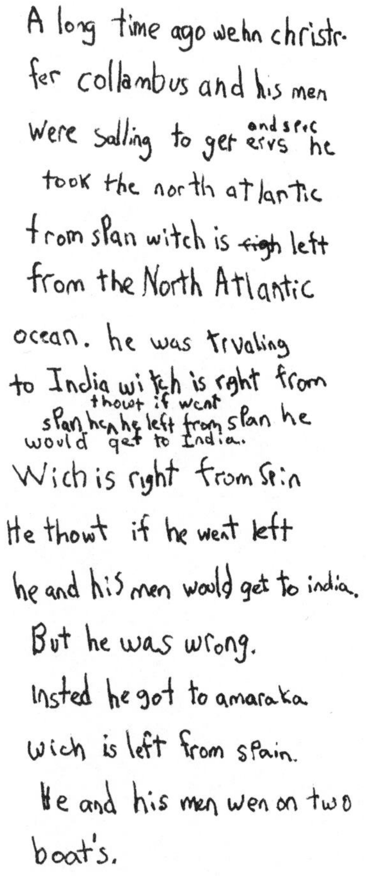

A long time ago wehn christ-
fer collambus and his men
were salling to get and spic he
took the north atlantic
from span witch is righ left
from the North Atlantic
ocean. he was trvaling
to India witch is rght from
span henhe left from span he thout if went
would get to India.
Wich is right from Sein
He thout if he went left
he and his men would get to india.
But he was wrong.
Insted he got to amaraka
wich is left from spain.
He and his men wen on two
boat's.

Figure 8 – 2

Translation:
A long time ago when Christopher Columbus and his men were sailing to get spices he took the North Atlantic from Spain (which is right left from the North Atlantic Ocean). He was traveling to India which is right from Spain. He thought if he went left from Spain he would get to India which is right from Spain. He thought if he went left, he and his men would get to India. But he was wrong. Instead he got to America which is left from Spain. He and his men went on two boats.

revision is enjoyable: reading, talking together, cutting, pasting, adding on. The thinking in revision is not unlike the thinking involved in drafting. Children discover more to say, only now, they invent ways to insert their additional words in the original text.

Because revisions fit easily into the seven-year-old's developmental level and interests, the process of revision catches hold easily in second-grade classrooms. Although the children need assistance from teachers in order to develop revision strategies such as those used to insert information in texts, they revise independently and eagerly. Some second-grade classrooms begin to resemble verbal carpentry shops, where children splice and sort and arrange their materials. In other second grades, children write their pieces and then move on to new ones. They rarely return to a text in order to rework it. Sometimes teachers say to me, "My children rarely revise their pieces. Is that OK?" I tell them we need to remember that our goal is not for children to cut and paste their drafts. It is, instead, for them to extend what they can do as writers. What we need to ask ourselves is not, "Are they revising?" but rather, "Are we extending what they can do as writers?" If second graders write often, if they write for an audience, if they are encouraged to focus on content as well as on form, and if they have opportunities to reread and reflect on their texts and their subjects, then I am confident that for them, second grade can be a time of tremendous growth.

third grade:
deliberate, concrete
processes

In our study, "How Children Change as Writers," Don Graves and Susan Sowers focused on young children, while I focused on the middle childhood years, following the day-to-day changes in eight children as they moved from third grade through fourth. I remember well my first days as a researcher in Mrs. Howard's third-grade classroom. The children had been through a traditional writing program in second grade with a teacher who paid attention to the two ends of composition only (assigning topics and correcting papers). Undoubtedly the starting point for their development in third grade would have been very different if they had come from writing-process classrooms. What I remember most about those first days in third grade was that, when the children finished their pieces, they would bring them to Mrs. Howard and plaintively ask: "Is this okay?" Sometimes they would add, "I think some words are wrong," or "I know it is messy."

What a contrast this was to the first-grade classroom where, when children finished a book, they often waved it overhead singing, "Oh Mrs.Giacobbe, I finished my writing and I'm very proud of it. I think it should be published!"

I didn't hear that song in the third-grade classroom, at least not in September, and I couldn't help but ask, "What happened to these voices, so booming in first grade and so plaintive in third!" I remember looking at their pieces and asking the same question. First graders tended to pour themselves onto the paper. Each page bore the imprint of the author's personality. The third-grade stories, on the other hand, seemed conventional, cautious, wooden. The children's first pieces were about dolphins, a topic assigned to them by their language arts textbook. In one story after another, the youngsters wrote: "Once upon a time there was a dolphin. He got lost. He couldn't find his mother. Finally he found her and they lived happily." As I watched the children write these tales, it seemed that mechanics occupied much of their attention. If they reread their pieces, it was usually to check for misspellings or missing punctuation. If they made any changes on a draft, these were usually changes in wording or in penmanship. The concern for correctness and convention that I saw creeping in during second grade had reached tremendous proportions by the time these children were in third grade.

In the preceding chapter, I pointed to parallel developments in children's art. Howard Gardner writes that when drawings made by seven- and eight-year-old children are juxtaposed with those made by younger children, a striking contrast emerges. "Works by the older children," he says, "feature a kind of precision, a concern for detail, a command of geometrical form which are lacking in the attempts by the younger artists. Yet, one can't help but feel," he also says, "something vital which is present at the age of six has disappeared" (Gardner 1980, 143). Gardner calls the missing quality "a certain freedom, flexibility or exploratory flavor." Writers would call it *voice*. It is easy to lose our voices as we grow up.

Somewhere between first and third grade, the children in Mrs. Howard's classroom had learned to plunk reasonable correct words into a reasonably correct form and to ask only, "Is this okay?" They had learned to take few risks and they were finding few rewards. For these children, the challenge and playfulness had gone from composition. In my book, *Lessons from a Child* (1983), a chronicle of one child's growth during third and fourth grade, I describe this as the third-grade plateau. "It seemed that having learned to write politely and with detachment, many children were no longer learning to write well" (13), I wrote, and I speculated that in our society, many people never get much beyond this plateau. Their writing becomes more correct, more conventional. Around third grade, writing development for many children slows to a halt. This is no surprise, for learning spurts usually occur because of personal involvement, a willingness to take risks, and opportunities to wrestle with more demanding challenges. When children begin to crank out correct, safe little pieces of writing, they short-circuit their opportunities to learn.

Yet writing development need not grind to a halt in third grade. Providing we find ways to rekindle in children the energy for writing and the willingness to take risks, middle childhood can be a time for tremendous new growth in writing.

Rehearsal

The first thing we can do for children in the upper elementary grades is to help them understand that writing is more than a display of their spelling and penmanship; it is a chance to create and to share their creations. In third grade, as in second, the most important task during rehearsal is for writers to realize that they have something to say, something others want to hear. Many third graders care very much about their audience. One boy recently put his list of possible topics inside a "voting box" and carried it from classmate to classmate, asking each of his friends to vote for a favorite topic. Although other children will be less obvious about their concern with audience, the third graders I know take their readers' responses very seriously. They like to share potential topics with a friend because in doing so, they learn how much they have to say.

Initially, many eight-year-olds will choose giant topics. They will want to write catalogs of information on subjects such as my family, summer, school, pets, my life. No wonder children run out of topics if their first topic is "my life." What will their next topic be—"my death"?

During rehearsal, then, I try to help these children focus their topics. This is not as simple as it may sound. It took me many drafts of *Lessons from a Child* before I finally found my focus, and then I had to rewrite the entire book in order to highlight that theme. For third graders, however, focus usually has more to do with limiting the dimensions of a topic than with highlighting one aspect of it. They tend to interpret focus as "having a tiny thing to write about." For example, eight-year-old Marisa begins writing all about her trip to Jones Beach. She strings together everything that happened. Then a friend asks what her focus will be and Marisa selects one small event and tells it in detail. For Marisa, rehearsal means choosing a topic and deciding where in the sequence of events to begin and end the story.

In his newest book, *Write to Learn*, Don Murray (1984) claims that rehearsal accounts for the bulk of his writing time. He discusses many of his rehearsal strategies, such as brainstorming titles for a piece about his grandmother, and illustrates how these strategies help him plan what he will say. During rehearsal, Murray drafts endings, maps alternative structures, anticipates his readers' questions, and gathers telling details. But can children do all this? Murray's ideas on rehearsal made me wonder whether children—and third graders in particular—can solve anticipated writing problems before beginning a draft.

Although Mrs. Howard's third graders became exceptionally skillful writers, none of them accomplished many tasks during rehearsal. They listed alternative topics, and they chose one from their list, usually with an eye toward their audience. But they rarely anticipated their audience's questions or shaped and reshaped the potential piece before putting pen to paper. Nor did they weigh possible endings in their mind's eye or think through alternative forms. It may be time-consuming to write a draft and only then revise it with an audience in mind, but my hunch is that third graders find *revision* easier than *rehearsal*. The steps involved in revision are simple, concrete, and straightforward.

Yet I may be saying this because revision was stressed in Mrs. Howard's classroom. It was stressed, quite frankly, because at that time Donald Murray stressed revision. Since then, Murray has shifted his emphasis from revision to rehearsal. I need now to observe third graders in a room where both rehearsal and revision are stressed before concluding—as I am tempted to do—that many eight-year-old children can do more through revision than they can through rehearsal.

Drafting

For the third graders I know best, their topics usually involve incidents from their lives. This is largely a function of their teachers' emphases on focused personal narratives, yet the way in which third graders approach narrative writing may reflect their development as writers. These eight-year-olds often write tightly structured pieces that proceed, step by step, through a chain of events. Notice how in the following typical pieces, everything is given equal attention. There is very little commentary or elaboration, and time moves along at an even pace. The writers do not speed past some things and linger over others. Instead, the narrative, like time itself, marches steadily on.

HERO
by Kristen

I got on the bus. I couldn't find a seat to sit in. The only place I could find was one with a boy sitting on it. And as I got on the seat he said "Get out and sit somewhere else."

"I can't," I said. My little brother Matt came up to him and hit him on the head lightly with his lunchbox. The boy jumped over to the next seat. I was ashamed that I couldn't handle it myself. My brother sat down with me. I was glad he did it and I thanked him.

MY DOG
by Michelle

When we came back from our vacation our dog was still at the vet. We called the vet to see if we could pick him up. The man at the vet said our dog was in the animal hospital. We went there.

*The man at the animal hospital said they would have to put him
to sleep. We could not watch them do it.*

We buried him in our back yard.

There is something very similar about these stories. In both of them,
it is as if the event rather than the mind of the writer has shaped the
story. Kristen and Michelle do not alter the passage of time in order to
skip quickly past some moments by saying, for example, "Three days
later. . . ." Nor do they linger over a single moment in order to develop
it further by saying, for example, "As I thought more about it . . ." or
"At the time, I didn't notice that. . . ." Their stories reflect the chronology
of life-events rather than their responses to those events. In third grade,
stories such as these are not unusual.

I am not doing justice to the tremendous diversity that exists in a third-
grade classroom, or in any classroom. My hope is that these tentative
generalizations will help readers perceive the exceptions, and that my
observations will invite readers to make their own observations; to see
their own trends, patterns, and diversities. Just as we are more observant
of differences among trees when we know the characteristics of various
tree families (Graves), I hope my observations about third graders will
help teachers become more aware of the unique character of each of their
children.

Although Ari's story is similar to the other two, it seems clear that
unlike the other writers, Ari has broken away from the march of time in
order to include background information for her readers. She does this
twice: once in placing the event within a setting, and once in explaining
about the eyesight of an alligator. It is interesting to note the similarities
between her ending and those in the other two pieces.

WHEN AN ALLIGATOR CHASED US!

*I was in K.I.S.G. with my Mom, sister and grand-parents. We all
walked to the pond and around it. All of a sudden we saw something
moving across the pond. It was long and scaly. It was an alligator.
It came out of the water slowly and started licking its chops and staring
at us. When an alligator chases you you are supposed to run zig-zag
because an alligator's eyes can't go zig-zag. They can only go straight.
I was so scared I couldn't run zig-zag. So I just ran straight into the
car. When I was in the car I turned around and looked at the alligator.
It just turned around and went back into the pond.*

Rebecca's piece, "Wonder," is both similar to and different from the
others. The piece is a chain of events, and yet the author has done several
things that are very different, as readers will see for themselves:

WONDER

I stare blankly at my math. "How do I do this?" I wonder. I scold myself: "Rebecca! You've done things like this lots of times!" But I can't remember how to do this. I try to force my brain back to a little while ago. I can't remember. I ruffle the pages of my math book, looking for when I did something like this before. Nothing. I turn back to my empty math paper. My mind is erased.

Rebecca, more than the others, has slowed down and concentrated on one single moment, moving in very small steps through the sequence of events. Also, in writing this piece she has clearly gone back and relived the experience. There is a strong sense of point of view in the story. Rebecca is telling *her* story rather than just the story of an incident. She moves easily between outer events and inner responses to them. She writes:

I stare blankly at the page. "How do I do this?" I wonder. I scold myself . . .

Readers will notice that Michelle's piece about her dog's death was written from the point of view of "we."

When we came back from our vacation our dog was still at the vet. We called the vet to see if we could pick him up. The man at the vet said he was in the animal hospital. We went there.

"We" cannot think or feel, and therefore it is not surprising that Michelle tells only the outer sequence of events, and that, in contrast to Rebecca, she moves through time in larger steps.

Eight-year-old Christopher's story may be the most sophisticated of all, since he used detailed narrative to make general points and shifts between one time frame and another. He seems to control the passage of time rather than being controlled by it:

I REMEMBER BARBETTA
by Christopher

When I was six years old, I had a dog, a brave dog named Barbetta. I loved her almost as much as I loved my parents. One morning I decided we should go out in the snow. My father got the sled and I woke Barbetta. She licked me and I hugged and kissed her. She put out her paw to shake my hand when she saw the snow. I gave her the rope in her teeth. She waited for me while I was getting on the sled. She went slowly as she pulled and I picked up snowballs along the way. A few months later is was summer again.

Barbetta loved the sun. We went outside. I got my wagon and she jumped into it. I took her up and down the block. Then it was my turn. We played king. I was the king and she was my private guard. Then we went inside. The next day we went into the pool. Barbetta hated the water but she liked splashing it on me.

One night I heard whining and howling. I went downstairs and saw Barbetta crying. We were face to face. I was about to cry. I could not hold it in. I hugged and kissed her. She was hurt. I called my parents. They told me to go upstairs. I hid in the pillow. I was whispering and praying to God. This was one of the saddest days in my life. I thought she was going to stay alive, because she was brave and she also had my love. The next morning my mother came to my room with a sad face. She said in a soft voice, "Barbetta did not make it." She turned and walked out of my room.

Although Christopher's draft is exceptional, my purpose has not been to show what third graders can do as writers, but to illustrate my hunch that they often find it easy to produce one-track, systematic, and even-paced narratives. There is a chainlike quality to many of their pieces, which can be a strength and a weakness.

I often joke that third graders can do anything except in moderation. They can use exclamation marks—but they will use tons of them, developing a hierarchy of fat ones and thin ones to show gradations in excitement. They can write with dialogue—but often the entire piece becomes a stream of chatter. They can write with detail—but they are less good at selecting where to expand their texts with detailed information and where to summarize things in passing. It is easy to be exasperated by the way third graders overdo whatever they do, but it is probably more helpful to be fascinated by this phenomenon. My hunch, for example, is that in the following piece, Philip persists with sound effects and dialogue for some of the same reasons that Kristen, Michelle, and Rebecca each proceed, step by step, through a sequence of events:

THE SPLASHING ROARING RAPIDS
by Philip

Kersplash! "Oh boy I'm as wet as a . . . Oh no!" "A waterfall!" I said to my brother . . . "Uh bye." "Oh no!" I forgot! "I'm seatbelted! I'd better cover my head!" Ninety seconds later . . . "Whew." "We are lucky we missed that waterfall." Kerplunk! "We hit a rock." "We kept on going until . . ." Shlunk! "We hit the side of a cliff." "Awww it's over." "Now I know why they call it the Roaring Rapids." I said to my brother, "I'm soaked to the bone."

Once Philip began writing with dialogue and sound effects, it was difficult for him to make the transition back to narration. Transitions, which require distance, control, and an ability to shift gears, seem hard for these children. In *A Theory of Instruction,* Bruner has commented that children's thinking is often one-tracked:

There is a great distance between the one tracked mind of the young child and the ten year old's ability to deal with an extraordinarily complex world.

Intellectual development is marked by an increasing capacity to deal with several alternatives simultaneously, to tend to several sequences during the same period of time, and to allocate time and attention in a manner appropriate to these multiple demands (Bruner 1966, 6).

After several years of closely studying third graders, I suspect that Bruner's remarks pertain not only to their written products but also to their writing processes. When I first began observing Mrs. Howard's students, most of them wrote without stopping to reread and reconsider what they had written. They rarely interrupted themselves to reflect on their subject or their text, to plan ahead, or to consider alternative paths. For most of them, writing was a continual process of adding on. Their process as well as their products resembled a chain: X → X → X → X. Susie, for example, began the year by writing a long tale about a Chinese girl. It took many days to write the story, and every day Susie's method was the same. She'd reread the last few lines from the preceding day, and begin adding on. Other children worked on shorter pieces but, like Susie, they spent very little time looking back, toying with options, or reconsidering. What many of these children lacked, it seemed, was what Carl Bereiter (1982) refers to as "a central executive function" that would allow them to shift attention back and forth between reading, writing, talking, thinking, writing, and so forth. In oral conversation, conversation partners provide the switchboard that allows participants to oscillate between talking and listening. But these oscillations are not built into the act of writing; the writer must learn how to disengage from one process in order to engage in another. Although these third graders were competent readers, writers, questioners, talkers, planners and so forth, they were less able to shuttle from one activity to another and back again.

The important thing was not that Mrs. Howard's children wrote one draft only, but that they didn't stop to learn from their writing. The importance of *revision* is not the succession of drafts, but the act of "re-vision," of using one's text as a lens to resee one's emerging subject. When children merely add on and on and on, they do not stop to hear and see what their writing is saying.

In time, Mrs. Howard began encouraging peer conferences and revision, and many of the children began writing successive drafts. They often tried three or four possible leads before selecting one to begin a story. Seeing this, I assumed that they were no longer locked into merely adding on.

For them, as for me, writing involved a creative tension between writing and reading, between looking forward and looking back, between thinking of what one has already said and what one has yet to say. Or so I thought.

But when I looked more closely and more honestly at the children's early revisions, I found I had projected my own processes onto them. I assumed revision meant the same to them as it does to me, and of course, I was wrong. A pile of drafts does not equal a new kind of thinking. In fact, I found that for many third graders, their chainlike thinking persisted even during revision.

Revision

When I draft and revise a text, what is going on inside my head can be likened to a taffy pull. Different versions of my text—some written and some only sensed—exist simultaneously. Different ideas, voices, and forms (some written and some not) interact. This creative tension in writing can be illustrated by this diagram, first drawn by Donald Murray:

For most third graders, revision means something very different. Even when the youngsters make substantive content revisions, their revisions tend to be corrections. Their purpose is to make the text match the subject that was in their mind when they began writing. Often children will find that a draft doesn't match "what really happened." This leads them to insert information or to write a new draft, which is meant to be a more accurate or more complete version of the first. In the child's mind one draft is replaced by a second. This means that the two drafts do not exist simultaneously in the writer's mind, nor are they used as a lens for discovering new meanings, new subjects. Most of Mrs. Howard's third graders spoke of revision as a form of correcting:

The ending is boring so I will cross it out and try three others.

I put this word two times in a sentence so I'm going to change it.

How will they know where I am? I gotta fix it so they don't get confused.

Revision for these third graders can be illustrated by the same chain that illustrated their products:

$$X \rightarrow X \rightarrow X \rightarrow X \rightarrow X$$

Time marches on, and they proceed to write one draft and then another. Because they do not stop to probe, these children do not understand that the purpose of revision is not to correct but to discover. They do not understand that by attending to what is said and unsaid in one draft, they can discover new meanings. This changes with time and experience. Listen, for example, to the sense of open-ended experimentation in some of the comments Susie made about revision a year after she wrote her story about the Chinese girl:

I like this draft but I might be able to do it better, I'll see. I'll try it out and read it over, see what it says. I'm going to work around here, writing and changing.

I'm just going to try another draft, or another part of the story, or I'll start differently.

I can't think of anything to fix up in the draft so I'll put it away and write a whole new draft and see. When I write a new one, I might find out there are parts I don't like from this one.

What I want to do next is to add detail. . . . I'll take the details from these drafts and fit them together. No, no, I'll just work on draft 7 and make it fresh. If it turns out, I'll stay on it. Otherwise, I'll go back and take from the others.

When I asked Susie early in third grade if she liked to revise, her answer was, "Yes, if there's good reason. Like it's not neat or if you see spelling mistakes or you have the parts mixed up," but in fourth grade, her understanding of revision was quite different. "Usually I put down a sentence that isn't the one I like. It isn't even in the piece. I just put it down and I can go right through it. After I write so many drafts, I read them over and take parts. There is a special feeling about them."

If my discussion of third graders is more esoteric than the preceding chapters, let me say, first, that I recommend taking what I say with a grain of salt. I do not have the statistical data to support my generalizations. My hunches come from closely studying several children and from working with many others. As teachers, you have the same data base available to you. Take your children's folders home and look closely at their revisions. Ask youngsters to explain their thinking. See if your children are similar to these, and notice especially the range of differences in all of our classrooms. If you find that, within that wonderful diversity, many third graders view revision as substituting one draft for another, or as a form of correcting, my suggestion is to see the amount of growth this represents. For your children, as for Mrs. Howard's, it is probably a step ahead when they reread a draft, searching not for grammatical errors, but for ways in which they have inadequately represented the initial subject. Your children, like hers, have probably developed a set of revision codes that allow them to make additions and deletions. This, too, is progress. Although they may not use their writing to discover new meanings, they may approach a draft anticipating that there will be another, and this allows them to postpone their concern about neatness and spelling until a later draft. Again, this is progress.

Also, if we recognize the nature of our children's revisions, it can help our teaching. You may find, for example, that you inadvertently taught children that revision involves small content corrections. Encouraging children to skip lines in a rough draft, thereby leaving room for revisions, supports only a limited understanding of revision. And although it is more helpful to encourage them to star sections which do not work and to wrestle again with these sections, this, too, encourages them to view revision simply as a form of correcting. Why not also ask them to find bits of their writing—words, lines, passages—which seem essential, and then ask them to explore why these sections are so very significant? Perhaps these key sections, like the tip of an iceberg, represent unseen meanings. Or perhaps the entire piece is a bit like the tip of an iceberg, as when Pedro wrote about the day, years and years ago, when his father threw the cat out the apartment window to the pavement, ten stories below. Pedro's teacher was wise enough not to ask about the name of the cat or the color of the cat, but instead to say, "And now, twelve years later, you still think about that incident. Why is it on your mind now, Pedro?" and soon the two of them, teacher and writer, were looking over one draft to discover a meaning and a message the boy didn't know was there.

There are other ways to encourage students to understand the open-ended, exploratory value of revision. Instead of merely looking to see what they have left out or misrepresented in a draft, why not suggest that they list possible approaches to their topic, and then experiment with one of them? Why not suggest that after writing a draft, they gather together a list of untapped resources and then shuttle between writing and researching? Why not help them to consider a real audience for their draft and then to vary their voice, their information, and their language so that they communicate well with that audience. In such ways, we can nudge children toward larger, more open-ended revisions.

Then, too, if we recognize that third graders' revisions often involve little more than correcting different drafts, we can take this as our cue to extend our students' sense of what makes for good writing. Students will evaluate their drafts depending on their idea of what is valuable in writing. Many third graders, it seems to me, believe that their pieces are good if they are exciting, long, focused, and if they are full of sound effects, dialogue, and action. Their corrections often involve improving the draft according to these criteria. With help, children can develop a more flexible sense of what good writing is. Not every piece need have sound effects.

Children tend to overuse "Puff, puff," "Eek" and "Watch out!" just as they overdo a great many things. They also overdo the importance of "telling the true thing," by which they mean retelling the literal truth of an incident.

For Susie, and for many of her classmates, this was an absolute goal in third grade. But when Susie tried to tell exactly the true story of what happened when she learned to fly, for example, the resulting piece resembled the writer-based prose which Flower describes as characteristic of unskilled writers. It was as if Susie had gone over her memory with a magnifying glass, retelling each minute detail, but without any sense of the whole:

> *"Susie, what are you doing?"*
> *"Just trying to fly."*
> *"Well, if you want to fly, go outside and do it, you're making too much noise."*
> *"But what if I start to fly and I float over to China?"*
> *"I wouldn't worry about that if I were you. I'll be down in the cellar if you need advice."*
> *"Okay, Dad, I'm going out now."*
> *"Hey Susie, your sister wants to come too . . . so come on in."*
> *"Okay, Dad, I'm coming on in now."*

Susie's dogged pursuit of an exact one-to-one rendition of remembered events prevented her from stepping back to create the setting (for example, "my father and I were talking in the living room") or to provide background information (for example, "I was only six years old and determined to fly"). Her attention was focused on telling the true thing rather than on recreating an effective portrayal of the incident for her audience. Only at the end of third grade did Susie begin to realize that a "true" retelling of her memory was not necessarily enough. Her concern for truth began to vie with a new concern for audience. "I'm trying to think of what would fit with the real thing and look good on paper," she said. Another time, after writing exactly how her father got from the shower to the sofa where he snuggled with her, Susie looked critically at what she'd written. "I told the true thing, what really happened, but it doesn't have true feelings." She crossed out what she'd written. "I have to think how, with the same feelings, I can get my father to the sofa." These concerns mark an important step ahead for Susie. Before, she wanted to tell what happened, and if friends questioned her version of the event, she would defend it, as children often do, by saying, "But that is what really happened." But by late third grade, Susie viewed the qualities of good writing, such as truth, not as absolutes but as things to weigh in her mind's eye. She was growing beyond the one-track, one-dimensional thinking I see so much in third grade.

I have slipped from prescriptions back to descriptions. I have said that it is important to help third graders develop a more flexible sense of the components of good writing because many of their revisions will be prompted by the judgment that something is wrong with a draft. I have also said that most of their revisions seem to be a form of correction that can usually be illustrated by this diagram:

$$\text{\st{1}} \rightarrow \text{\st{2}} \rightarrow 3$$

But I was oversimplifying matters. As I mentioned in passing, there was another very common form of revision in Mrs. Howard's classroom: listing leads. When we experiment with different leads to a story, each lead represents a different tack toward our subject, each involves a different point of view, tone, or field of vision. But when I looked closely at many of the leads written in Mrs. Howard's classroom, it seemed that for her students, leads represented different points along a single chain of events. Usually each lead was farther into the narrative sequence:

1 We got up early, ready for our trip. I brushed my hair extra hard and ran down to breakfast.
2 After breakfast, we drove and drove until we got to Pennsylvania.
3 Finally we found a campsite. "Here's a good one," I called out when we saw the picnic table and the soft, dry spot for a tent.

This youngster chose the last lead, as the third-grade children often did. Lead-writing allowed her to select the point in the sequence of events at which her story would begin. This *is* an important decision, and the lead-writing strategy helped her realize she need not begin at the very beginning. Yet it is equally important to notice what the lead-writing strategy has *not* allowed this writer to do: She has not experimented with different approaches to her subject. Instead, she has proceeded along a single narrative track: $X \rightarrow X \rightarrow X$

Finally, let me comment on one more feature that seemed characteristic of these third graders' revisions. They did everything in a concrete, systematic way and wrote out everything in full. The children rarely considered sentences in their mind's eye. Instead, they wrote out every option. When they deliberated over topic choice, they usually listed their options, and often they even went through the list, starring the three best, then crossing out two, and then circling the one chosen topic. They thought with pencil in hand. The same thing was also true of their lead-writing. When I toy with different leads for a piece, my jotted notes may begin like this:

Until recently ~~more few~~
~~The group was~~ ~~I worked until the~~
~~the~~ Last march, several hundred
educations gathered in Cedar Rapids, Iowa,
for a . . .

My discarded fragments represent whole chains of ideas, tested and put aside. Third graders tend to toy with leads in a more concrete, deliberate fashion. They tend to write everything out in full. They might divide the page into four parts, for example, and within each, write out a possible lead. Only then did they look back, rereading each alternative and choosing. It is as if they saw the task not as exploring different leads in order to find a good one, but rather, as listing four leads. Similarily, when children made insertions in their text, they often deliberately set out to do this, and this alone. "I am going to read it over and add stuff, details," a child would say and begin rereading her text, adding codes which signify an insert. This is radically different from how I revise a text. My attention is on my meaning. I draw on revision strategies without thinking of them, just as I hold a pencil without thinking of it. My strategies overlap and blur. One moment I am writing leads, and then suddenly, I'm inserting information into one of them, or bolting down the page. In time, revision will also become second-nature for children. But this takes us to fourth, fifth and sixth graders, who are the subject of chapter 10.

10

fourth, fifth, and sixth grade: new flexibility

"Hey Diane, listen to these leads," Susie said, pulling her chair closer to her friend's. Susie read five leads aloud to Diane, and in doing so, she read them to herself. When she was finished, Diane responded with a question, but Susie wasn't listening. She'd picked up her pencil and was inserting missing information into her fifth and final lead. By the time Susie finished tinkering with the passage, Diane had returned to her writing, so Susie showed me the revised lead, pointing out the line she had added. Like Diane, I said little . . . but I, too, inadvertently helped Susie switch from writing to reading and reconsidering. Again Susie found a problem in what she had written. "How will they know I am fishing?" she muttered, not expecting me to answer. This time she wrote another draft of the lead, correcting the problem. "This is not the only time I ever worked on one little section really hard for a long, long time," she said to me. "But I got it right." This is the lead she had written:

LEAD 5—DRAFT 4

*Me and my father were
fishing at a lake. I
looked in the water and
saw a quick flash. It
was a school of fish
that looked like silver
dollars.*

93

This writing episode shows little resemblance to the forward moving, one-tracked process I described in the previous chapter. In working on her lead to "The Big Fish," Susie had alternated between writing, reading, redrafting, rereading, inserting information, rereading, and trying another draft, and in doing so, she had written 287 words and used eighteen revision codes (arrows, carets, coded insert marks, stars, etc.) She had also illustrated some of the ways in which children tend to change as they grow older and more experienced as writers.

The changes were largely brought about by teaching, but in this instance and others, instruction does not necessarily come from the teacher. Both Diane and I had extended what Susie did as a writer, and we had done so not by giving brilliant responses to her work-in-progress, but simply by providing her with an external executive function. Because she had the opportunity to read her emerging text to us, Susie dislodged herself from endlessly adding-on and began to reread, reflect on, and reconsider her draft, and to move back and forth between one process and another.

In the earlier grades, it would have taken more than these simple conferences for Susie to have made the revisions that by now she could make almost independently. As Vygotsky says, "What a child can do in cooperation today, he can do alone tomorrow" (Vygotsky 1962, 101). The revisions children make with a teacher's help in third grade, become part of their repertoire in fourth and fifth grade. With time, assistance, and experience, children find it easier to conceive of different ways to say the same thing. They develop a set of tools (codes and strategies) for making revisions, and it becomes easier to look back on their traces and to reconsider what they have already done. They begin also to internalize the questions that can be asked of an emerging draft. In this instance, all that Susie needed to nudge her towards a second version of her lead was the opportunity to read her work to someone else. Diane's presence and mine prevented Susie from merely floating along with the forward-moving tide of her composing process. Our presence nudged her to consciously direct her process. Flower and Hayes (1980), two of the most probing writing researchers, have found that unskilled adult writers often have a hard time shifting from writing to rereading and monitoring their own composing. It is not easy for them to say, "I'm going to just jot down whatever comes to mind" or "I'm going to list the subtopics, then choose one." For Susie, having friends at hand while she worked provided her with this external switchboard. Diane and I allowed Susie to become a reader of her own writing.

One change is related to another. In the upper elementary grades, the children I know best seem to become a little more capable of thinking through their options. Strategies that are first concrete, physical operations begin to be internalized as abstract mental operations. This evolution happens also in math. When young children first learn to divide twenty by four, we encourage them to deal with the problem in a concrete way. For example, they may solve it by dividing twenty cubes evenly among four people. Later, children do not actually need to hold the cubes and sort them into equal piles. Instead, they do it mentally. "Internalization means that the child does not have to go about his problem any longer by overt trial and error," Piaget writes, "but can actually carry out trial and error in his head" (1962).

In *Lessons from a Child*, I show how Susie internalized concrete revison strategies. The best example involved using (and adapting) the lead-writing strategy. Susie was working on a troublesome section in the middle of a fishing story. "I want to make the section where I catch the fish shorter; it should be quicker," she said. She sighed, cast her eyes about the classroom, reread the section several times, sighed again. No one came to her rescue, so she decided to adapt the lead-writing strategy to meet this new problem. On a separate bit of paper, she wrote numbers one to three as if she were writing leads. Beside the numbers one and two, Susie tried alternate ways of writing the section. Then she circled number three, and for a few minutes held her pencil still. Finally, she brought it to the paper and held it there, ready to write. Then she pulled away.

I asked, "What'd you almost write?"

Susie blushed, "I was going to say, 'Just then a quick jerk awakened me and I looked and saw my pole bending,' " she said, "But it's way too long." She was quiet again, her pencil dabbing occasionally at number three and her lips moving as she whispered other alternatives to herself. For the first time, Susie was internally considering ways of saying something.

In *Lessons from a Child*, I point out that by listing the numbers one to three in her margin, and writing leads beside two of the numbers and then pointing to the third, Susie built concrete scaffolding within which she could organize the alternative leads that crossed her mind. Each time she considered another option, her pencil tapped on number three. Bruner gives a similar example of the way in which a concrete operation can provide an internalized structure. He writes that, when children use the balance scale to solve math problems, they later solve problems by visualizing the structure of serial weights in their minds. "Such internal structures," he claims "are of the essence: they are the internalized-symbolic systems by which the child represents the world" (Bruner 1966, 36, 37).

Once Susie and other children internalize concrete revision strategies, these strategies become tools of thought for them, and they use them in easy, offhand ways. Now that she had a strategy for doing so, Susie began weighing possible options for endings, for titles, for problematic descriptive passages. Soon she did not need to list numbers in her margin at all. In a story about riding on a moped with her father, Susie wrote down:

I fe

and then crossed it out and wrote:

We

and then crossed it out. I later asked what she had been thinking, and her answer showed that those five letters represented several chains of thought, and the juxtaposition of free association and critical thinking.

"When I put down 'I fe,' I was wondering if I should do a little more about how I felt," Susie said, "or should I put more about tightening my grip and speeding down the hill. Then when I put 'we,' I was thinking whether I should make us approach the house or not."

"How do you decide?" I asked.

"I think how it would sound. Either I put it down or I just think it, and if it doesn't sound right, I think of a different way."

Five letters, but underlying them, sophisticated mental processes. Writing has become a means for thinking and rethinking. Now when Susie writes, she is no longer bound to the word at hand. She anticipates the ends of sentences and the conclusions of thoughts. When she works with words, she works also with potential words. In this way, writing has become for her a highly efficient, intense way of extending and critiquing her own ideas.

What does this mean for the teacher of writing? It means, first of all, that when children's revisions seem overly elaborate and wasteful of time and effort, we can trust that this will not always be the case. Revision strategies, like conference questions, are eventually internalized, becoming scaffolding for thought. Then, too, what children do once through revision they can later do through rehearsal. As children grow older, and more experienced as writers, they can do more and more in advance of writing. By the time she was ten, Susie was able to view her draft through the eyes of a reader even before she had written a word, and certainly before she shared it with a friend. She could listen to the sounds of the text even without putting that text onto paper. It is no accident, then, that I have not separated this chapter into the subsections of rehearsal, drafting, and revision. There is no line between them. What is done through revision can later be done through rehearsal and drafting, leaving room for new challenges to be tackled through the concrete, physical process of revision.

As children do more and more writing in their minds, their composing processes become more complex. Because they can test out an idea quickly and effortlessly, they may do more experimenting. Because they can consider possibilities without spending three days on writing a draft, they try out more of them. Their processes span more ground. As writers, they can zoom ahead in their mind's eye and then return to organize and arrange.

In fourth, fifth, and sixth grades, as in third grade, the amount of control over time and content evident in the child's writing processes parallels the amount of control and flexibility evident in the child's written products. If older children can shift easily between one strategy and another, between planning and remembering, then they can also produce narratives which are significantly different from those written by third-graders such as Kristen and Michelle. Amy's draft, for example, shows how she shifts between narrative and description, proceeding step by step through a time sequence but pausing to respond to events:

TURKEY DINNER
by Amy

My stomach growled savagely as I looked down the table. My grandmother was busily putting the things on the table. The turkey was right in front of me. The gravy sizzled in the pan. The juice trickled down the sides of the turkey. I looked at the mashed potatoes and sweet peas. The butter melted on the both of them. My stomach growled again and again. There were mashed turnips, which I didn't care for. There were cranberry sauce, carrots and rolls. My eyes wandered back to the huge turkey I couldn't resist. My hand snuck up and snitched a piece of turkey. "Mmmm" it was good. Finally the knife sunk into that delicious turkey. I ate half of it almost. When I was done, I sat back in my chair with a full stomach.

That Amy is an artist with a knack for noticing visual details is evident in her turkey story. The next piece, one of my favorites, was written by a fourth grader from a class for mentally retarded children. Randalio does not have Amy's precise vocabulary or literary sophistication, but his piece is a powerful and sensitive one, and he, like Amy, moves easily between the vertical and the horizontal dimensions of the story. He follows a chain of events and elaborates on those events. He also shifts from one time frame to another.

MY MOTHER WENT TO THE HOSPITAL
by Randalio

My mother went to the hospital. I started crying. A lot of things changed in my house.
My clothes smelled like perfume because my sister washed my clothes. And my pants were high waters because my sister washed them with hot water. I hate that all right. And how they ironed my pants! They ironed them wrong. I got so mad one morning because my pants were wrinkled. And the rice and beans tasted funny. And they treated me like a man. They hit me like I was a big man. They punched me, smacked me, threw me down the stairs, and they hit me with a spoon too. And they didn't let me go outside at three.
One Saturday my mother came home. We all hid behind the sofa. Then I gave her a big hug. And I asked if I could go outside. She said yes!
And then my pants smelled not like perfume, and they weren't high

*waters anymore, and they weren't wrinkled. And the food tasted good
and we all lived happily.*

The beginning of the next story provides yet another example of the
way in which many upper elementary school children are increasingly
able to control a sequence of events rather than being controlled by it.
Darren's story also illustrates the ease with which many upper elementary
students weave dialogue into their narratives. It is not new for Darren to
include dialogue in his drafts, but previously, he used dialogue in large
chunks. Now he moves in and out of it with grace.

BUG YEARS

*In 1980 and 1981, I caught bugs with my brother. Bugs were my
favorite things. But we made a big mistake. We put the purple guys
and the green fast guys in one jar. "Oh, no!" my brother called out.
The purple guys, the powerful ones, had killed the green fast guys.
My brother smacked the purple guys. But they pinched him. Then he
taught them not to pinch.*

*We also had wolf spiders which were strong, but not as strong as
the purple guys. My brother said, "Don't put the wolf spiders with
the purple guys" and I agreed. The wolf spiders were hairy ones, and
their favorite meal was potato bugs. Whenever the potato bugs were
nasty to my brother, we fed them to the wolf spiders. We didn't usually
do that because it was a shame to see the cute potato bugs die . . .*

It is not surprising that the growing sophistication in children's processes
and products is echoed also in their growing sophistication about the
components of good writing. As I mentioned in the preceding chapter,
many third graders seem to believe that there are absolutes in writing.
Because he thought stories should have action and excitement, eight-year-
old Birger rewrote even his squirrel report to make it more exciting.
Because they believe stories should be focused on one thing, most of the
third graders I know best would not have written about wolf spiders,
potato bugs, and "fast purple guys" in the same story. In fourth, fifth
and sixth grade, however, children often develop a more complex understanding of good writing. We saw this in Susie's discovery that she
must "tell the true thing that happened," but also give her audience
necessary background information. A year later, she took this lesson a
step further when she discovered that sometimes the Truth of an event
can best be conveyed by skipping some parts and taking poetic license
with others. In fourth grade, Susie told me that the favorite part of one
story was "true but not true." She explained, "I liked the part when I
was getting off the plane and I could tell by looking at Jill that she was
just as excited as me. It didn't really happen, but I know she *was* excited

and I wanted to put in that I looked at her and saw she was excited, to show how we felt . . . . It's much better now; as I read it over I can almost tell the exact feelings I felt then."

Similar changes occurred in Susie's understanding of good endings. In third grade she had been very clear about "The Right Way" to end stories. "Endings shouldn't just go off," she said and indeed, her endings reminded me of a knot tied onto the end of each piece. She ended "Learning to Fly" like this: "The next day I planned to try again and just keep on doing it until I flew. So I tried and tried and I'm still trying." A year later, in fourth grade, when Susie wrote about falling out of a bunkbed, she said, "I usually have a little line to end it, like 'I'll never sleep in that bunkbed again!' but I think, for a change, I won't put that in." Instead, she ended the piece with her mother consoling her. By the end of fourth grade she realized that her options were broader still. "Endings can leave them hanging," she said. "Usually they don't, but they can." Once again, Susie had seen that there are no hard and fast rules, and that the rightness of any choice depends on a multitude of factors.

When I look back at my own writing to see what I have done, my judgments are usually intuitive. I am apt to say, "It looks good" or "It sounds wrong" rather than justifying my judgments according to rules. From my successes and failures in previous pieces of writing, and from my own reading, I have developed an intuitive feel for what works in a text. Many things have become second nature for me. The same is true for experienced upper elementary school writers. By sixth grade, it is second nature for these children to write with precise bits of information. Their first drafts are detailed and fluent. Then, too, by fifth and sixth grade, these children find it easy to start at a point in the middle of the narrative. When Monica writes about the day her bird died, she no longer feels it necessary to begin with getting the bird. But if she wants to include such information, she probably knows how to weave it into her narrative about the bird's death.

Although I do not hear many children talking about "voice," this is another quality of good writing that seems to become second nature for many upper elementary school children. It seems that many nine-, ten-, and eleven-year-olds enjoy pretending to be a particular person when they write, and with each role, they are able to use a new voice. Instead of simply writing an all-about report on Africa, Todd wrote his piece as if he were a reporter on a safari. In his book of health tips, Eric assumed the voice in his mother's books on astrology and miracle diets. As students grow in competence and confidence, they find new ways to integrate writing into the rest of their lives.

11

---

early adolescence: the best of times, the worst of times

Although my research has focused on the upper elementary school years, I am most at home talking about young adolescents. I suspect this is not only because my first teaching experiences were with this age level, but also because I can poignantly recall my own adolescent years. They were passionate times. I remember when an ex-convict spoke to hundreds of us on a church retreat. I felt certain he was speaking specifically to me, and for weeks afterward, everything in my life bristled with spiritual significance. I had been called to a special mission. In my diary, I listed the ways I would improve myself. At night, I would lie in bed going over my list, grading myself on each item and resolving to do better. I still have those diaries, and when I read them I can feel all over again what it was like to be thirteen. On March 16, 1965, I wrote, "As Mommy put it, there are some things I like and excel in, and some things I detest. I like English, plays, projects, kids, creativity, riding, and gym. I dislike homemaking, health class, spelling, clothes, and politeness." It was an understatement to say "I like English, plays, projects"—actually, I *lived* for them. When I was in the school play, I would set my alarm for five o'clock A.M. and ride my bike to school in order to attend play practice. On weekends, I would round up all the neighborhood children for my own playhouse. We wrote scripts, made scenery, sold tickets, and produced elaborate plays and marionette shows. My zeal for drama was inextricably linked with my devotion to Miss Armstrong, my seventh-grade English teacher. In a spiral notebook, I listed everything I knew about her, and at the end of the year, I solemnly presented it to her.

My best times came when I felt as if I belonged. This sense of self was precarious, though, and it was easily shattered. I will never forget the time when the members of our gym class divided into pairs and I was the odd one out. Or the time when Allison Able suggested I didn't need a costume to play the part of Abraham Lincoln's mother, since the dress I had on looked old enough to have been hers. I cried myself to sleep that night. I can still remember thinking, "When I am thirty, the pain will be gone. It can't last forever."

Those were the best of times, those were the worst of times. They were, above all, crucial times. Erik Erikson (1964) describes adolescence as a turning point which is animated by increasing energy and increasing vulnerability. During those years, the young person constructs a sense of personal identity. It is a time for trying on selves, for discarding some and choosing others. It is a time for self-awareness, choice, pain, and self-definition. The adolescent learns to say, "This is who I am."

Twenty years have passed since the day when I wrote that I loved English, plays, projects, kids . . . and hated spelling, homemaking, health class, and clothes. But if I were to make a new list today, it would not be very different from the list I wrote as a thirteen-year-old. Each of my current interests can be traced back to the days of junior high, and most of them can even be traced to specific teachers. Although the connection between teachers and students is crucial at every grade level, it is nowhere more true than during the middle-school years. Nancie Atwell points out that David Halberstam (author and Pulitzer Prize winning journalist), John Bushnell (Chief of Mission at the American Embassy in Buenos Aires), and Ralph Nader (consumer advocate) were all in the same seventh-grade social studies class. Halberstam has written about their teacher, Miss Thompson. "She taught with genuine passion," he writes, "encouraging young people at a delicate moment to think they could be anything they wanted." Adolescents need mentors like Halberstam's Miss Thompson and my Miss Armstrong.

Shirley Brice Heath has gone so far as to suggest that the single most important condition for literacy-learning is the presence of mentors who are joyfully literate people. The best middle-school teachers I know demonstrate what it means to be joyful readers and writers. They, like Miss Thompson, teach with genuine passion. "Our true authority does not come from detention slips, grade books or lesson plans," Nancie Atwell emphasizes. "It comes instead from the fact that we are writers and readers" (Atwell, forthcoming). Nancie's eighth graders are given the opportunity to live, work, and learn alongside a joyfully literate person.

I tell my kids, 'Writing, reading, and teaching them to you are my life.' I write with my kids. I show them my drafts, I ask for their responses in conference. I tell them writing is a new habit but it is one that is changing my life. I read with my students. I show them what I read and I talk about and loan my books. I tell them reading is an old habit, one that shapes my life and gives it so much meaning that I don't know if I could go on living if I suddenly couldn't read. I am demonstrating the truth. I love these things so much, I can't imagine my students won't love them too. (Atwell, forthcoming)

Nancie Atwell not only demonstrates the power of reading and writing, she also invites her students to become equally involved in the world of written language. This invitation, Holdaway says, is the flip-side of mentorship. The toddler sees dad sweeping the kitchen floor and thinks, "That looks like fun," and so the child makes his way over to where his father is working and unsteadily reaches for the broom. The father, welcoming the little one's "help," hands the broom over, and soon the baby is pushing the broom about the kitchen as if it were a truck, knocking things right and left. This, Holdaway says, is developmental learning. The child sees the bonded adult happily engaged in an activity, and the child wants to participate. The adult makes room for the child to join in, encouraging the learner to approximate the activity as best he or she can. Thus the baby "reads" by holding the book upside down and backward, and the youngster "saws" by scratching at the plank with the wrong side of the saw blade. In a similar way, Nancie's eighth graders approximate the richly literate life their teacher leads. In a uniquely adolescent way, they do what good readers and writers throughout the world do.

Nothing I have said so far should be startling. It is only common sense. *Of course* adolescents need teachers who demonstrate that reading and writing can bring tremendous joy to life. *Of course* adolescents need the chance to do what readers and writers do. The only surprising thing is that most junior highs are deliberately structured so that neither of these takes place. Jim Squire reports that in seven hours of instructional time, students spend an average of seven minutes on real reading (1984). Goodlad (1984) and others report that for 80 percent of the school day, students sit passively and listen to their teachers talking. There is a paucity of demonstrating, showing and modeling on the part of teachers, and of constructing things, acting things out, and carrying out projects on the part of students. This is particularly true in English classrooms, where activities are the same throughout every year of school. Students fill in dittos, copy down and memorize definitions, do drill work, answer questions on excerpts they have read, and listen to their teachers' interpretations of books. It is no wonder students rank English as their least favorite subject (Goodlad, 1984, 113). If we recognize, as Frank Smith points out, that we *are* teaching and students *are* learning all the time, then it should come as no surprise that our students learn to dislike reading and writing. Clearly something needs to be changed.

Although turning traditional classrooms into writing workshops is never easy, it is particularly difficult in the secondary school, where the givens of the school day conflict with the structure of writing workshops. At least in the elementary school, teachers and children have the entire day together, and it is feasible to reserve an hour a day for a writing workshop. But most junior-high teachers spend only forty-five minutes a day with their students, precious minutes often dominated by a preset curriculum full of prescribed units of study and assigned readings. Even when teachers do have the responsibility for designing courses of study, they must take into account many not-too-subtle pressures. Districtwide exams test discrete items such as definitions of alliteration, the characteristics of the sonnet, the sixteen uses of the comma. Then too, most middle-school teachers work with more than a hundred young people each day, and it is not uncommon for classes to change every ten weeks so that, when teachers do finally know their students, it is time for everyone to change classes. I do not think any of us in the field of composition can work effectively with junior high school teachers until we recognize the reality of their junior high school worlds.

But recognizing the reality of those constraints is one thing and deciding to work within them is another. We cannot afford to accept the norms of most junior high schools docilely because they contradict not only what we know about reading and writing but also what we know about adolescence. Our young people need time in school for reading and writing. Their lives are such that there is little time for reading and writing outside of school hours. Adolescents also need time to build relationships with adults who are joyfully literate because it is during adolescence that young people construct a sense of personal identity, deciding, "This is who I am," and "This is who I want to be." These decisions are based, to a large degree, on relationships with people who act as role models.

I cannot recommend one "correct" way to build in time for reading, writing and relationships. At one school in the Bronx, language arts is given a double period, which allows teachers to begin each day with a forty-five minute reading workshop, followed by a forty-five minute writing workshop. At Great Neck Middle School, Nick Aversa team-teaches with a social studies teacher. They use reading and writing as tools for learning about topics that relate to both social studies and literature. Other teachers find that their writing workshop can be made a viable part of their educational program if they devote chunks of the year exclusively to writing. Students may, for example, spend the first eight weeks of school in an ongoing writing workshop. Because classes are only forty-five minutes long, these workshops cannot be divided into mini-lessons, writing, and whole-class share meetings. Instead, some teachers devote one day a week to whole-class share meetings or schedule small response groups during the last twenty minutes of several class periods. The bulk of class time is devoted to the workshop itself. The important factors are that time is structured in simple, predictable ways to allow students to plan their writing strategies, and that writing is done during class time so that students can receive feedback on their work-in-progress. In most secondary classrooms, the demands of the curriculum eventually squeeze writing into two days a week, but it is important that the workshop begin with larger stretches of time. Later, students will write drafts at home so that class time can be reserved for writing conferences, response groups, and mini-lessons.

The structure and purpose—the exoskeleton—of these workshops do not vary a great deal from those of their elementary school counterparts, but because any workshop is characterized by the people who work within it, the flavor of the middle-school writing workshop reflects the distinctive character of its adolescent members. There is something unique (and at times problematic) about the combination of adolescents and the writing workshop.

Our instinct, I think, is to shy away from the volatile combination of adolescents and writing. We cannot imagine all those big adolescent bodies and those big adolescent passions being let loose in our classrooms. We are certain teenagers will not want to put their private lives onto paper anyway. We suspect that teaching writing is easier with younger children, and it probably is. But everything that makes adolescence into a difficult time also makes it into a time when writing can be particularly important.

I began this book by saying, "There is no plot line in the bewildering complexity of our lives but that which we make and find for ourselves . . . Writing allows us to turn the chaos into something beautiful, to frame selected moments in our lives, to uncover and to celebrate the organizing patterns of our existence." My thesis for that chapter and indeed, for the entire book, is that, as human beings, we need to write because writing allows us to understand our lives. But it is during adolescence that we have a special need to understand our lives, to find a plot line in the complexity of events, to see coordinates of continuity in the midst of all the discontinuity. Writing can play a crucial part in the task of identity formation.

When adolescents feel that they can trust their teacher and their peers, they often choose to write about incredibly powerful topics. Recently, a colleague introduced a class of seventh graders to the notion of topic choice. While the topics in a third-grade room might include "a visit to Aunt Babsy's house," "the day I got an A in math," and "buying new shoes," one boy in this class described how he walks through shopping malls, looking over each passing man to see if he could be the boy's real father. A girl told about returning from a long vacation with her family and finding that, because she'd gained a lot of weight on the trip, everything was different. "I can't believe my best friend doesn't want to be my friend any more," she wrote. Another student described the feeling he sometimes gets when he stands at the chalkboard doing a math problem and has the peculiar sensation that he had stood before at that same chalkboard, doing that same problem. He has the same feeling sometimes when he is browsing in a bookstore and is haunted by a sense of "I've done this before." Each of these students was writing in order to make sense out of his or her own life.

The reason-to-write is equally apparent when students write fiction. Bowen, a basketball player, writes stories about jocks who seem to have a cocky self-assurance, but underneath feel inadequate and afraid. Sumi, a bright student who is alienated from mainstream social life in her class, peoples her stories with teenagers who keep to themselves. James brings the turbulence of his home life into his fiction, writing stories in which the protagonist shoots the members of his family and feels no remorse.

Of course, not all adolescents embrace writing as a way of finding meaning in their lives. Some will hide behind trivial topics. Some will resort to retelling television programs. Still others will groan and complain at the thought of writing. "Boring," they'll say. "Do we have to write?" "Is this going to be graded?" The forms of their protest will vary, but teachers need to remember that these layers of bravado or apathy often shield youngsters from the vulnerability and confusion they feel. Adolescence is a time of tremendous change: physical, emotional, psychological, and intellectual. It is a volatile time, one that is marked by wide swings of emotion, which seem to come and go for no reason at all. Often the adolescent is so painfully self-aware that merely having to write a sentence on the chalkboard causes feelings of shame and inadequacy. Writing is, by definition, an act of self-exposure. As Shaughnessy describes it, "Writing is but a line which creeps across the page, exposing as it goes all that the writer does not know. . . . Writing puts us on the line and we don't want to be there" (1977, 7).

When our students protest against putting themselves on the page, we need to realize that the protests may not come from laziness. Many young adolescents are ashamed of and humiliated by their writing. They cannot write without envisioning red marks taunting them from the margin side-lines. Their goal is to avoid error.

No one can write well or learn well when fear and shame are so pervasive. Therefore, if we do nothing else, we need to help young people see writing as a safe medium, a place for exploration and discovery, and to see the writing class as a supportive community. We need to do this for students of all ages, but I want to stress two aspects that are particularly important in working with adolescents. The first centers around error. When first graders invent their own spellings and use punctuation marks in unconventional ways, we find it charming. When eighth graders do the same, we are no longer charmed. The errors scream out at us; we can see little else. Mentally or on paper, we begin red-penning each error as we make our way down the page. Soon we are overwhelmed by the chaos of mistakes. We despair. "This kid is too far behind to catch up," we think. We forget the statistics that show how many students enter middle school without ever having the opportunity to learn the craft of writing. We think our students must be slow learners, and we decide, "This kid will never catch on." Our prophecy becomes self-fulfilling. Students sense our despair; they feel our hopelessness. Our fears confirm their own. In chapter 20, I discuss editing. Although that chapter relates to every grade level, the issue it considers is particularly important in the secondary school, where concern about error can overshadow everything like a heavy grey cloud.

There is a second issue of special relevance to adolescent students: criticism. We need to be certain that the writing class is a safe and supportive environment so that students will be willing to share work in progress. Middle-school students often balk at the idea of reading their drafts aloud. "Do I have to?" they ask. "Will *you* read it for me?" Once again, it is important for us to recognize that this behavior is not a reflection of a "bad attitude," but rather of fear. Often the fear is well founded. Adolescents can be brutally critical of each other. In some classrooms, they will tease a student for writing "Daddy" rather than "Dad" and roll their eyes when an unpopular classmate reads aloud. Even in very effective writing class-rooms, adolescents are hard on each other. The students I know best delight in pointing out illogical sections in a friend's story. "How could he have carried the basket with a broken arm?" they ask. "Why would he take a cab if he was poor?" When we direct their attention to the story itself, they tend to evaluate their peers by their own criteria. If Christa prides herself on how well she sets the scene, then she is quick to notice José's failings in that department. If Pedro's story is exciting, he'll complain that his friend's has no action. Then, too, students' responses to each other are often based less on the draft than on the writer's place in the classroom social scene. Loud, chubby Miles is the class clown. Whenever he reads his work to the class, he does so with a show biz flair, and his work is greeted with copious laughter and approval. Meanwhile, Lisa, a withdrawn, quiet girl, who is a far more capable writer than Miles, invariably receives responses which are perfunctory and bland.

In many middle-school school classrooms, small response groups and peer-conferences seem to be safer, more productive settings for giving and receiving responses than the whole-class share meetings. Some teachers assign students to response groups, bringing together students of varied strengths who nevertheless like each other. In other classrooms, students select their own response groups. In still other rooms, students do not work in groups of four or five; instead, they find peer-conference partners as they need them. The configurations vary, but the importance of col-laboration is indisputable. We know that writers need readers, and that these readers are necessary while the work is still in progress. We know, too, that adolescents need peers. When Goodlad asked junior high school students, "What is the *one* best thing about this school?" their most frequent response was "my friends." "Sports activities" ranked a distant second, followed by "good student attitudes." These three choices accounted for 62 percent of the responses in junior highs. A greater percentage of students said, "Nothing is important about school" (8 percent) than said the classes they're taking (7 percent) or their teachers (5 percent) are most important. These results have been confirmed by other studies. Recently, National Family Options conducted an extensive study of students in grades seven through twelve and found that, when students were asked why they like school, friends (80 percent) and sports (31 percent) ranked as the two top choices (1984).

In discussing these and other statistics, Nancie Atwell says that we can look at these figures and remark on just how shallow adolescent kids really are, or we can recognize that students are valuing the same things in school that we adults value in our jobs. If a survey of adults were conducted that asked, "What is the *best* thing about your job?" most of us would probably say "my colleagues'" or "my friends." Relationships *do* matter in life, and this may be particularly true for adolescents.

When these students are encouraged to collaborate, to pool their energies in the reading and writing workshops, they bring a fierce amount of enthusiasm and dedication to the classroom. As Nancie Atwell points out, "If we know social relationships come first for adolescents, then it makes good sense to bring them into the classroom and put them to work. We need to give these relationships a legitimate forum" (forthcoming).

Yet middle school teachers often resist the idea of student collaboration. "With all those hormones going wild," these teachers say, "group work becomes a time for touching legs under the table and for whispering about who likes whom." They view the notion of a workshop, with opportunities for movement and talking, as a risky idea. It is easier to keep the kids sitting passively in rows. Teaching in secondary schools, Goodlad found, is characterized by a narrow range of instructional activities favoring passive student behavior (128). It seems likely that student passivity and the low emotional tone in classrooms serves an implicit function of maintaining control. Years ago, Silberman (1970) emphasized that it is hard to fault teachers for this concern over order and quietness, and Silberman's words still ring true:

> If teachers are obsessed with silence and lack of movement . . . , it is in large part because it is the chief means by which their competence is judged. A teacher will rarely, if ever, be called on the carpet or denied tenure because his students have not learned anything; he most certainly will be rebuked if his students are talking or moving about the classroom, or—even worse—found outside the room, and he may even earn the censure of his colleagues as well. Nor will teachers receive suggestions from supervisors as to how to improve their teaching methods and materials; they will receive suggestions for improving "discipline." Thus, the vows of silence and stillness are often imposed on teachers who might prefer a more open, lively classroom. (144)

I have come full circle. I began by saying that writing is an act of self-exposure and courage, and that we must create safe and supportive classroom environments so that our students can take the risks necessary to learn to write. It seems fitting to add the corollary: teaching writing is also an act of self-exposure and courage. Teachers, too, need support if they are going to take the risks necessary. They also need to believe that the writing workshop is very, very important to students because it is not easy to bring the writing workshop into middle schools. Even if students have been writing happily for years, as adolescents, they and their teachers must discover reasons for writing all over again. Some students will want to write because they fancy themselves becoming journalists, poets, and novelists. With encouragement, these students will invest the same energy in writing that I once invested in drama. They will see a movie or a play with their parents, for example, and, inspired, take on projects of similar scope themselves. At home over a weekend, they will set out to write a screenplay, a book of poems, a novel. But many other students during these years will have aligned themselves with fields other than writing: math, science, music, or sports. This means that levels of student investment in the writing workshop can vary tremendously unless we help all youngsters see the essential role writing can play in their lives.

To convince adolescents we need to believe ourselves. We need to ask, "*Why* is it important for kids to write these personal narratives, these poems and stories?"

Don Murray's answer is the best one I know. He says we write, above all, to learn.

Why write?
  To be surprised.
  The writer sits down intending to say one thing and hears the writing saying something more, or less, or completely different. The writing surprises, instructs, receives, questions, tells its own story, and the writer becomes the reader wondering what will happen next. (Murray 1985, 7)

I am not convinced that the young children I know best follow their writing to new, unexpected meanings. I am not convinced that second, third, and fourth graders see unexpected patterns, connections, and meanings in their emerging texts. Perhaps they *can* do this, I do not know. Certainly middle school youngsters can write-to-learn, but in our Writing Project, we have only just begun to recognize that we need to demonstrate the teaching power of writing. Recently, Shelley Harwayne launched a writing workshop with a class of eighth graders. Generally we begin these initial workshops by brainstorming several topics we might write about (perhaps a haircut, an experience with a pet, or a moment in a relationship).

Shelley realized that this can give students the impression topics are decided before writing a draft, and she wanted, instead, to show them it is through writing that we discover what we have to say. Therefore, she came to the workshop with a draft in hand. "I wrote this last night," she said and then she read the piece to the students who gathered around her. It was a personal narrative depicting the events that occurred after Shelley gave a workshop in Denver. On the way to the airport, the people who hosted her visit decided to show her the city. Shelley hardly noticed the sights because she kept anxiously glancing at her watch, sure that she would arrive at the airport and find it too late to check in her baggage, or that the nonsmoking section would be full and she'd have to sit amid the cigarette smoke. And indeed, when Shelley arrived at the airport she found that the regular section on the airplane *was* full. But the narrative ends happily because Shelley was moved into the first-class section. The peanuts came in a ceramic bowl rather than a tinfoil package. For dinner she had shrimp scampi, the napkin was linen—and it was a lovely experience.

It was also a lovely draft, full of telling details and a sense of drama. But when Shelley read it to the eighth graders, she said, "I know it is OK, but I can't help but think—so what?" Then she went on to say that as a writer, she knows the piece of writing should be important to her. "All this piece does is tell about one day," she said. "I need to think about whether this topic matters to me, and if so, why." Shelley ended by realizing that the incident in Denver said something about herself, something she had never realized. "I ruined that whole afternoon in Denver because I worried so much. I am such a pessimist, I always expect the worst . . . and look at the wonderful surprise that life brought to me!"

As Shelley moved around the workshop conferring with students, she continued to demonstrate the teaching power of writing. She watched as Pedro reread his draft. "Did anything surprise you?" she asked.

"Yes," he told her. "I'm writing about how when I babysat for my three-year-old nephew, he punched me and gave me a black eye. But guess what? I'm *happy* when I read it. This kid can do *anything* to me and I still think he is the greatest. I guess that's because I'm the only one I know who has a three-year-old nephew and I'm so proud of him." For Pedro, a quick story about his black eye turned into a discovery and eventually, into an important piece of writing.

Shelley's mini-lesson could have been part of the previous chapter. There is no reason to think that upper elementary school children cannot learn to probe their topics as Pedro has done. Yet I think that adolescents have a special need for their writing to add up to something important. Younger children are often happy to crank out little pieces of writing, one after another, but for middle-school students it seems especially important that at least some pieces of writing are treated as major projects. Pedro ended up spending several weeks on a character sketch of his nephew. In a small spiral notebook, he jotted down the details about whatever his nephew did and said. Then he set to work writing a collection of small pieces on his nephew, storing each piece in a big manila envelope that Shelley had given him. Eventually he began to see themes emerging, and his final character sketch explored these surprising connections.

Pedro's writing process is a testimony to the new intellectual powers of an adolescent. Like many of his peers, Pedro is able to distance himself enough from concrete details and specific incidents to see larger themes. Although Pedro was able to do this because Shelley nudged him to turn a little piece of writing into an important project, it is natural for adolescents to look for the significance in events, to view a subject from a variety of perspectives, to shuttle between one point of view and another. In the first part of her piece, for example, thirteen-year-old Liz sees connections between two phenomena and begins to abstract from her experience:

I met a person a few years ago who became one of my closest friends. She was witty, intelligent and lit up the room with her personality.

We probably became friends because we were so much the same. We had the same interests and ideas, for instance, and we liked the same kinds of music. We enjoyed sports, acting and also we had the same opinions of certain people whom we both knew. This similarity became so extreme that we started to say things at the same time and we had the exact same reaction to things. My other friends seemed less important now that I had my one Friend.

It got to the point where I thought one of us might get tired of the other and so she did. I'm not sure if it was that she actually got tired of me or she just wanted other friends. In any case, the way she dealt with it was to drop our friendship completely.

Other students show a similar ability. Gene, for example, uses sensory details to create a larger impression. He writes, "The hospital was big, glaring with bright lights, and it gave me a cold feeling in my chest." Adolescents not only have an ability to perceive underlying themes in concrete details, they also have a desire to do so. By probing into the significance of life-events, they can build their writing on a foundation of meaning.

Writing will also be meaningful for these students if it connects with the purposes and interests that energize their lives. Just as I poured energy into the scripts for our playhouse productions, so, too, Joshua writes endless letters in an effort to get materials on Dorset sheep, and Ben sends passionate pleas asking his state senator to vote against increased military expenditures. Adolescence is not only a time for projects, but also for causes. Many young teenagers become intensely involved in ideological movements. Writing can play a part in all of this, and in doing so, it taps a tremendous energy source.

But students of this age level not only need to write with passion, they also need to write with skill. Howard Gardner suggests that these middle-school years form a kind of "sensitive period" during which skills must be developed at a rapid rate so that by the time students reach the age of fourteen or fifteen, they are already accomplished enough in their craft to withstand the rise in their own critical powers (*Art, Mind and Brain*, 90). But Gardner also feels that in the upper-elementary and middle-school years, children seem supremely equipped to learn just about anything. He quotes V. S. Pritchett who has written in *The Cab at the Door* (102), "That eager period between ten and fourteen is the one in which one can learn anything." Gardner adds, "If one has any doubts about the particular learning facility of this period, he should travel with a preadolescent to an exotic land and note who picks up the language, and without a trace of an accent" (214).

If these students can learn French or Spanish by traveling to France or Puerto Rico, they are as quick to learn the techniques of written language by immersing themselves in literature. Imitation seems to be part of the process of scouting around to find oneself. Many adolescent writers try on first this style and then that one, almost as they try on sets of clothes. "Is this me?" they seem to be asking. "What will using this style say about me?" Sometimes students lose their own voice in this process and end up writing muddled, pretentious stories, such as Chris wrote after reading Steinbeck's *Of Mice and Men*. Chris's story begins:

> *The flat, dissipated land stretched endlessly among the blackish trees of a summer long gone by. On the run-down farm men were talking, stripped of everything but stories and anecdotes which they told in a brilliant and eloquent manner. Inside, the swaying breeze flirted with the stained curtain and memoirs of an old man were laid upon a worn-down chest which had crumbled almost to dust in the years.*
>
> *The ending of the book he had wished would be good, but it was not. The man rolled over and looked at the clock. It much resembled him, for it could be described as a time bomb ready to explode.*

Like a kid dressed up in his father's clothes, Chris has taken on a style that doesn't fit him. If he has a chance to bring his writing to a small response group or a whole-class share session, Chris's classmates will probably ask about his tone.

If Chris feels that his classmates are criticizing his writing, he may react, as many adolescents do, by crumpling up the draft and saying, "I knew it wasn't good," or "What do *you* want me to do then?" OR he might say, "See, I can't write fiction." As hard as these students are on each other, they are even harder on themselves.

Adolescence is a time of extremes and of wide swings of mood. One day the writer will tear up a draft rather than reworking it, another day, the writer will pour endless energy into revision. One day the writer will want to show the world what he or she has done, the next day the writer will be very private. One day the writing workshop will be "boring," the next day, "fantastic." These are the best of times, these are the worst of times.

III

writing conferences

12

---

let youngsters show us how to help them

A student waves his paper overhead. "I'm done, I finished my draft," he says. Giving it to the teacher, he asks, "Now what should I do?"

The question, of course, is what should *we* do. We want our students to do what real writers do, and in part this means knowing what it is to do their best and then make their best, better. What can we say? We skim the draft anxiously. The student, shifting his weight from one foot to the other, asks, "Can I copy it over into final draft?" It is a familiar scenario in writing classrooms, and it is a scenario I often begin with when speaking on the topic of teacher–student conferences.

At a recent workshop, I played the role of student. "Here is my piece, I'm done," I announced and, with an overhead projector, I displayed the draft (Figure 12-1). Hands went up as members of the audience took the part of the teacher. "What did the hospital look like?" one woman asked. Another wondered, "What did you do when you visited your grandfather?" Still others wanted to know what it had been like when my grandfather was alive. One person disagreed with the implicit message in these conferences and said she would ask if the draft was done, did I plan to revise it? After many such responses, someone timidly said, "This probably isn't the right response but to tell the truth, I'd hug the child and say I was sorry her grandfather died."

Why is it so difficult to give a simple human response? I think it is because we try so hard to be helpful we forget to be real. We forget to listen. I used to think listening was easy, that you just sat there and

One tim my gan Fath
Was in The Hbtl
He dinH. git badr.
SoHe Wet to God
I Mid my gan Fath

Kornelia

Figure 12–1

Translation:
One time my grandfather was in the hospital. He didn't get any better. So he went to God. I miss my grandfather.

waited while the other person had a chance to say something, and then you talked. But I have come to realize that listening is the hardest thing I do. In *Lessons from a Child*, I make an analogy between listening and playing tennis:

> *I once thought watching the ball in tennis was easy too. When I was a kid, my mother used to shout from across the net saying, "Keep your eye on the ball." I remember thinking, "Obviously you watch the ball." Obviously you listen.*
>
> *But the other day on the tennis courts, I watched the ball—and it was an entirely new sensation. I was mesmerized by the ball; watching it come over, as if in slow motion, then the bounce, the climb; then it hung, suspended for an instant. Why was that day different? Because I wasn't apologizing for my bad shots or tidying my hair or pulling my shorts down so I wouldn't look fat or remembering to step into the ball. I wasn't thinking about myself (132–33).*

When we first learn to confer with writers, we often worry so much about asking the right questions that we forget to listen. We focus on asking the questions that will draw out more information, not realizing that it is listening that creates a magnetic force between writer and listener. The force of listening will draw words out; writers will find themselves saying things they didn't know they knew.

Our first job in a conference, then, is to be a person, not just a teacher. It is to enjoy, to care, and to respond. We cry, laugh, nod, and sigh. We let the writer know she has been heard. We tell the youngster we are sorry about her grandfather. Sometimes that is enough. Sometimes the purpose of a conference is simply to respond. Other times, if the moment seems right, we try, in a conference, to extend what the youngster can do as a writer.

Because I believe that writing is a process of interacting with one's emerging text, it is important to ask questions of students that help them interact with their work-in-progress. I try to act as a backboard, sending the ball back into the student's court. I nudge students into "re-vision," into looking through what they have said to see what they can discover. After reading a draft, I may say, "Let's see, what have you said so far?" Then the student and I survey the piece, highlighting the large chunks of meaning. By doing this, I see what has been said, but I also help students "re-see." This should become part of the writing process; they should shuttle between the roles of involved writer and detached critic.

Of course, this is not the only question to ask, nor the only lens that can help writers learn from their writing. We can also engage students in asking themselves other questions:

How do I feel about it so far? What is good that I can build on? Is there anything that disturbs me, that doesn't fit or seems wrong.

What am I discovering as I write this? What has surprised me? Where is this leading?

What is the one most important thing I am trying to convey? How can I build this idea? Are there places where I wander away from my central meaning?

How will my audience read this? What will he (she) think as he (she) reads along? What questions will he (she) ask? What will be his (her) response to the different sections of the text . . . to the whole?

What might I do next? Would it help to try another draft . . . to talk with someone . . . to put it away . . . to reread it several times . . . to try a new genre . . . to keep on writing . . . or what?

It is easy to list questions in a book and harder to ask them in real classrooms. The questions put the spotlight on the writer, and too often, as teachers we hesitate to give away control. We look at a student's rough draft and have the urge to take it over, to make it match our expectations. I find that my own writing block vanishes the instant I see someone else's draft. My fingers begin to itch. I envision my ideal version of the text, and I know exactly what changes I would make to bridge the gap between what the student has written and what I would write. Buried three lines into the piece I spot the perfect lead sentence. I notice where the pace breaks down and envision just how I would remedy the problem. However, while I do not take pen in hand to rewrite the student's draft because I know better, I can be manipulative and coy. "I'm wondering if you see a different way to start your piece?" I ask. "Is there a different sentence down around here which might work better?" If the youngster doesn't catch my hint, I may even read the piece aloud, saying "Listen and see if you hear where the action picks up." Then, of course, I use my voice to signal the "right" answer, and pretty soon the student's text has become my own.

But it is not my piece of writing. It belongs to somebody else. If we, as teachers, ask questions and make suggestions so that student texts end up matching what we had in mind—what have we accomplished? Better bulletin boards, perhaps. Longer lines during the writing workshop. The only real lasting result of such conferences is that we teach students to be dependent on our evaluations, on our advice. But we will not always be there when our students write. The underlying notion of the writing process is that students need to become critical readers of their own texts. Our job in a writing conference is to put ourselves out of a job, to interact with students in such a way that they learn how to interact with their own developing texts.

If we can keep only one thing in mind—and I fail at this half the time— it is that we are teaching the writer and not the writing. If the piece of writing gets better but the writer has learned nothing that will help him or her another day on another piece, then the conference was a waste of everyone's time. It may have done more harm than good, for such conferences teach students to be dependent on us.

There are many ways in which, without meaning to do so, we take over ownership in a writing conference. Sometimes, for example, I find myself holding a student's draft in my hands: the piece is, quite literally, out of the writer's hands. Worse yet, I sometimes find myself reading a student's piece with pen in hand, or standing above a student while I ask about the draft. These may seem like small points, but our actions can convey more than our words.

Body language during teacher-student interactions can help convey respect for the writer. I try to draw my chair alongside the writer's desk, or to crouch beside it. I hope that I look less at the writing and more at the writer, since it is the writer who needs to look at the piece. When I am at my best, my body language says, "I am teaching the writer, not just the writing."

Of course, sometimes it is a sham. I may display all the right body language and still take the piece of writing from the student. One indication that I am doing this is the feeling I sometimes get that the spotlight is totally on me. When the student approaches me for a conference I think, "What am I going to say? What am I going to ask?" as if the student is a blank slate and it is up to me to find something brilliant to say to begin the conference. I should know better. When I remember that someone else has just written the draft, as I have just written this chapter, I realize that the best way to begin a conference is by asking "How's it going?" or "Where are you with this?" or "How can I help you?"—anything that puts the ball back in the writer's court and gets the writer showing me how I can help. When a patient goes to a physician, the physician doesn't begin with clever or brilliant remarks. The physician begins instead by listening: "What hurts?" "How can I help?" We need to begin writing conferences in a similar manner.

Then, too, I take control—and most of us do—by asking specific content questions that pull the writer toward things in which I am interested. "Oh, tell me about your dog," I ask, "What kind of dog is he?" I pump for specific bits of information that the writer will then, I hope, add to the text. Yet who is to say that the writer wants to expand upon these things? We may want the writer to add information, but it would be far better to ask broad questions that invite the writer to choose what is important: "What are you getting at in this story? What's the main thing?" Then our specific questions can expand upon areas the writer has deemed important.

I also take control with my compliments, my evaluations, my assessments. "I like the beginning—the ending is less good," I say. Soon writers learn that *they* are not the critical reader of their text: I am. Yet the writing process must involve evaluation. Standing back to critique is a crucial part of writing. Revisions are often prompted by a writer's own evaluations of his or her text. Our students need to be critics of their own writing. Instead of doling out our evaluations, we need to ask them questions such as "How do you feel about it?"

The issues I am raising are tricky ones, and there are no absolutes. It is easier to demonstrate effective writing conferences than to write about them, because the tone of a voice, with its subtle inflections and pauses, or a touch says so much. Nevertheless, I hope this discussion has provided a framework for a more detailed look at writing conferences. In the next four chapters I am going to address different tacks we can take in the writing conference:

- Content conference.
- Design conference.
- Process conference.
- Evaluation conference.
- Editing conference.

I will not discuss editing until later. Let me say also that these distinctions are a fiction. In real life, they overlap and blur together. Yet I think it will be helpful to look at them separately.

13

content conferences: teacher-student and peer conferences

I often tell people that much of what I know about responding to writing has come from Donald Murray. When they hear this, people nod their heads as if to say, "I understand." But I wonder if they do.

The most important things I've learned from Murray have not come from his wonderful books and articles, but from what he did for me thirteen years ago when I was a fledgling teacher. Teaching was hard for me. I was what you would call a "two-bag teacher." Every night I'd lug two of those giant canvas L. L. Bean bags home, each one full of papers to correct, and I'd stay up until all hours of the night going over them. But it wasn't those long hours that made teaching hard for me, it was the little seed of embarrassment I felt over being an elementary school teacher. Amazing as it sounds, I used to go to parties and hope no one would ask what I did. Every year I spent Christmas vacation writing essays to get into graduate school, and then I'd think better of it.

One day I wrote something other than an application essay. Somehow I got up the nerve to send that piece to Murray, whose book I was reading, and to ask if he would help me make it better. Murray wrote back saying yes. That Saturday, and as it turned out, one Saturday a month for the next two years, I drove two-and-a-half hours to the University of New Hampshire for a fifteen-minute conference with Murray and then drove two-and-a-half hours back to Connecticut. As a teacher of writing, I often think back to that: five hours of driving for a fifteen-minute conference! What did Murray teach me that was so important?

He taught me I had something to say. He was fascinated by what I knew about classroom teaching, and his interest helped me believe in my profession and in myself. I began to know that I had a unique and powerful story to tell. Of course, years later, I realize that Murray makes everyone feel this way. But I also realize that there is no greater gift a writing teacher can give than to help another person know he or she has a story to tell. The teacher of writing is a student of students. Listen to Murray's description of his teaching:

> *I am tired, but it is a good tired, for my students have generated energy as well as absorbed it. I've learned something of what it is to be a childhood diabetic, to raise oxen, to work across from your father at 115 degrees in a steel drum factory, to be a welfare mother with three children, to build a bluebird trail, . . . to bring your father home to die of cancer. I have been instructed in other lives, heard the voices of my students they had not heard before, shared their satisfaction in solving the problems of writing with clarity and grace.*
>
> *I feel guilty when I do nothing but listen. I confess my fear that I'm too easy, that I have too low standards, to a colleague, Don Graves. He assures me I am a demanding teacher for I see more in my students than they see in themselves.*
>
> *I suppose he is right. I do hear voices from my students they have never heard from themselves. I find they are authorities on subjects they think ordinary. . . . Teaching writing is a matter of faith, faith that my students have something to say and a language in which to say it (Murray 1982, 157).*

The writing teacher takes lessons from children and, in doing so, helps them know what they know. If it seems I am speaking of content conferences in elevated terms, this is as it should be. They are at the heart of teaching writing. Yet what actually occurs in a content conference is neither elevated nor unusual.

Each morning, when youngsters tumble into the classroom bearing their small treasures and their elaborate news, we hold content conferences. Yung-su has an invitation to Stephanie's birthday, Tamara will be staying after school for gymnastics, Kendra has five possibilities in mind for her new kitten's name. These are the topics children will write about if we confirm their importance.

Kendra tells me about the Name-the-Kitten contest she has scheduled for her family. In great excitement I respond that Kendra could write a whole book about naming her cat! She is delighted. Meanwhile Tamara not only wants to tell me about her gymnastics stunts, she wants to show me, and then, to teach me. When I groan, she laughs, claps her hands, and tells me that in her next book, she is going to write the directions for doing a cartwheel.

A friend, listening to these conferences, comments, "They don't sound like writing conferences. They are just conversations: kids and teachers talking about writing topics." And of course, that is the point. In content conferences, we do not ask brilliant questions or give astute advice.

Yet even these, the simplest, most natural forms of conferences, are not as easy as they sound. Youngsters do not always come to a conference convinced they have something to say. We sometimes have to draw information from them. Or the reverse is true: too many children are too eager to tell us their stories. The lines grow long and no one is writing. The constraints of classroom teaching are such that we need to listen efficiently as well as sincerely. Then, too, it is one thing for a youngster to tell us about his or her topic, and another thing for the child to write it. Let me put these problems and their solutions into context by showing two effective content conferences.

Eric crumpled up another sheet of paper and added it to the discarded drafts which already littered the floor around him. "I've got nuthin'. I'm out of stories, I'm out of trips."

"I'll tell you what," Eric's teacher, Mrs. Gerwin, said, crouching next to his desk. "Why don't you and I make a list of things you know a lot about, things you're an expert in."

"Nothing. TV, that's all," Eric said, "and baseball. That's all."

"Oh, that's right, you play baseball!" Mrs. Gerwin said, her voice filled with interest.

Eric nodded. "Almost made a home run last night," he muttered. "Got to third."

"In one hit? Tell me about it, what happened?"

"When I stood up to bat, I had the feeling it'd be a lucky one," Eric said, his resistance melting. "I took hold of the bat and I said to myself, 'stay cool' . . ."

Sliding a clean sheet of paper in front of Eric, Mrs. Gerwin interrupted to say, "Eric, would you put that down—just how you said it to me." And she repeated his words, looked expectantly at his paper until he'd started writing, then moved on to another child.

Eleven-year-old Sumi paused in the midst of writing, and stared into space. Drawing her chair alongside Sumi's desk, Mrs. Thornton asked if she could interrupt. "How's it going?" Sumi slid her story toward her teacher and looked down at her hands as Mrs. Thornton quietly read the draft.

My father died when I was three but my sister was twelve and my brother, ten. When I see pictures of him holding me, it's like he is a stranger. In the same picture is my brother and sister only they knew him well. They never talk about him except to say, "You would have liked him." When I see other kids with their fathers, I wonder what it would be like to be his daughter.

"Sumi," Mrs. Thornton said, pushing a strand of hair from the girl's face. "I'm glad you are writing about this. I can tell how special your father is to you, even though you never got the chance to know him."

Sumi nodded. There was a long pause before she began to talk. "When people ask me how it feels not to have a father, I tell them it doesn't matter because I never knew him. But when I see my sister and brother with him in pictures, I feel sorry for myself because I didn't get to know him like they did. I sort of feel cheated."

"I'd feel the same way, Sumi," Mrs. Thornton said. They were quiet for a moment and then, touching Sumi lightly on the shoulder, Mrs. Thornton said, "I'm going to leave you now because I don't want to get in the way of what you are doing. It is so important, the things you have been saying. I'll be back, my friend."

Although Eric and Sumi were each in different places, Eric facing the blank page and Sumi working her way into a draft, their conferences were similar. I call these content conferences because in both conferences, the teachers focused on the subject. They did not focus on the writer (How was it to write this piece? What are you going to do next?) or on the text (What have you done so far? What do you like best about it? Do you think you could add onto that?). Instead, the teachers responded to and asked questions about the content, and in this way, helped the youngsters add onto (or begin) their drafts. This is an extremely common pattern in teacher-student and peer conferences, and for this reason, it is important to consider why some of these conferences are more successful than others.

If a conference is going well, the child's energy for writing increases. The child should leave the conference wanting to write. Eric and Sumi's energy increased, I believe, because their teachers focused on what they *did* say. The energy level would have been very different had their teachers rushed to elicit more information. Compare Mrs. Thornton's response with the way many well-intended writing teachers might have responded to Sumi's draft:

MRS. THORNTON'S RESPONSE	MANY OF OUR RESPONSES
"Sumi," Mrs. Thornton said, pushing a strand of hair from the girl's face. "I'm glad you are writing this. I can tell how special your father is to you, even though you never got the chance to know him."	*"It is too bad about your father, Sumi," the teacher said, her eyes flickering over the draft as she searched for places where more details were needed.*
Sumi nodded. There was a long pause before she began to talk. . . .	*"Um, Sumi, you told about seeing photographs of your father. What did he look like in the photographs?"*
"I'd feel the same way, Sumi," Mrs. Thornton said, and then,	*After Sumi answered, the teacher said, "Do you think you should add*

touching Sumi lightly on the shoulder, Mrs. Thornton said, "I'm going to leave you now because I don't want to get in your way. It is so important. . . ."

that? When I read your piece, I didn't know about it."

Sumi nodded dutifully, and the teacher again scanned the page. "Another thing, you never told your brother and sister's names. Don't you think that might help? . . ."

Is it any surprise that some content conferences are successful and others are not! Some empower the youngsters, making them feel like experts, while others pull them down, making them feel that their drafts aren't good enough.

Although in the example above Mrs. Thornton did not ask a single question, there are times when it is helpful to ask content questions. Initially, these questions should be broad enough that children are able to select which aspects of the topic are most important. Even then, children will often summarize their information in one or two quick sentences, as Eric did when he said, "I almost made a homerun . . . made it to third," or as a child did recently when she described her day at the park, saying, "We had a lot of fun playing on the swings and then we came home." Usually I respond by circling back to what the child has said, encouraging the youngster to include more detail. I might say, "You made it to third base! What happened?" or "You played on the swings? I remember the last time I did that, it was terrific fun. Would you tell me about it?" If the youngster still responds with broad generalities ("We just swung"), then I try again. "It is hard for me to really picture it when you tell about it so fast, in one sentence. What was it like for you?"

When content conferences work well, children not only realize that the details about their topic matter, they also learn that in order to write well, they must keep their eye on their subject. Just as it is important to keep one's eye on the ball in tennis, and to focus on the melody rather than on the fingering in playing the piano, so too, writers know that when they focus on inserting dialogue, using metaphor, and adding descriptions into their writing instead of concentrating on their subjects, the resulting texts are often contrived and lifeless. Powerful writing comes from looking deeply and honestly at a subject. Content conferences can help students relax about their style and technique in order to better focus on their subjects—and their pieces of writing usually improve as a result.

I am reminded of Amy, the class artist in Mrs. Howard's third grade. Amy wrote incredible first drafts, and I believe she did so because she had learned through drawing to focus on her subject. Amy could pick up her pencil and without lifting it from the paper, draw the contours of a sleeping cat. She wrote as she drew. "When I write, it is like I have a movie in my mind. I can see the fox, curled up in his stump, and I keep my eye on him. The words just click off of me. It is like I am a typewriter, clicking them off." This is the lead that resulted when Amy kept her eyes on the fox, curled in his den:

A beam of light shone through the crack in the red fox's den. The fox opened his eyes just a crack and looked around his den. It was a cozy stump . . .

Audience awareness is another aspect of writing that children can learn through content conferences. Sometimes we cannot respond to a child's story because we do not understand it. When we have *real* questions, not trumped up ones meant to elicit revisions, we must ask young writers these questions, because it not only shows them that their information is valued, it also helps them anticipate their audience's need for information. In this conference, listeners ask for clarification, and as a result the writer's energy increases.

The cluster of first graders listened as Charles, a stout youngster with dark curls framing his face, read his story to them.

Me and my friends ran in the football field. Then we went to the Hornell's house. When we got to the Hornell's house we ate dead pig. Then we went to our house. I watched TV with my dog. Then I went to sleep. The End.

"You told us all about what you did," Sharon said to her classmate. "How you ran, went to the Hornell's house, and . . ."

"Ate dead pig!" Scott added. "Yucky, yucky." The children laughed and Charles beamed, proud at his unexpected luck. Charles was a solemn fellow and it was rare for children to laugh at his stories.

Mr. Osborne asked if anyone else could remember more of what happened in Charles's book and Jerome raised his hand. "He went home and watched TV with his dog. It was a good story, he told it in order, what he did."

"But what is dead pig?" Scott wanted to know. "On your plate did you have a pig with ears and a nose and a curly tail? Did it say oink?"

"It was a big ugly thing and it was cooked and it was brownish. There was a nose but Mr. Hornell cut it off. It was like a different kind of ham."

"That's important information, Charles," Mr. Osborne said, adding, "Some of us were a bit confused about that part." Charles nodded and said he'd add about the dead pig. The class then talked about ways Charles could use arrows or carets to insert the information in his text.

It is worth noting that Charles's conference ended with a discussion of ways he could add information to the text, and Eric's conference ended with his teacher sliding a clean sheet of paper in front of him, saying, "Why don't you put that down." Other content conferences will end with the child compiling a list of subtopics, or taping a second sheet onto the bottom of the first, or stapling paper together to make a book with chapters.

As a content conference concludes, the focus usually shifts from content to process, from "what do you have to say?" to "what will you do next?" In Charles's conference, it was the teacher who made this switch, and his peers who asked the content questions. "What is dead pig?" Scott wanted to know and his question is a reminder that even very young children can take over the teacher's role, acting as conference partners for each other.

"Our job in a conference is to put ourselves out of a job," I have said. When teachers respond to the content of student drafts, children will respond in similar ways to the work of their friends. Without peer-conferences, teachers feel like Pied Pipers. A huge line of children follow the teacher wherever he or she goes. This line causes chaos, and it pressures the teacher so that conferences become hurried, tense, and less effective. Peer-conferences are important for another reason as well. When children ask questions of each other, they learn to ask questions of their own emerging texts.

"I tried peer conferencing and it didn't work," teachers tell me. "The children couldn't do it."

"If you tried math and it didn't work, would you give up?" I ask in response. If the children couldn't do the math, we would show them how, we would help them. Yet somehow we expect children to confer well with each other without our guidance.

On the second or third day of their writing workshops, the teachers with whom I work usually introduce children to peer-conferences. By then most of the children have finished their drafts. Accustomed to the one-draft-only pace of our schools, children come into a workshop writing in single, quick spurts. By the second day, all around the room, children will be jumping out of their seats, saying "I'm done," "I'm done," and teachers will find this a good time to introduce the class to peer-conferences. As I mentioned in chapter 7, the teacher might begin that day's workshop by saying, "Yesterday I talked with you about being writers. Today I want to talk with you about being writing teachers. There is not just one writing teacher in this room—there are thirty of you. Every one of you needs to become a writing teacher."

Recently JoAnn Curtis, one of the teacher-trainers in our Writing Project, said this to a group of students who were new to writing process. On the chalkboard she had listed a simple framework for peer conferences, and she told the class that they would begin by conferring (as a group) with one writer. Because I was researching the interaction between JoAnn and the classroom teacher, who was watching this demonstration lesson, I copied JoAnn's list from the chalkboard:

1   The writer reads out loud.
2   Listeners respond, or if the piece is confusing, the listeners ask questions, then respond.

3　Listeners focus on the content, perhaps asking questions about it. The writer teaches them about the subject.

4　The focus shifts to the text. What will the writer do next and how will he or she do it?

Alejandro had finished his first draft, and JoAnn, following step one, asked him to read it aloud. After he finished, JoAnn asked, "Who listened really well? Can you tell Alejandro what you heard, what you liked?" We find that when peer-conferences are introduced, children often do not listen well to each other. If they are asked to retell what they heard, this not only highlights the need for good listening, it also gives the class a second chance to hear the piece.

On this particular day, Alejandro called on Jason to retell the story. "I heard that your cousin was swinging you and a dog came and scratched your cousin and then you flew and banged your head on the dresser, the pointy part, and got stitches."

The class giggled, and Alejandro squirmed. Immediately JoAnn Curtis became very somber. "What concerns me is that you are laughing and it isn't a funny story," she said. "Alejandro is telling about how he got hurt." Nothing is more important than helping children honor each other's efforts, and this issue needs to be addressed the moment it comes up.

This time a youngster protested. "We weren't laughing at how he got hurt," he said. "We were laughing at the funny part when he said he flew through the air."

"OK," JoAnn said, "because some parts weren't funny at all and you have to be very careful of an author's feelings." Then she asked the class for their responses to the story, and for their questions. Because this ritual was new to the children, JoAnn didn't expect them to ask open-ended questions or to follow a line of questioning. For now, she only wanted the children to experience the gestalt of peer-conferences. Later, on another day, she would help the children improve particular aspects of their conferences.

Ramon's hand was up immediately: "How many stitches did you get?" he asked Alejandro.

"Three."

The next child pursued an entirely new tangent. "Did you ask your cousin to swing you or did he just start swinging you?"

"No, I guess I asked him," Alejandro said.

"Whose fault was it that you hit your head?" Jason wondered.

"It wasn't anybody's. It wasn't the dog's fault because he didn't know what was happening, he just walked up to my cousin and he had this person flying at him."

"I couldn't picture how he was swinging you."

To answer this, Alejandro stood up and demonstrated. At this point I finally realized the cousin had held his ankles and swung him around in a circle "like an airplane." Alejandro described the event again. "My cousin was swinging me and he fell and hit his head and I went flying."

There were other questions: what was the dog's reaction when he saw a person flying at him? How far did you fly? After a few more minutes of discussion, JoAnn interrupted to ask Alejandro whether the questions had helped him.

"I liked them," he said.

"How have they helped?"

Alejandro thought for a minute. "They ask you all these little questions so I could tell more. You aren't going to tell all the little parts unless they ask you, unless they are interested in it."

"What will you do now?" JoAnn wondered.

"Copy it over neat."

JoAnn said, "Alejandro, here is something I want you to consider. During the workshop today you *could* write what we call another draft, explaining things so much more." Then she added, "When I first heard your story I had a hard time picturing it but now I can see in my mind what happened. Later, if you want, you will have the chance to think about the parts which might not be that clear. I can help you."

Then, JoAnn told the children that when they needed help, they could act as conference partners for each other. The class reviewed the format for these conferences and the children returned to work. A few minutes later, I joined Jerod and Arthur who were sitting on the floor along the edge of the classroom. Jerod had already heard Arthur's draft and he was responding to it.

"A cage? You took your cat to the park in a cage?" Jerod said.

Arthur nodded. "Yeah, a bird cage."

"Why?"

"That's the only cage we have. He'd run away."

Jerod was surprised. "He would?" Arthur nodded. "Why don't you tie something around his neck?"

"I did that one time, some string," Arthur answered. "You still got your cat?"

Jerod nodded. "Yeah, I got him sooner than you did so he is still small."

"If I ever come to your apartment this year, I might bring my cat."

"They might fight."

"Then we could write a really long story," Arthur said, picking up his draft.

"Oh, it's good, Arthur. Your story is good. 'Cept I think you should tie something around its neck," Jerod said. The conference ended without switching from content to process. The focus never returned to the draft, and Arthur did not make changes on his piece as a result of the interaction. It is easy to dismiss such a conference as "just talk." And perhaps it was. But writers know that writing can be a lonely activity. My phone bill skyrockets when I am writing: I need to "just talk." Arthur probably gained from the interaction. Also, of course, this was their first conference. Children will learn ways to help each other in a conference when they have had more practice in peer conferences and when their teacher has helped them in teacher-student conferences.

In time, the children will sense for themselves the difference between successful and unsuccessful conferences. Perhaps the class as a whole will talk about the need to let a writer choose which aspects of a topic are most important. I've seen teachers asking the author to go into the hall for a minute while the class learns about being good writing teachers. When the author is out of the room, the teacher says, "Children, your job will be to find what matters to this author, and to get the author talking about whatever that is. How will you find out what interests the author?" Only after the class has considered and chosen a way to begin the conference does the author return. "We learned a lot from your piece," a child might say, "but we weren't sure; of all the things you wrote, which was the most important thing to you?"

Another time, the teacher might help children ask open-ended questions. "I'm going to be the author," a teacher might say. "You respond to my story, ask me questions, and if you ask an open-ended question you will feel the difference. I'll probably give a much fuller response and you will notice that I am more interested in what I am saying." In the discussion which ensues, the children who ask yes/no questions receive blunt, dull responses. Those who ask open-ended questions receive more elaborate, energetic answers.

A word of caution. There is a danger in too much emphasis on "the skills of peer conferences": responses quickly become "canned" and mechanical; children perform on cue; they act a part. From time to time, it helps to focus on the skills of responding to writing, but too much is not helpful. Above all, conferences should be natural. They should be full of good listening and honest reactions. Perhaps the best way to extend peer conferences is by participating in them: listening, modeling, and gently guiding.

In the following whole-class share meetings, we see teachers doing just that. Six-year-old Ricardo took his seat in the author's chair and waited until his first-grade classmates grew quiet. He looked at the teacher, and she nodded for him to begin. With great ceremony, Ricardo opened his paper and began to read:

I want to be an astronaut. [There was a pause as he reread something quietly.] I want to be an archeologist because you find bones. The end.

Several hands went up, and one child asked, "Why do you want to be an archeologist?"

"Because they find bones."

"Yes, but they have to give the bones to their bosses."

"I know what you mean 'cause they give dinosaur bones to their museums but then they get rich. The museums give them gold."

Another hand went up. "Why did you want to be an astronaut *and* an archeologist? And where are you going to get the things to wear to be an astronaut? Buy them?"

"Yeah, buy them, but I got a little mixed up because the words sound the same, and I read it wrong."

"So what do you want to be?"

"An archeologist who finds bones and takes them to the museum and gets rich."

At this point the teacher said, "Class, pretty soon we are going to end this conference. What do you think you might say to Ricardo that will help him when he goes back to his desk?" This teacher knows that share meetings can be more than show and tell sessions, that they can be instructional.

One youngster said she'd ask Ricardo what he was going to do next. Ricardo responded, "Write a new story because I don't have any more space."

The teacher repeated what Ricardo said to the class and asked if any of them had ideas about how he could add more space to the original story. Soon Ricardo and Brian had agreed to work together, adding more "space," and presumably, more words to Ricardo's story.

In a sixth-grade-classroom, Robert began the share meeting by telling his friends he didn't know if his draft was good. "Tell me what you think," he said, and read this aloud:

The man in the pet store handed us a mouse with golden hair and black eyes. It was in a carrying box, in the corner. It looked confused and frightened with its ears up and its long tail wrapped around itself.

Then the mouse jumped out of the box and landed on the floor. My sister grabbed the mouse and put it back in the box, and we walked out of the pet store. We had one more stop to make, so we went into the clothing store. I felt a little sorry for the mouse so I lifted the box lid. The furry mouse looked up at me with a black-eyed gaze. Without a second to spare, the little fur ball jumped out of the box and landed on the cold floor of the department store. I grabbed it. The mouse gave a pitiful squeak and squeezed through my hands. I tried to snatch that pipsqueak again. Then my sister got into the act. She grabbed the mouse . . . and dropped it. "You stupid," I yelled. I grabbed the mouse, he bit me through the skin, and then I threw the little twerp into the box."

By this time, the children were laughing with delight at Robert's tale of woe. Their hands shot up: "It was a cute story," "I loved it," "It was great," they said. Then the teacher intervened. Directing her question to the class, she said, "Can I ask you to tell *why* it was funny or cute or great. What made it so?"

"It was funny, Robert, when you called your sister 'You stupid,' " one child said.

Another added, "And the words you used, like black-eyed gaze." After other specific responses, the teacher asked the class if they had questions for Robert.

"What did you name your mouse?" one youngster wanted to know.

Robert shook his head. "We didn't get that far. I don't think names are that important for a mouse."

"Have you kept him as a pet?"

"No, we gave it to the snake," Robert answered, and his classmates gasped.

"When you write your next draft, are you going to tell about giving the mouse to the snake?"

"That is another story, it isn't what I wanted to tell about in this one. Are there any other questions?" Robert asked.

"How come you opened the lid?"

"Because I felt sorry for the mouse."

"If you felt sorry for him, how come you fed him to your snake?" And so the discussion went, one child amplifying and referring back to what others had said, and Robert engineering the entire discussion. The teacher had done her job well.

14

beyond content conferences

Graves once said, "You can tell a good writing classroom by the presence of the children's own interests in the room," and he was right. Soon the bulletin boards will boast photographs of Jerod's cat and Robert's snake, stories of Sumi's father and a map of Morat's trip from Russia to America.

Even more important, a workshop hum will fill the room. "Every child has a story to tell," Harold Rosen has said, "the question is, will he tell it to you?" In good writing classrooms, clusters of children are everywhere, writing stories and sharing them with each other. In each cluster, one youngster teaches the others about his or her topic. As a result of these content conferences, the stories grow longer and more full of detailed information. Their length results at first from piecemeal additions. Ricardo adds another line to his one-sentence story. Robert turns "My Golden Mouse" into a book, and part two features his snake as the villain. With arrows, Alejandro inserts details into his piece. Sumi's story of her father becomes very long, very bittersweet.

At first, length comes from revisions, but soon children approach their drafts with plans to include detail. They pace themselves so they no longer finish their stories in a single line (We played in the park and then we came home). From the start, their stories are detailed and fluent. Students also begin to notice gaps in their texts; they have internalized a sense of audience. Seven-year-old Heather reread each page of her book. "I'm having an individual writing conference with myself," she said in a prim, matter-of-fact voice. "On each page I ask myself the questions the other

135

kids would ask me." Then Heather opened her book. "Here I wrote,

I HAVE A HORSE.

The kids would ask me if I ride it, so I'm going to add

I RIDE MY HORSE EVERY DAY
UNLESS IT'S RAINING.

Amazingly, throughout the country there are now hundreds of classrooms where children of all ages have learned to internalize their audiences' content questions. Like Heather, these youngsters carry on an internal dialogue as they write: they ask themselves the questions that have been asked of them in content conferences; "What else can I say?" "What can I add here?" "Will this be clear?" Then they share their drafts in peer conferences and whole-class share meetings, and their friends ask more questions about the content. As a result, writers see how to add more information to their initial texts.

Finally, the children bring their richly detailed drafts to us. Eager to nudge youngsters toward revision, we elicit still more information. "What else happened?" we ask, "Can you tell more?" Of course there is more; there is always more. And so the youngsters dutifully tape on sheets of paper and insert more information into their texts. The pieces become longer, as if length is the ultimate goal. In truth, long pieces clog up the entire system in many writing workshops. Everything takes longer: peer conferences monopolize the workshop; teacher-student conferences become slower, and the lines, longer; editing takes forever; significant revisions become less likely; share meetings grow tiresome, and the quantity of writing replaces quality.

One can always add more to a draft. But the essence of writing is selection, not addition. When a child writes fluently and with a sense of audience, is there not a point at which it becomes counterproductive to eke out yet more information? What are we teaching children anyhow; to write by committee? Do we want our youngsters to believe that good writing is constructed, like a machine, through piecemeal additions, through repairs? Why must everybody's good ideas and everybody's key question be grafted onto a piece of writing? The added hunks of information stick out awkwardly, like extra appendages, and destroy the balance and form of a piece. For a time, this awkward, gangly growth may be necessary. But as time passes, children are ready to move on to new challenges. The question is—are we ready?

What I am suggesting is that we need to guard against an attachment to revision for revision's sake. There is nothing inherently good about making additions to a text, nor is there anything inherently good about revision. It is not helpful for teachers to trump up content questions in order to push children toward revision. The process of piecemeal revision should be a provisional one. In time, children outgrow the need for it. What is done first in revision later becomes part of rehearsal. Our children need to move on to new territories, to new frontiers, and we as teachers need to go with them, knowing that today's frontier will become tomorrow's homeland.

I do not want this chapter to negate the preceding one. Content conferences are at the heart of the writing workshop. If I could, I would suggest that only experienced writing teachers read this chapter, because I believe that the best and simplest way to begin a writing workshop is by celebrating what children know and by helping them to develop their pieces so that they convey more information to their audience. Yet I also believe that content conferences should be balanced by design, process, and evaluation conferences, which I will discuss in the next chapters, and that as writers develop, content conferences must become more sophisticated.

In the conferences cited thus far, writers have learned how to answer their readers' questions. They also need to know how to stir their readers' imaginations, to tug at their curiosity, to carry their readers into the secondary world of the story, to instill in their readers feelings of wonder, alarm, tenderness, and hurt. Elbow suggests in *Writing With Power* that our responses to writing must include more than content questions. We need to let writers know our experience of reading a text. We need to give writers "movies of our mind," as Elbow says. This is his example of one student's response to a text:

First I was open and sympathetic to what I thought you were up to. But then without noticing I drifted into resisting what you've been saying. Something made me feel "Wait a minute! There are things that don't fit!" Somehow I became an adversary. . . . (Elbow 1981, 257).

When writers are given movies of their readers' minds, the writers can reshape their texts so as to instill certain feelings in the readers.

Some teachers use conferences to help youngsters inspire and move their readers. When Bradley brought his draft to his teacher for a conference, he prefaced the conference by saying, "I told it all, the whole thing. I got a lot of information in my story." Then, in a monotone, he read the draft aloud:

When my father was gone, me and my brother put a wooden match on and then I put it out with my foot. We did this a lot of times but one time I couldn't put it out. Things started to burn. I put the burning things in the sink and I turned on the cold water faucet a little. I went next door to my grandfather, Uncle Leo, and looked at the house on fire. I sat on his sofa near the window. The end.

Mrs. Holton stared up at Bradley. "This happened?" she asked, amazed that she'd never heard of it until now. Bradley nodded and then told her more about the fire. When he was finished explaining, Mrs. Holton, still shuddering at the thought of the fire, turned to the paper. "You *did* tell a lot of information this time, Bradley. I'm impressed with the details." Then she continued. "But Bradley, sometimes an author needs not only to include information but also to convey a feeling. You know how sometimes when you read a story, you *feel* sad . . . or when you watch television and you are spooked? Is there a feeling you want to get across to your reader in this piece?"

"How scary it was, because it was the scariest time of my life."

Putting the draft aside, Mrs. Holton looked at Bradley. "Will you *tell* it to me so I can feel how spooky it was. What happened? Make me *feel* the scariness, like on a TV program."

Bradley cleared his throat. "My father left and so me and my brother got some matches out . . ." Then he paused. "No, that's not exciting enough." He made one or two other false starts, and then Mrs. Holton interrupted him.

"Maybe if you make it into a fiction story, as if it was about someone else, like, "One day, a young boy . . .""

Bradley lit up at the idea of fiction. "One day, a young boy watched as his father drove away. Then the boy said, 'Ah ha, now I need the matches,' and he began looking for them. He searched through one kitchen drawer, then another. Finally he found them. . . ."

A few minutes later Mrs. Holton slid a clean sheet of paper in front of Bradley, and he began spinning his tale on paper. When Bradley was finished, he and his teacher talked about the larger lesson he'd learned in the conference. "What I learned is that I have to decide on the feelings, the moods, and build up to them," he explained, and "feelings" was added to the list of "Things To Notice," which Bradley kept on the inside of his writing folder.

In the content conferences cited earlier, listeners asked writers about their subjects, and writers added the information to the text (see Figure 14-1).

Figure 14 – 1

As the one-way arrows suggest, the focus in these conferences moves from the subject (What really happened?) to the text (Did you tell that? Do you want to add it?) It is significant that the arrows go in one direction only. In the simplest content conferences, the text is not used as a way to re-see the subject. The writer does not probe, explore, discover, test or change the subject through the act of writing. It is preset, and in the conference pre-existing information is merely moved to the printed page. It is the *listener* who learns about the subject in these conferences, not the writer. The purpose in most content conferences is to elicit what the writer *already knows* rather than to engage the writer in further exploration. Revision is interpreted to mean repairing and extending the piece so that it is more congruent with the pre-existing topic, rather than re-seeing the subject through an early draft. Even my graduate students read their drafts as if they were opaque. They look at drafts and see only drafts; they do not see through them to their still emerging meanings. For them, revision consists simply of making small improvements on the page.

For most writers, the purpose of writing is to think, to learn. My drafts become a lens, helping me see my subject with a new perspective. Murray describes the process this way: "I use language as a tool for seeing and understanding," and again: "We do not write what we know so much as we write *to* know. Writing is exploration" (Murray 1984, 228).

Our content conferences, then, need not focus on what a student knows about the subject. They can focus instead on what students have yet to know, on what they are discovering. "What surprises you as you write?" we can ask. "What new connections do you see in your ideas?" "Where is this leading you?" Above all, we can ask, "What are you learning?"

For a time, our students will shrug and say "I dunno," just as previously, when we asked them to tell more about swinging in the park, they shrugged and said, "I dunno, it was fun." But they have found ways to go beyond a one-line description of the park, and in time, they will also find ways to go beyond a one-line description of what they are learning.

Finally, content conferences emphasize the bits of specific information out of which a text is constructed. Good writing not only conveys information, it is also a work of art. It must try to achieve balance, form, and grace. In our conferences, then, we need to help writers discover what they have to say, but we also need to help them say it well.

15

design conferences: balancing content with form

Teaching, like writing, is a process of rough drafts and revisions. Pulling in, pushing back; creating and criticizing, we ask the same questions of our teaching that we ask of our writing:

- What have I said so far?
- What am I trying to say?
- How else could I approach this?
- What am I learning?

I have often asked these questions of my teaching. I have listened to my answers and made revisions in my "text." This chapter represents one such revision.

I never used to speak of design conferences. Until recently, I said we can focus on the *content* of someone's writing, on their writing *process*, or on their *evaluation* of their emerging text. The design of a piece was, in my mind, determined by the content. Once Amy formed a clear picture in her mind of the cozy stump in which the red fox lived, she had only to find a way to begin the piece, and the words would click out as if from a typewriter. She might leave out information or jumble her facts, and these would be repaired in another draft, but the basic structure of the text was, in my mind, determined by topic choice. She needed only to try to tell what she knew about her chosen topic in the clearest and best way possible. Her goal was for her text to match her subject (see Figure 15-1).

Figure 15 – 1

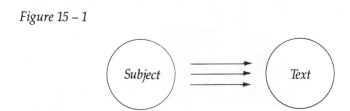

Similarly, if a youngster wrote about his adventure at the beach, my assumption was that in writing the piece, the child would retrace his memory of the day and tell all the significant aspects of the adventure. I would not have thought to ask, "How did you decide which sections to describe in detail and which to summarize in passing?" It was the shape of the *topic* which concerned me more than the shape of the *text*. I encouraged teachers to help students think about the dimensions of their topic. "A good subject has focus," I told teachers. I encouraged them to ask students questions or make comments that would help students narrow their topics:

- What is the one thing you most want to get across?
- You know so much about this topic! Of all that you have to say, what is the most important point?
- What was it about this topic which made you choose to write about it?
- You have told about a great many things. One thing I do after I write a draft to look over it once and ask, "What is the most significant thing to me? How can I make it significant for my readers?"

When teachers made comments and asked questions like these, children soon internalized them and responded in similar ways to their own drafts and those of other children. Birger paused midway into his draft. "In my first story, I wrote two stories in one," he said. "Now I am always thinking, 'is this one story?' 'Is this two stories?' " When Sangwa began her piece, she called it "All My Pets." Several lines into it, she paused to reread the draft and to ask herself focusing questions. She ended by telling only about the day she traveled by subway to the fifty-first Street Deli and left her cat to live there beside the garbage cans in the alley. Sangwa had learned to move in "small steps" through a chronological sequence of events. She included little details—the faint meows she heard coming from inside the cardboard box as she sat, holding it, on the subway, and the late afternoon chill she felt as her cat, Muenster, disappeared into the empty alley. It was a powerful story.

Other children focused their topics in similar ways and the structure of their writing resembled Sangwa's. Diana told about her visit to the eye doctor and how she felt when she heard she would need glasses. Hasun retraced his trip to Manhattan. Brett described the first moments in his softball game.

Some children wanted their pieces to encompass bigger topics. "I am going to tell about my WHOLE trip to Puerto Rico," Julio announced. With his teacher's help, the youngster decided to turn his piece into a book with chapters, each focused on one portion of the trip. Chapter 1 would be about waking up, chapter 2 about packing, chapter 3 about breakfast, chapter 4 about driving to the airport and so on. Julio's teacher gave a mini-lesson on leads and as a result, Julio abandoned chapters 1 to 4 and started his book with the flight to Puerto Rico. In the mini-lesson, the teacher had made a timeline of her own story on the chalkboard:

MY MOUNTAIN CLIMB

- *Waking up on the day we were going to climb the mountain.*

- *Having breakfast.*

- *Driving to the mountain.*

- *Climbing up it.*

- *Reaching the top.*

- *Climbing down.*

- *Getting home.*

"Where do you think I could begin my story?" she asked the class. The response was unanimous: she could begin with waking up. "Anywhere else?" the teacher questioned and soon the class realized the piece could begin anywhere, and that if it began with returning home, the piece might become a flashback.

Mini-lessons such as this one give children tips that can help them write effective narratives. When teachers emphasize limiting the topic, the quality of the children's writing improves dramatically. Their pieces become more dramatic and follow a logical sequence, and they are written with telling detail. Teachers who have never worked with children in this way may want to do so because it is a good base from which to move as we work with our children's writing.

My concern in this chapter is that we don't move from this base. In some classrooms, teachers have seized upon focus as the cure-all. Children crank out pieces to fit a formula. Someone recently said to me, "The question will be, can you survive success?" She was worrying that if our teacher-training ideas became too popular, they could end up as another orthodoxy, but her question also holds true for our methods of teaching children. Success breeds orthodoxy. Six years ago, when I observed children at Atkinson Elementary School, their writing tended to be personal narratives. They built their stories out of little details, and they decided where in the sequence of events they would begin and end. The pieces that resulted, like Sangwa's and Julio's, were powerful. Now children in writing process classrooms everywhere write similar pieces. What have we done?

In some classrooms, all the energy that could have gone into introducing children to a world of written forms has gone instead into hurrying them toward focused chronological pieces. The results are often caricatures of good writing. Roberto loves watching sporting events, but after he applies the "focus treatment" to his topic, he ends up with a piece describing the last ten seconds of one football game. Carmel's grandmother has died, and she is filled with good memories of her, but she wants to write a focused piece, and so she tells about just one small incident. Sarah writes about the death of her thirty-six goldfish, and then, in an effort to narrow her topic, she tells about the death of just one fish.

These children have not learned to experiment with the design and shape of their writing, but only to focus their topic. Focus has come to mean one thing only: selecting a smaller event. No one mentions thematic focus. Roberto does not know he could focus his piece around the reasons he loves watching sports. Carmel is unaware that she could eulogize her grandmother in a piece filled with wonderful memories of her. Children's written products have suffered because of our narrow view of focus. More importantly, the process of writing has suffered.

We have taken away part of what it means to write. Writing, by definition, is an act of composing meaning. When we see the author's task only as the retracing of memory or the translating of an incident into print, we remove the composing process from writing. Where is the art, the discovery, the creation in this process? Where in this diagram (Figure 15-2) do we see room for the author's mind?

I am writing this book out of personal experience, but I am combining all that I know and feel and believe in with my memory of incidents and events. I am connecting my ideas with my experience, my research with

Figure 15 – 2

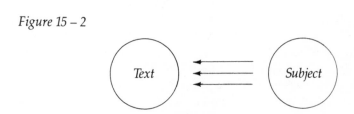

my teaching, my information with the information of others, my past with my present (Murray). *This* is a composing process. I am not restricted to recording what I know or reporting what I did. I am generalizing, organizing, synthesizing, predicting. Our children need the chance to do the same.

They will fail at it. It is easier to follow the structure of an event than to impose order on a topic. And yet, as Faulkner says, "You have to write badly in order to write well." While he was talking about the need to write terrible rough drafts in order to write good ones, I think it is not only within a piece that we need sometimes to write badly, but also within our lives as writers. It probably comes down to an issue of trust. Perhaps it is because I finally believe in children as writers that I no longer want to provide them with a formula for success. I am less worried that if they write badly they will not also write well. Children need to be learners-of-writing more than they need to be producers-of-good-writing. My hope is that writing classrooms can provide children with safe environments so that they can move out beyond the modes in which they have succeeded and try new, strange ways of writing. Perhaps we can help children take risks in their writing, even risks we may no longer be willing to take.

I hope teachers will continue to help children focus their topics and redefine and limit the boundaries of their subjects. But in our design conferences and in our mini-lessons, I also hope we will issue invitations to children to experiment with the shapes and forms of writing. Our purpose should be not so much to help them produce well-ordered products but to invite them to try the groping, shaping, ordering activities that are such a part of writing. For young writers, "form" is more important as a verb than as a noun.

What do we say in design conferences? There are so many possibilities it is hard to be specific. One thing we can do is to help children see that form is not built into a topic. It is, instead, chosen by the author. Although chains of events have a ready-made organization, even in a narrative the writer must shape the piece. When Sangwa brings her draft to a conference, we can help her step back and reflect upon the design of what she has written so that she can see how she has moved chronologically through the sequence of events. Perhaps she can even map the design of the piece:

$$X \rightarrow X \rightarrow X \rightarrow X \rightarrow X \rightarrow X$$

Especially if this is the way most of her pieces are structured, it may help Sangwa if she brainstorms other possible designs. She may realize for example, that she could have given greater attention to some moments in her narrative and less to others:

```
        X              X
       XXX            XXX
   XXxxXXXXXxxxxxxXXXXXxxxxxx
```

She may see that she could have composed her piece out of "snapshots," perhaps beginning with a glimpse of life with the cat, and then one of letting the cat go in the alley. Sangwa could also have written the piece in an altogether different mode, perhaps as a letter to a friend, a poem, a song, a piece of fiction. Those options are still open to her, since revision often means restructuring a piece. Perhaps now that she has put the sequence of events onto paper, she can select another mode if she writes another piece on the topic.

When Sangwa realizes her choices, she also realizes her power as a writer. The structure of a piece is determined not by the topic but by the author. An author creates the shape and form of a piece, critiques it, and re-creates it. The responsibility is hers. Our job as teachers is to put ourselves, and our writing formulas, out of a job. It is to ask questions that will invite children to claim their decision-making power, and to help children become conscious creators of meaning. Therefore, especially as children become a little older and more experienced as writers, we ask design questions:

- How did you decide on this particular mode? What others did you consider? What are you going to do next in terms of the form of this writing?
- Do you think the shape and pace of your piece works? Where does it work well? Where does it work less well? What could you do next?
- Are there places where the reader may be misled by your digressions?
- Have you chosen the most significant aspects of your topic? How can you keep these in the forefront and put the rest into the background?
- What have you left out? skimmed over? expanded in detail? How else could you have rationed out your attention? Do you think another way would work better?
- What is the balance between parts of your piece? How else could you have done this?

This chapter represents a recent revision of my teaching ideas. It has not been filled with the faces and voices of children because I have rarely seen children struggle with the issues I describe here. Yet I sense that for some teachers, and for some classrooms, design conferences will add a great deal to writing workshops.

Those who know my work, and the work of my colleagues, will see that design conferences are just one of several new areas of concern. In this book, I also place a new emphasis on literature, on the forms of writing, on mini-lessons, and on poetry. My hunch is that these elements are interwoven, that each depends on the others, and that taken together, they represent a new vision of what is possible in K–8 classrooms. For a time, it was amazing just to find that even very young children could draft and revise their own writing, and confer with their peers about their personal narratives. Now it seems crucial to extend what children can do by inviting them to become joyful participants in literate cultures. I not only want young writers to write, share, and rewrite their stories, I also want them to admire and learn from the work of other authors, to try diverse kinds of writing, and to use and adapt the techniques they find in the literature they read.

16

process and evaluation conferences: teach the writer, not the writing

On the closing day of last summer's writing institute, Aida Montero, one of the participants, brought down the house with an unexpected skit. Wearing the name tag CALKINS, Montero stood at the podium and looked keenly at the audience until the room grew quiet. Then she began to speak, saying "People, listen carefully. This is important." Her speech lasted about four minutes and during that time, she repeated the line, "Listen carefully, this is important" about twelve times. The laughter was uproarious, and I was humbled. I felt like the third grader who punctuates each sentence with at least one exclamation mark and uses a whole line of exclamation marks for emphasis. I feel the same way about these chapters. I know I have said that content conferences are at the heart of teaching writing and that design conferences are crucial. Bear with me when I now say that process and evaluation conferences are also crucial. I have clustered them together in one chapter in a valiant effort to avoid saying one more time, "Listen carefully, this is important."

I have also paired process and evaluation conferences because my understanding of both originated during my first experiences as a researcher. At Atkinson Elementary School, I wanted to document what my case-study subjects did during writing, what they thought, and what they tried to do. With assistance from Giacobbe, Graves, and Sowers, I developed a repertoire of questions. They were research questions, not teaching questions—or so I thought.

PROCESS QUESTIONS

(a sampling)

How did you go about writing this? Did you just pick up your pencil and write straight through or did you stop and think, or reread? What made you stop?

What problems did you run into while you were writing this piece? If I'd been watching you, how would I have known you were having problems?

How did you go about finding a topic? Once you found the topic, did you start writing right away or what?

How is your process of writing changing?

I notice you made some cross-outs here. What led you to do that?

What will you do next? What are your options?

EVALUATION QUESTIONS

(a sampling)

How does this piece compare with the other pieces you've written this year? Which is the very best? next best? What makes this one the best? Could you make it even better if you wanted to? Are there ways?

Are there places in the piece which you think are especially strong? Where are they? What makes you think these are especially good sections?

What makes a piece of writing really good?

Of all the kids in the class, which one writes in a way you especially like? What makes you like his or her way of writing?

Of all the authors you read, which one writes in a way you especially like? What makes you like his or her writing?

What do you think would make your writing even better? What are the strengths of your writing? the weaknesses?

Over and over, I asked these questions. I wanted to see how children's answers changed over time, and they did change. But I have come to realize the teaching power of those research interviews. Process and evaluation questions allowed me to understand children's growth in writing, but they also allowed me to nurture that growth. There is only a thin line between research and teaching. It is enormously helpful, I think, when teachers want very much to understand children's writing process and their criteria for evaluating a written text. Carl Rogers has helped me recognize that such understanding is both rare and powerful: "I have found it of enormous value when I can permit myself to understand another person." Rogers goes on to explain:

The way in which I have worded this statement may seem strange to you. Is it necessary to permit oneself to understand another? I think it is. Our first reaction to most of the statements which we hear from other people is an immediate evaluation, or judgment, rather than an understanding of it. When someone expresses a feeling or attitude or belief, our tendency is, almost immediately, to feel "That's right"; or "That's stupid"; "That's abnormal"; . . . Very rarely do we permit ourselves to understand an individual, to enter thoroughly and completely into his frame of reference (Rogers 1961, 18).

When we ask process and evaluation questions of children, the children teach us about themselves and their writing. These insights about our children provide the grounds for our teaching.

It is the most natural thing in the world for the master potter to watch an apprentice at work, noticing what the student does and does not do with the lump of clay. Yet writing teachers are more apt to focus on final written products than on the processes that produced them. In a recent workshop, I asked teachers to jot down the names of their students and then to write key words describing each student's composing process beside each name. Many of the teachers wrote "good with descriptions," "strong vocabulary," or "writes bland, general pieces." They tended to write about the students' products, not their processes. I had expected that they would write notes on how one student spent almost no time at all in rehearsal and invariably ended up thinking the topic "stupid," and how another student approached a piece with elaborate plans, often written out in full. I envisioned comments about the help students seek out for their writing and the uses they make of that help, but there wasn't a single teacher who reported on how his or her students wrote. This is an important reminder: we are more apt to talk about the topic or the text than about the writer, yet it is when we know how our students go about writing that we can best help them improve their strategies.

In chapter 3, I drew an analogy between a writing teacher and a tennis coach. The coach watches how someone plays the game and then helps that person see which strategies are effective and which are not. "You are stepping away from the ball," the coach says. "Try stepping into it."

When teaching children to write, we cannot always watch how they play the game. In a process conference we give children the chance to teach us about how they write. "I have heaps and heaps of drafts," Diane tells me, "because every time I start anything I botch it up and have to copy it over. Then I end up botching up the next draft, too, and so it goes." Diane has given me a glimpse of her writing, and by following up on her casual comment I will learn a great deal more. "What do you mean, you botch it up?" I might ask, or "Have you always written heaps of drafts or is this a new thing for you?"

As a researcher, when I wanted children to teach me about their composing process, I often found it helpful to use their drafts as the basis for our discussion. Students would bring all their drafts to our interview (our process conference) and then, after spreading the drafts out on the table in front of us, we would use these drafts as a way to reconstruct the students' processes. Birger's first bit of writing for his research report, for example, was a tattered page of notes labeled "Transportation." "Tell me about it," I said to him.

"Oh, that is from the book," he said, "the encyclopedia." He went on to explain that, when he learned he was to write a report, he went immediately to the town library, where he'd gotten out the encyclopedia and written notes on "everything." The notes looked like an abbreviated version of the encyclopedia, but Birger assured me they were in his own words. "Whenever I came to a big word, I changed it to a small word . . . like here, it said 'There were numerous railroads crisscrossing the state' and I wrote, 'Lots of railroads crisscrossed the state.' " Then, in school, Birger's teacher suggested that "Transportation" might be too big a topic and encouraged Birger to choose one specific thing about it. Instead, Birger changed his topic to squirrels.

"See, I was thinking of topics here," Birger told me, pointing to a small list of words in the corner of one of his papers. "I thought of these topics: snakes, rivers, squirrels. I would have had snakes but Brad had that topic and he didn't want me to do it."

Next, Birger showed me six pages of notes and explained where they had come from. His teacher had suggested that students read the easiest books first and work gradually toward the encyclopedia. Birger felt funny sitting in the town library with a "baby book" in hand, so he hid it inside a huge volume of the encyclopedia.

In this way, Birger and I slowly reconstructed the way he went about writing his squirrel report. I learned about his methods for writing and for research. I began to understand his view of revision ("I read it over and the sentence was too long. In this next draft I shortened it. I added a period.") and of writing in his own words ("Whenever I came to a big word I changed it to a small word.") From all this, I gained a sense of the logic behind his decisions and the ways I could help him.

I was not the only person to benefit from this conference. When students are asked to describe their writing processes, they often become aware of them for the first time. In anticipation of process conferences, children monitor their writing strategies and soon, they consciously revise those strategies. Becoming aware of their thinking process gives students a new dimension of control over their writing. Simply having the words—handles—to talk about their writing strategies makes it more likely that children will consciously select ways of going about writing. In her book, *Children's Minds*, Margaret Donaldson stresses this link between awareness and control:

The point to grasp is how closely the growth of consciousness is related to the growth of the intellect. . . . If the intellectual powers are to develop, the child must gain a measure of control over his own thinking and he cannot control it while he remains unaware of it (Donaldson 1978, 129).

In her research on the differences between skilled and unskilled writers, Linda Flower claims that skilled writers approach writing by planning not only what they will say, but also what they will do. These plans allow a writer to set priorities and to organize ways of solving a problem. They become the writer's defense, Flower says, against the deluge of competing concerns during writing. The writer can say, "I'm not going to worry about being precise right now, I just want to get down the gist of things." Alternately, the writer can say, "I want to be certain each word is right; then I can build up from a strong base. I'm going to spend today just working on the beginning."

Once they are aware of themselves as writers, children no longer "just write." Listen to the way these children describe their processes:

Now I'm going to reread my story, trying to make parts longer like Susie did in her piece. I'm going to add on at this part when I come out of the garage to the accident. I'll tell about when I was walking across the driveway, how I heard sounds, like the vet with the siren, and I smelled the air. It wasn't bad air and I remember thinking, it was hard to believe a part of me had just died, the air smelled so nice and clean. I'm going to put all that in, spreading it out with more detail.

Birger, age 8

I pretend I am my audience. I read it to myself and then I see if it's good or bad.

Ramon, age 5

I get my topic from my feelings. I felt lonely yesterday and I wanted to write it out of me. I wrote fast, just getting it all down and the strong feeling made the words come.

Regina, age 11

I suspect that it was because these children have had a researcher at their side that they are this articulate and this aware of writing strategies. Most classrooms do not host a researcher, and it is rare for teachers to have the chance to sit with one child and reconstruct the life-stages in that youngster's piece of writing. Yet it is well worth our time to do this. We can also find other ways to learn about, and to help our students learn about, their writing processes. Sometimes whole-class or small-group activities such as these can help focus attention on methods of writing:

- Students can conduct surveys to learn how their peers go about writing. They can ask classmates, for example, where they got their topics, how much time lapsed between finishing one piece and beginning the next, what portion of their time went to gathering information, and how they would classify their revision strategies (large or small, additions or subtractions, across drafts or within a draft, etc.) The information gathered could provide the basis for whole-class discussions.
- For many of us, recent books and articles on the writing process have heightened our awareness of the components of writing. Upper elementary school and junior high children could read these sources. In some classrooms, children have gone so far as to write their own articles.
- One fifth grade class was studying flow charts in science and decided to make flow charts of how they go about writing. Later, in response groups, the diagrams became a starting place for discussion.
- In *Writing with Power*, Peter Elbow portrays different kinds of writers. Students (and teachers) will see themselves in his portraits. These sections of the book can be read aloud in mini-lessons or used as the basis for discussion in response groups. Children may want to write their own portraits of themselves as writers. If they want to show how their writing strategies have changed over time, they may want to write autobiographies of themselves as writers.
- The class can compile a list of process questions for students to answer in peer-response groups:
  What problems do you run into when you were writing?
  How did you go about solving those problems?
  How has your writing changed over time?
  What kind of revision do you usually do?
- Researchers have found one of the best ways to learn about how someone goes about writing is to ask that person to carry on a running monologue during writing. The person says everything he or she thinks during the writing. Teachers or students might compose aloud while they write on the chalkboard. Later the class can reconstruct what the writer did during writing and reflect on what worked and what did not.
- The teacher can show the class a strategy he or she uses during writing (changing from one genre to another, taking a key section and spreading it out with more details, dividing a piece into subsections, reading the piece aloud to hear how it sounds, etc.) Over the rest of the school year, students might take turns sharing strategies which have been particularly helpful to them.
- Class members might keep process logs in which they record how they go about writing and how their processes are changing. These could

become dialogue journals in which the teacher writes back, or they could become the source of discussion in peer conferences.

- When they finish a piece of writing, students could be asked to write a short piece about what they learned from the writing and what they plan to do differently another time. Alternatively, this could be done once a month, or before an Authors' Day, in which case the students would look back on all the pieces of writing they had done in the recent past.

Any of these activities could be a helpful tool for learning about students' writing processes, but let me caution against using *all* of them. If the activities are to be a forum for thinking about one's writing process, then they must become part of the backdrop of the workshop. If they are always changing, always new, they themselves become the focus of attention rather than a tool for focusing on something else. I urge teachers to use one or two of these activities often, over and over, rather than attempting to do a little of everything.

My emphasis in this discussion has been on ways we can help students become more reflective, more conscious, and more in control of their writing processes, and also on ways *we* can become more aware of what strategies work and do not work for our students. But, picking up on the metaphor I used in chapter 3, the tennis coach does more than watch, listen, and videotape: the coach also gives pointers. "Try stepping into the ball," the coach says. The writing teacher can make similar suggestions. Sometimes these suggestions will be astute, well-timed, and tailored to the individual, emerging after a great deal of listening and observing. At other times they will be simple suggestions, meant mostly as a way to keep writers on task and to encourage them to move on to new challenges. In my experience, these little process conferences comprise the majority of the conferences. This is especially true at the beginning of the year, when the writing workshop is just getting underway. Listen to what Shelley Harwayne says as she works with a class of fourth graders who are new to the writing process.

When I arrived in this classroom, Shelley had just finished her mini-lesson and the children were dispersing to their desks. "I don't know what to write about" one boy told Shelley, and behind him another boy echoed the same comment. Shelley sympathized. She told the boys that she sometimes gets stuck on what to write about too and that it helps her to call up a friend and talk about it. "So why don't you two try talking and see if that gives you ideas," she suggested, steering them toward the edge of the classroom. End of process conference number one.

Now the questions came from everywhere. "Can I use pen?" "Do I need yellow paper?" "Should I write in pencil?" "Do I need a table?" "Can I use cursive?" "How long should it be?" The children clustered around Shelley, calling out for her attention. At this point, Shelley asked the class to stop for a moment and when the group was very still, she quietly told them about the questions she had heard. "What do you think I am going to say to these children?" she asked the class. Then she turned to the youngsters clustered near her and while the rest of the class observed, she gently and firmly said, "You are the authors. You are in charge of your own pieces. Do you need to come to me with your questions or can you, as authors, make up your own minds?"

The children returned to their work and soon the clatter in the room subsided into a hum. Shelley noticed a little girl who sat chewing on her pencil, thinking. Shelley stood alongside the girl's desk, and I joined her, clipboard in hand. The girl asked, "Can you write one story all bunched up?" Shelley looked puzzled and asked the youngster to explain. The girl said, "I want to write about my two cats, Tom and Tiger, and about my robin and my trip I went on."

"Are they all one story or are they different stories?"

"My cats are one story and also my robin that I have out my window," the girl said. "That's the 'My Pets' story. The trip is different."

"Congratulations," Shelley said to the girl. "You just did what writers do all the time. You started with a bunch of things and then you asked, 'Do they go together or not?' " Shelley went on to say that the girl now had a story with different parts in it, and she asked whether the girl wanted to write the parts together, or in different chapters. The girl chose chapters. Shelley showed her the table of contents in a book, and then as the girl began making her own list of chapters we moved on.

"What are you up to?" Shelley asked Yusef.

"I'm figuring out how to write it," he said.

"How to write it?" she repeated, unsure of what he meant.

"Yeah, the title."

So Shelley and Yusef talked for a while about titles. Yusef told us he'd been thinking about the title for two days and had nothing down so far.

Shelley touched the boy lightly on the arm and said "Yusef, I have two different suggestions. First of all, some writers do spend a long time on titles. But I think it might help if instead of just sitting, you list every idea that pops into your head . . . brainstorming, like we did before." Then she said, "Other writers don't worry too much about titles until they have written the story, and you also might want to try that option— either one." Shelley moved on before the boy had chosen his next move.

The two boys Shelley had sent to the conference alley were still there and so Shelley urged them back to their desks, saying, "It is good to keep track of your time in conferences. We try to keep it to about five minutes."

At the far edge of the room, one child had a heap of crumpled drafts on the edge of her desk. Shelley talked with her about free writing. "In free writing, you put anything that comes to mind onto the paper without worrying," she explained. By then there were several students clustered around us saying, "I'm finished." Shelley spoke with them first about interrupting her conferences, then she asked one of the children whether anyone had heard his story. The boy shook his head, no, and so Shelley and the next child in line agreed to become the boy's conference partners. For a few minutes they listened and spoke with the writer. By the time the conference was over, other children who were waiting for Shelley had also joined the spontaneous response group. Before leaving, Shelley helped the group review the steps they had just taken in the peer conference. Shelley suggested they divide into pairs and help each other. "I'll come around and admire how well you work together," she told them and proceeded to do just that.

This was only the second writing workshop these children had ever experienced. Once the workshop is well underway and children know how to "carry-on," teachers will spend less energy rushing from child to child like the stunt man at the circus, who gets plates spinning on sticks and then watches until one begins to totter. The purpose of process conferences will change, and children will begin chatting with each other about their writing process just as I do with my colleagues.

Morat, a sixth grader in Rose Napoli's classroom, interrupted his friends during writing time to say, "I need your help. Where do I start my story? My father took my cousin and me on a boat trip, but if I start the story in New York then I have to tell the whole thing to Florida and it will be boring."

Before the others could respond to Morat's problem, Hasun pulled a homemade map from his notebook and slid it over to Morat, who took the map and explained to me, "He's drawing my illustrations because I'm not such a good drawer." After scrutinizing the map, Morat decided Hasun wasn't such a good drawer either. He gave the map back to Hasun with orders for a second draft. The Great Lakes were too big. Now Morat returned to his initial problem, and this time Joseph had an idea. "Try about six beginnings," he said, "and see if one turns out." Morat sighed, but agreed. "Once I get a good beginning it is like a corkscrew," he said. "The rest just comes pouring out." So he set to work . . . and later announced he had decided how to start the piece. "It's good. I'm starting with action, with how when we board the ship and they take pictures. I'll start with 'Smile. . . .' " But now there was a new problem: Morat couldn't recall the exact sequence of events and he wanted his story to be true. Hasun suggested he bring in a calendar and see if he could recall how he spent each of the days, but Morat interrupted this suggestion to say, "I got an even better idea."

The next day when I approached the group, there was a great deal of whispering. Apparently Morat had brought in a diary from the trip, and in sharing the little pages with his friends, he'd also shared his secret with them: a movie star's daughter was aboard the ship, and the voyage turned out to be a True Romance.

Pointing to me, Joseph said, "Show her what you did, Morat. You are real fast. You are something else."

Morat blushed and handed me four of the five pages. "The other one is too personal," he apologized. The first page went like this:

July 6:   I met a girl. We had coke on the rocks. I am in love. I'm talking hearts and flowers. You should see her in her bikini.

That day, Morat shuttled between the diary and the story. Once he looked up to say, "Oh, no, I made a booboo." He had left out an incident. Joseph skimmed the diary-version and announced that it was an important omission, and so he headed over to the writing corner for scissors, tape, and extra paper.

"When I left stuff out of my story, I pasted on more paper," he said, and set to work helping Morat do the same. Together they added some space to Morat's story.

This time Morat didn't look up from his paper until the workshop was over. Surveying his work, he said, "This story has everything. It is a real good story. It has romance, excitement and music."

It may not be clear what all of this has to do with process and evaluation conferences. Morat and his friends seem to be "just talking." A closer look, however, shows that these youngsters have, in fact, been suggesting, trying, and evaluating alternative writing strategies. In a very natural way, they have collaboratively developed writing methods. They have been chatting about ways to use source materials, to find a lead, and to insert information in a text. They have also been talking about their evolving criteria for good writing. "This is a real good story," Morat said. "It has romance, excitement and music." Earlier, he redrafted his lead in order to begin the piece with action, and he tried to limit his topic so he wouldn't end up writing a boring story about the whole trip. Throughout his drafting and revision, then, Morat has been evaluating his emerging text.

Morat has probably learned to shift between creation and criticism because his teacher often asked him to do this in evaluation conferences. "How do you feel about your draft?" she would ask, and if he answered with a single phrase—"Good"—she asked for a more specific response. "What do you like best about it?" she might say, or, "Is there anything that doesn't seem to work?" By asking these questions, she put the responsibility for evaluation onto Morat's shoulders, and she involved him in the ongoing process of evaluation. In this way, it became second nature for Morat to shuttle between writing and rereading, between experimenting and critiquing.

Writers need to be critical readers of their own writing. Thomas Mann describes talent this way: "At bottom it is a compulsion; a critical knowledge of the ideal, a permanent dissatisfaction." Our sense of the ideal instructs our judgments about our texts. Children not only need strategies for evaluating their writing, they also need an understanding of what makes good writing. It is important for us to ask questions that invite children to discuss, share, refine, and extend their ideas about good writing. If a child is struggling with his or her beginning, then, we can ask, "What makes a good beginning?" If a child worries whether his or her draft is exciting, we can ask, "Is it important for every piece to be exciting?" or "What kinds of things add excitement?" When a child says he or she *loved* reading a book, we can ask "What was it about the book which made it so perfect?"

It is not only through the conference that we can help children develop a sense of what good writing is. A feel for what works in writing comes also from reading, listening to, and discussing literature, and from learning what others have discovered about the craft of writing. This leads us to our next two sections, on teacher input and reading-writing connections.

section

IV

high teacher input

17

don't be afraid to teach

In the town next to ours, an open-space elementary school has been converted into a traditional school building, complete with self-contained classrooms and institutional-green walls. It was no surprise to me that these changes were made. Any mention, these days, of open classrooms conveys images of laissez-faire teaching and unstructured chaos. I do not think the reputation of American open-classroom schools is entirely unwarranted. At their best, these progressive schools are excellent; but the best has been rare. At their worst, they deserve the criticism they receive. David Hawkins describes the problem this way:

What Dewey called "the supremacy of method" is subtly wrong. . . . There are some truths that require at least two sentences. The first truth may well be that the art of inquiry is educationally more fundamental than the facts and truths established by that practice. But the second truth, no less important, is that the art cannot grow except by what it feeds on. . . . Method consists in using knowledge to gain further knowledge, . . . and the mind equipped with method and no content . . . is an absurdity (Hawkins 1974, 10–11).

Hawkins argues that the greatest art in teaching is the art of combination and he includes in this the combination of high teacher input and high student input. Many open-education teachers, in their enthusiasm for process and for student input in the curriculum, seem to reject formal

163

instruction entirely. Yet when students are deeply absorbed in their subject matter, formal instruction can bring students to new levels of understanding, and teacher-interventions can lead them to probe, test, and learn. As I visit writing-process classrooms around the country, it seems to me that they fall into one of four categories. Mary Ellen Giacobbe has helped me to see that a graph, borrowed from Edward Chittendom, illustrates these categories (see Figure 17-1).

Classrooms where writing is taught through ditto sheets and language arts textbooks belong in quadrant one. In these classrooms, published materials lead students into whatever writing they do, and neither the students nor their teachers invest much energy in written work.

Many teachers will probably identify with the second quadrant: high teacher input and low student input. During my first years of teaching, my classroom would have fallen into this category. I wanted to be a creative, committed, and skillful writing teacher, and so I spent long hours writing story starters and responding at great length to everything my students wrote. It never occurred to me that I was one of the only people in that room investing a great deal of energy in writing.

When I first learned about the writing process, my classroom switched into the high student input, low teacher input quadrant. Many writing-process classrooms fall into this quadrant. The teachers have read Murray, Elbow, Macrorie, Calkins, or Graves, and they have heard us say that students should select their own topics, that writers need ownership over the process, and that students want to confer with each other as well as with us. All of these things are happening in the third-quadrant writing classrooms. Students write up a storm and eagerly share their work in response groups. Many students willingly revise. They write in a range of genres, and they write for a variety of purposes. Teachers are amazed at the interest in writing. But the curious thing is that often the writing

Figure 17 – 1

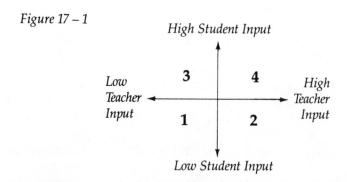

does not improve with revision, or even over time. Students are apt to write rough draft after rough draft, but they do not know how to hone their strengths or to select what works best in their pieces. Because they lack a sense of what good writing is like, they have no compass to steer by as they write. Meanwhile, out of fear of "taking ownership," teachers desperately avoid teaching. Sometimes, on the sly, they make coy comments such as, "I wonder if there is another sentence you could use as a lead?" This, of course, convinces the students that their teachers have the "right answers" but are hiding them, and so the students try all the harder to wrangle judgments and suggestions out of their teachers.

We might avoid these problems if we created classrooms in which there was high student *and* high teacher input. Ideally, both teachers and students should bring all of their skills, wisdom, and energy to the teaching-learning transaction. We should not relinquish our identities as teachers in order to give students ownership of their craft. If we have a tip to give about good writing, why not give it? If we think students need instruction in quotation marks, why not teach them? We need not be afraid to teach, but we do need to think carefully about the kinds of teacher input which will be helpful to our students.

18

mini-lessons:
an overview

My belief in mini-lessons comes from my own background. My parents were "project people." They believed the nine of us should each have our own projects—and so Joan entered her dog in obedience trials, Ben raised a flock of sheep, Steve played in jazz bands, and I explored the swamp on a homemade raft, or later, wrote and directed plays for the neighborhood children. My parents balanced their interest in projects with an interest in achievement. In whatever our area of interest, they provided us with the best available instruction. I have come to believe in this balance. I learn best when I am deeply absorbed by a topic and when this involvement is guided by well-timed tips from experts.

I learned to write through a balance of high teacher and high student input. I was working in England at the time, teaching in the British Primary Schools and living in the basement of a Cotswold manor house. I had never written for publication, but what I was seeing in the schools seemed so important that I fancied myself writing a book about it. Every day I spent hours poring over my manuscript, investing every ounce of heart and soul into it. Then, in the late evenings, I read great literature, and finally, for a snippet of time before going to bed, I read about the qualities of good writing. It took me three weeks to read Zinsser's *On Writing Well;* I could only digest a few bits of advice at a time or my mind would begin to swirl with too many pointers to remember as I worked on my writing. I read slowly, and took the time to integrate each new bit of information. If I read about leads while I was in the midst of writing a chapter, I'd

167

tuck what I learned into the back of my mind and draw on it, either deliberately or unconsciously, when I began a new chapter.

I want students to experience the balance that was so valuable to me. This is one reason for my belief in mini-lessons. Then too, just as I have come to believe that there is something powerful about the ritual of beginning every football game with a huddle, or opening every program of "Hill Street Blues" with a meeting in the police station, I find that the ritual of beginning every writing workshop with a whole-group gathering brings form and unity to the workshop. In theory, mini-lessons are wonderful.

In practice, they often represent the worst part of a writing workshop. When I bring visitors to see the writing-process classrooms throughout New York City, I sometimes deliberately time our visits so we avoid the mini-lesson. A colleague recently suggested that it might help to change the title, "mini-lessons," to something with less traditional overtones. She explained, "As soon as teachers hear mini-*lessons*, we think of aims and motivations, and of discussions to elicit information from children. What title would be more accurate? Nutshell meetings? Writing huddles? I would want the new title to convey the simplicity and brevity of a good mini-lesson.

About a year ago, I observed Shelley Harwayne teaching a writing workshop. Afterward, I told Shelley that her mini-lesson was fabulous. Apparently this comment perplexed her because as far as she knew, she hadn't given a mini-lesson that day. At the time, Shelley said nothing to me about her confusion. At home that night she reread her notes. "What could Lucy have meant?" Then she realized that instead of what she perceived as a mini-lesson, she had begun the workshop with a quick tip. She had said to the children, "Can I ask just one thing of you before you begin your writing? When you open your folders today, and every day, would you reread what you have written? Before you add to it, have a little conference with yourself. Ask yourself questions: how you feel about the piece, whether there are ways you could make it better. All right, take out your folders and, first, read them to yourselves." To my way of thinking, this was a perfect mini-lesson. Shelley had given students a strategy they could use often. She had not interrupted their ongoing commitment to writing with an elaborate assignment. Best of all, instead of a long whole-class discussion on rereading, she simply told them about this strategy. The mini-lesson had not become a maxi-lesson.

Then too, I would want my revised title for "mini-lessons" to let teachers know that there is nothing wrong with a three-minute lecture. Teaching through recitation is deeply ingrained in most of us. In one study, Hoetker (1982) found that English teachers ask questions at the average rate of one every 11.8 seconds. But mini-lessons become diffuse and clumsy when teachers persist in the question/answer mode that is so pervasive in our schools. To illustrate my point, let me describe a mini-lesson on titles and then show how that lesson might look if taught through recitation. In the first version, the teacher might say something like this:

Last night I was thinking about the titles you are using for your pieces and it occurred to me that if your piece was about your dog, many of you—without thinking twice—would put the label "My Dog" on the top of the page. You wouldn't stop and think about how to change that label into a title *which might catch the reader's eye.*

I mention this because it may help you, as authors, to think about the titles of the books you are reading. *Jerome is reading a book about two dogs but instead of calling it "Two Dogs," the author, Wilson Rawls, has named it* Where the Red Fern Grows. *It is a curious title, isn't it, but if you read the book you will understand why he selected it. Cynthia's book is about a journey taken by three children but instead of being called "The Trip," it is called,* The Lion, the Witch, and the Wardrobe.

And so, children, when it comes time for you to work on titles, think hard about a good title. You may want to go to the library and look at the titles there, or you may want to brainstorm a lot of possibilities before selecting one for your piece. Or perhaps it isn't important for you to think about titles now, and that is OK too.

If there are any of you who want to work on titles today, why don't you stay after the mini-lesson and we'll form a title-group. The rest of you, off you go. Let's have a good day.

The same lesson, taught through recitation, might begin like this:

The teacher has a book with her. She holds the cover up towards the class as she says, "Last night I was thinking about a part of your writing we haven't talked about." Pointing to the title of the book in her hand, she says, "the what, class?"

The children respond in chorus, "The name."

"Title, we call it," and the teacher writes title *on the chalkboard. "It occurred to me that instead of giving your pieces catchy titles, you do what?"*

"Hand it in," Robert guessed.

"Yes, you do hand it in and class, I am glad you're now remembering to put your pieces in the box called 'Final Editing,' but before you hand it in, what do you write? (Pause) Not titles, but labels. You are labeling your stories, telling what they are about. If your piece is about dogs, what would you probably call it, Sarah?"

Sarah has evidently not been following the discussion. She fumbles for an answer, and so the teacher calls on two more children. The second one guesses correctly, "Dogs," etc.

When I listen to recitation mini-lessons, I often find them hard to follow. I often cannot supply the correct answers, and I spend so much time raising and dismissing incorrect answers that I do not follow the teacher's train of thought. Worse still, the mini-lessons drag on and encroach on the time reserved for writing.

Although I find the question/answer format cumbersome, an even more serious problem occurs when people want every student to interrupt whatever he or she is doing to use that day's mini-lesson. For example, in some classes, on the day in which titles are the subject of the mini-lesson, every child is expected to list ten possible titles for his or her piece. Although there are certainly occasions when it makes sense to ask every child to do something—as when Shelley suggested that every child take a moment to reread his or her draft—I think more often, mini-lessons will only be suited to what several children are doing. We need to think of mini-lessons, then, as ways to add information to the class pot. If five children pick up on an idea when it is presented, that idea is in the room. When those five children share their work in peer-conferences and share meetings, the ideas are recirculated. Meanwhile, other children have tucked the ideas into the back of their minds, and they will draw upon them when they are needed.

But all of this avoids the main question: what does one teach in a mini-lesson? People often suggest that I write a book of possible mini-lessons. I will not and cannot do this. I am not in the classroom day by day, and I do not know the rhythms of those classrooms. I cannot know whether children in one room are cranking out purposeless little pieces, or whether the writing folders are sloppy, or whether a child has just turned a personal narrative into a beautiful letter. Only the classroom teacher knows the pulse beat of a class. Mini-lessons are meant as a time for teacher-input, not for my input.

Perhaps, however, I can give teachers the tools and the confidence to invent their own mini-lessons. In the next chapter, I want to suggest categories of mini-lessons and within each category, several possible examples. I will address these categories, although there are many others:

- Early Writing. In this section, I suggest several mini-lessons that are particularly suited to kindergarten and first-grade youngsters. Many of the other mini-lessons are also applicable to this age group.
- The Launch. The hardest days in a writing workshop are the first ones. This section contains transcripts of two "launches" and a list of other ways to begin writing workshops.
- Topic Choice. Although topics are an ongoing concern throughout the year, they are of particular importance at the start of the year. I describe a number of mini-lessons in detail in this section.
- Conferences. I hope this section encourages teachers to develop mini-

lessons that help students confer well with each other and with themselves.

- Classroom Procedures. A writing workshop is only as good as the management system that supports it. Mini-lessons can help create and sustain that management system.
- Rehearsal and Revision Strategies. Children often do not know what to do when we ask them to rehearse for writing or to revise their pieces. It is helpful to demonstrate specific strategies such as mapping, listing titles, changing modes, etc.
- Qualities of Good Writing. I think it is extremely helpful for children to think about and learn about the components of good writing. In this section, I try to recommend ways to convey these qualities without turning them into diehard rules, and I suggest some of those that seem particularly suited to K–8 children and their writing.
- Literature. Talking about good writing is often not as powerful as immersing oneself in it. Some of the most successful mini-lessons center on reading and celebrating good literature.

19

*tools to help teachers
create their own
mini-lessons*

Early writing

Mini-lessons can help young children understand the functions and power
of print. For example, I sometimes gather together a class of kindergarten
children and, showing them examples of environmental print, I ask them
to read what the print probably says. The letters on the milk carton
probably say "milk" and the letters on the can of peas probably say "peas."
Usually I end the lesson by switching from reading environmental print
to writing it. I ask children what word I should write on a tagboard label
hanging on the door, and soon the children and I have labeled the library
area, the hamster, the coat hooks, and the math manipulatives. At the
end of the mini-lesson I generally ask whether some children want to
write more labels during the writing workshop, and the others go off to
their drawing and writing.

A natural follow-up for this mini-lesson might be for me to draw a
picture and then, sounding out words, to label different parts of the
picture. Then I could encourage children to label parts of their own pictures.
Alternately, if two or three children had made the breakthrough and were
writing words (perhaps with scribble-writing or initial consonants only),
I might celebrate and share these in a mini-lesson. Still another mini-
lesson might involve the children in brainstorming the sorts of writing
they might do in the block area (road signs, maps, titles to the buildings,

etc.) or the playhouse area (phone messages, grocery lists, labels for each child's room) and so forth.

Although many young writers will need very little help with spelling, some will need to learn how to listen for sounds. In mini-lessons, I sometimes encourage children to stretch out a word, listening slowly to the component sounds. Recently, after gathering together a group of five-year-olds, Martha Horn, one of the teacher trainers in our project, brought out a miniature chalkboard and told the class they were going to be spellers. "Does anyone have a special word we could spell together?" she asked. The children suggested spaghetti, Tyrannosaurus Rex, and hippopotamus, and then the class worked together to say the words slowly. "Watch my hand, and see if you can say it as slowly as my hand goes," Martha said, stretching out the word with her hand. "Stretch it like a rubber band," she urged, "and listen to the sounds." Then she asked, "What sounds do you hear?" and transcribed the children's guesses on the chalkboard. Her purpose was not to arrive at correct spellings, of course, but to model the process of spelling words. For this reason, if a child called out an incorrect letter, Martha did not correct the youngster.

Soon many children write whole sentences and use those sentences to tell stories, write recipes, compose poetry, and so forth. Mini-lessons can provide a forum for sharing those breakthroughs. Ideally, the mini-lessons should support the less able youngsters while also celebrating and raising the upper level of what children are doing. I particularly liked the way Shelley Harwayne did this on her third day with kindergarteners at P.S. 10. Once the children had quieted down, Shelley said, in her softly energetic voice, "This morning I looked on my bookshelf and saw some books. I thought to myself, 'These authors are doing just the same things as the children at P.S. 10.' " Then, holding up a picturebook she said, "In Tana Hoban's book, she put a picture on each page and one word to tell about the picture." Then Shelley held up a child's writing. "Here is a piece by Sylvia and see, she too has written one word to tell about her picture. She has written 'family' " (spelled FME). In the same way, Shelley showed the class that another young author, Marigold, wrote like Richard Scarey, whose books have lots of labeled pictures on every page. She concluded, "Marigold is doing just what Richard is doing," and then she turned to the final comparison. "I have one more book to show you. This book is called *The Little Bird* and it is written by Dick Bruna. After Dick drew a picture, like many of you are doing, he put some words to tell what is happening in the picture. On this page, he wrote, 'A little yellow bird flies in the air looking for a place to build a nest.' " Then Shelley likened this to Alex's work, showing that he, too, had written a sentence to tell what was happening in his picture. The mini-lesson ended with Shelley congratulating the children on being authors, and sending them on their way.

I have also seen effective mini-lessons in which the teacher begins by telling her children about a visit she took to another writing classroom. By showing samples of what the authors in that room were doing (books with chapters, tiny three-inch square books, poetry, class newspapers, etc.), the teacher encouraged her youngsters to move in new directions.

If many children are uneasy about invented spelling, I sometimes begin a mini-lesson by asking children, "Who is the boss of your book? Who makes the decisions?" Once we establish that each child is the boss of his or her writing, I ask, "Who decides whether you will write with pencil or with marker?"

"We do!"

"Who decides whether you are going to write a big, big book or a very little book?"

"We do!"

After a series of such questions, I come to the crucial question, "Who decides how you will spell a word? If you come to the word 'rattlesnake,' who decides how to spell it?"

"You do!" The children will often answer, which gives me the chance to tell them that no, *they* are the boss of their spelling, and they must not come to me for spelling decisions. "Just do the best you can and don't worry. You are the boss of your writing."

Literature can also be the source of countless other mini-lessons. For example, the teacher might read several pages from a book aloud to show children that writers usually make sure that their words match their pictures. Another day, the teacher might simply read a beautiful passage aloud and in this way, set the stage for the writing workshop. Then too, children can talk about the titles of their reading—and their writing—books, or they can notice page numbers, or think about the ways in which stories end. The teacher might bring in many different kinds of books, ranging from Kunhardt's *Pat the Bunny* to Mayer's wordless books, encouraging young writers to realize that they too, can write different sorts of books. The primary-school teacher will also find that most of the mini-lessons described in the next sections of this chapter can be adapted to the needs of very young children.

Launching the writing workshop

Teachers often ask what I recommend for the first day of writing workshop. In this section, I include a verbatim transcript of the way the teacher trainers in our Writing Project often launch writing when we use demonstration lessons to train teachers in New York City classrooms. I developed this launch six years ago when I first came to New York City, and since then we have been continually refining it. This particular transcript records Shelley Harwayne's work in a sixth-grade classroom. At the beginning of the transcript, Shelley had just come into the room. She glanced around at the children, seated at their desks. "Boys and girls, could I ask you to clear your desks of everything?" When the children had finished this, Shelley said, "In a moment, I am going to ask you to come and sit with me, but when you come, please remember to push your chairs in and to come quietly." Shelley, meanwhile sat on the floor. When the first group of youngsters (row one) came to join her, she motioned for them to pull in close, and to sit on their bottoms, not their knees. When all the children had gathered, she again waited for their total attention before beginning to talk. "We will begin every writing workshop by gathering together like this. There are a couple things I want to ask of you during these meetings. If you whisper to each other or if you all start talking at once, I won't be able to appreciate the things you have to say. So I will ask you not to talk out in the meeting. And second, if you are wearing those sneakers with Velcro straps, could I ask you not to play with the straps during the meeting? In many classes I go into, there are a few children who play with their sneakers and I cannot listen really well when there are those sounds."

From the change in her body posture and in the tone of her voice, it was evident that Shelley was now done with her introductory remarks and ready to begin. "My name is Mrs. Harwayne, and I am a teacher and also an author. All of you will be authors today, so it is important for us to think, 'What does an author do first when he or she is going to write?"

"Even before that," Shelley responded, and continued, "The author begins by thinking of his or her topic, and all of you will be thinking about that today."

Immediately I saw worry lines on the children's foreheads as they glanced back and forth at each other. It was as if they were thinking, "But I haven't gone on any trips and no one has died." It often seems that our children have watched so much television they are convinced a story will only be interesting if it contains two murders, a suicide, and a trip around the world.

Shelley, wanting to show children that little, everyday topics are worth writing about, continued, "Let me tell you what I was thinking of writing about. The other day my daughter, who is eleven, was in an awful mood. "Come on and play with me, Mom," she kept begging, but I was busy making banana bread so I said no. She kept begging and begging, so finally I scooped up a big handful of walnut shells and tossing them to her, I said, 'Here, play with these.' I never thought she'd buy the idea, but she vanished, and an hour later, she reappeared. She had taken the lid of a shoebox and flipped it over to make a tray, and on the tray was this wonderful collection of walnut-shell animals. With yellow pipe cleaners she had made a giraffe, and with paper ears she had made a bunny. I was so proud of her, and I might write about that."

Then Shelley quickly mentioned other options (one involved a hair cut, another an incident with her cat). She gave several examples in order to demonstrate the brainstorming she does prior to settling on one topic, so that the children would get a sense of the range of options open to them. Then she quickly said, "I am going to ask you to think of things that really happened to you, things you do and things you know about, and to tell them to the person sitting beside you." For a few minutes the room was filled with happy chatter. Quieting the children, Shelley asked, "What did you come up with?" and then called on several children.

Their topics were reasonably focused and so she did not carry the mini-lesson one step further, as we often do, by helping children focus their topics. If children select topics such as summer, my family, and school, I often ask the class to listen well to the question I ask. Then I ask one youngster, "Of all that you have to say about summer, of all the things that happened to you and all that you know and feel, what is the one thing you want to focus on in this piece?"

But Shelley did not do this on this particular day. Instead she simply heard several topics and then reported, "I learn so much about you when I hear your stories. I didn't know Miguel is from Peru, or that Marigold gets bad earaches when she goes on the airplane. . . ." The children interrupted Shelley with giggles. They thought Marigold's earaches were very funny. Shelley responded by becoming serious, almost stern. "Can I stop you?" she said. "When I tell a funny story and you laugh, that is OK. But when I tell a sad story, you should not laugh. Instead, we need to feel with the person. OK, children?"

Then Shelley turned back to the job at hand. "In a bit I am going to get you started, but first, here are some rules, and these will apply to every day in writing workshop. Would you put your name and date on the paper, and please don't erase. Just cross out. This is a rough draft and no one expects it to be perfect. Don't ask for help with spelling! Just take a guess. It is the story that matters for now. Off you go. . . ."

Six or seven teachers observed Shelley on the day she gave this mini-lesson and about a week later, one of them asked if Shelley would do some demonstration teaching in her class. "But don't tell the walnut-figures story," she warned, "I already told that one." It turned out that in trying to model her lesson after Shelley's, the teacher pretended *her* daughter made walnut shell animals. How afraid we are to invest ourselves in something! Now, whenever I tell teachers about a launch, I ask them to brainstorm what stories they might tell the children, and then we consider which of their ideas might be most effective. I encourage teachers sometimes to model functional writing, such as a sympathy letter to a friend, or the notes for a talk, or an article for the local newspaper. We wrestle with the issue of fiction. Although later I stress the importance of fiction, I generally begin the workshop by modeling stories which highlight the day-to-day details of life: how the dog crawls into the bed when it thunders, what it is to watch our forsythia begin to bloom, the day I found a beautiful rock in the water and carried it for nine miles before noticing that when it was dry, the colors grew dull. When modeling, I generally do not share topics that involve big events, or ones that center on retelling a television show or a movie. These topics are not taboo, but children already overuse them.

Recently, my colleagues in the Writing Project have helped me to see that we can launch a writing workshop by demonstrating how writers often use their early bits of writing as a lens for discovering what they really want to say. We can gather students together and say, for example, "I wrote this little piece of writing a while ago and then I fixed it up, copied it over, and put it away. But when I reread it the other day I realized that it doesn't get at the really important thing that I wanted to say. So I put it aside and started brainstorming. . . ."

I hope that it is evident from this example that just as staff members in our Writing Project are continually adapting our ways of launching writing workshops, every teacher too, can invent his or her own ways to bring writing into the room. In our Writing Project, when staff members begin a workshop, we are generally demonstrating how to do this for observing teachers. For this reason, we need to squeeze the introduction to the writing process into a single class. Most of my readers do not have this constraint. You may want to begin the workshop by allowing time, day after day, for children to tell true stories to each other, either as an entire class or in small response groups. At the end of a week, each child could select one story to put into writing. You may want to begin by telling how a well-loved author went about composing his or her book, and suggesting that children could begin writing using a similar rehearsal strategy. Alternately, you could ask youngsters to bring objects in from home and, working in pairs, interview each other to find out the stories behind those objects. Whole-group meetings could be used to demonstrate and teach interviewing skills. After several days, you could encourage children to write these—or other—stories. Or you might begin by telling children that on Wednesday of the following week, a very special thing would begin: the writing workshop. In preparation for the workshop, you might devote twenty minutes a day to readiness activities: discussions of potential topics, introductory remarks about the routines of the writing workshop, opportunities to watch the teacher in the midst of writing.

I hope these suggestions serve as an invitation, encouraging you to invent and adapt your own ideas for launching the writing workshop.

Topics

When I lead writing workshops for adults, as I often do in conjunction with our summer institute on the teaching of writing, I find that a surprising number of my mini-lessons deal with the issue of topics. I know the reason: I want my students to have successul writing experiences and it seems that when they find the right topic, half the battle is won. The reverse is also true: I have the hardest time helping writers when their drafts are those which Macrorie describes as "all style and no content." For this reason, even after a launch which deals largely with topic choice, I am apt to spend the second day (and perhaps the fourth, and tenth) on topics.

At our Institute last summer, I began the second day's workshop by saying, "At home, I thought a lot about what I could say today that might help you. I tried to put myself in your shoes, to imagine what writing is like for you. I thought about how, for many of you, this kind of writing is very new. You have done a lot of teaching about the characteristics of good writing but less actual writing. This can create an imbalance." I tried to explain. "I worry that rather than approaching your writing by thinking deeply and honestly about your subject, you will approach it by trying to produce a 'good' text. I worry that your focus will be on writing impressive descriptions, a strong lead, a forceful ending and so forth." Then I referred to how Elbow, in his book, reminds us that the way to empower our words is not through "techniques" but through letting words be an extension of ourselves. Elbow likens this to the blind man with his cane. If the blind man focuses on the place where his cane meets the edge of the sidewalk, then the cane becomes an extension of his arm and it is as if his fingertips are feeling the edge of that sidewalk. But if the blind man's focus is on the way he holds the cane, then the cane becomes an awkward piece of equipment (Elbow 1981, 368).

I ended the mini-lesson by saying, "Try to remember that this is also true for your writing. Let the focus of your attention be on your subject rather than on trying to write an impressive piece. This means taking some risks but, as Faulkner says, "If you want to write something really good, you must risk writing a great deal that is really bad."

Another day I began the workshop for adults by reading aloud a passage from Peter Elbow's book, *Writing with Power*. I suspect the passage, one of my favorites, might have meaning for upper-elementary and junior high school children, and so I quote it here:

New and better ideas . . . don't come out of the blue. They come from noticing difficulties with what you believed, small details or particular cases that don't fit what otherwise feels right. The mark of the person who can actually make progress *in thinking—who can sit down at 8:30 with one set of ideas and stand up at 11 with better ideas—is a willingness to notice and listen to these inconvenient little details, these annoying loose ends, these embarrassments or puzzles, instead of impatiently sweeping them under the rug. A good new idea looks obvious and inevitable* after *it is all worked out and the dust has settled, but in the beginning it just feels annoying (Elbow 1981, 131–32).*

I ended the mini-lesson by encouraging teachers to probe their topics, to deal with the contrary feelings, the exceptions, to lift up the rug. "In this way," I said, "you will learn from your writing, and the piece will be more textured and have more insight as a result."

Another year, when working with an advanced group of teachers who were interested in writing articles on teaching composition, I began by giving the teachers an inventory, and I could imagine giving a similar inventory to a class of young writers. When working with the teachers, I simply read through a collection of questions, and after each question, I gave time for them to jot down silently whatever came to mind. These are some of the questions:

- What are some of the discoveries you've made as you've been teaching writing?
- Good writing is based on something we know and care about—list some of the things you have cared very much about in the teaching of writing.
- Trace the journey you have taken in learning to teach writing. What were the turning points? The high moments? The crucial lessons?
- Look back over what you've mentioned thus far. What stands out—from this list, or in your mind's eye—as a possible topic?
- What do you already know about this topic? What don't you know?
- What images, memories, or anecdotes does the topic evoke?
- If you were going to make a movie about this topic, how might you begin it? What would the opening scene show?

Thus far, my illustrations in this section have come from my work with adults. I have done this partly in an effort to elevate mini-lessons, to show readers that mini-lessons are not gimmicks for children. They are as important to my graduate students as they are to children. Also, I want to leave my readers with some work to do, and one challenge will be to find ways these mini-lessons can be adapted so they are appropriate for children.

Finding topics is a multifaceted problem and mini-lessons can be developed to deal with each facet. I can imagine mini-lessons that help children see that the seminal issues in one's life are not "used up" once they have been written about: topics such as a relationship with a sibling, wishing for a pet of your own, or wanting to have an area in which you excel are quarries from which many pieces of writing can be mined. The range of pieces any one child writes will probably be broader if the youngster circles back often to readdress the salient topics of his or her own life.

There will be times during the year when many children feel as Greg did, when he said, "I am broke. I am out of space stories, I am out of war stories . . ." and on these occasions, a mini-lesson might deal with the issue of what to do when you are, in Greg's words, "broke." The class could brainstorm strategies for finding a topic and post this list on the back wall. Included on this list might be: free write, take an interest inventory, confer with a friend, make a list of bad topics and hope a good one pops up on it, reread one's folder to see if previous pieces could be revised, think of an area in which you are an expert, notice what the other kids are writing about, and so forth. Or in a mini-lesson the teacher might encourage everyone to begin keeping a list of potential topics inside their folders. For a few minutes, the children could work in pairs, helping each other come up with the beginning of a list.

Recently I watched a simple lesson in a kindergarten classroom. The teacher, Carol Seltzer, told the class that she was excited by their topics. Then she simply asked youngsters to tell their classmates, in one sentence, what they were writing about. The lesson was particularly effective because each child stood to announce his or her topic. One by one, these youngsters jumped to their feet and, sticking their chests out proudly, said, "This is a make-believe story and I'm writing about how a puppy drowned," "I'm writing about when I had a bad dream and I was all alone on the ocean," "I have a three-months cat," or "I went on a house tour." Of course, children who did not have ideas for their writing got ideas from those who did, and the class as a whole enjoyed knowing what others were doing.

Shelley Harwayne recently gave a mini-lesson on topics. She was teaching in a third grade classroom in which the children were in the "when-I" stage: when I went to Great Adventure Amusement Park, when I visited my aunt, when I went to the movie, when I went to Florida. Shelley wanted the children to realize that they could write about the tiny details of life, so she began the mini-lesson by reading aloud a poem called, "Jumping on Mama's Bed." Then she said, "Can you imagine that this writer actually thought of jumping on Mama's bed as a topic?" "It is such a little thing—jumping on Mama's bed—but you know, sometimes the little things that happen almost every day but are still very important to you, can make wonderful topics."

The class decided to call these "un-topics," and then they shared possible un-topics with each other. "I could tell about my mother's face when she is mad at me," one said. "How my baby brother throws food off his plate onto mine when we are eating," another suggested. "How every time I go to play, I take one thing out and put it on my bed, then another thing out, and soon my whole bed is covered," still another child suggested.

Brian's un-topic was, "I could write about when I shut myself in my closet and play." The children seemed puzzled, so Brian began to explain in more detail. Closing his eyes and feeling the air with his hands, he said, "On this side of the closet is my mother's fan, and there are lots of coats over here." Brian gestured with his hands as he talked, as if reliving the scene in the closet. "Over here, I make a little space between the toy chest and my mother's fan, and that is where I put my teddy bear."

"Isn't there a light in there?" the children asked.

"Oh, no! It is a dark castle. I can't see. I just feel, and I keep my teddy bear close to me. He is my subject and I am king." Brian was ready to write.

Conferences

Earlier in this book, I described the way I would probably introduce peer-conferences in a classroom. "There are thirty-two writing teachers in this room. Everyone of you must be a writing teacher," I might say. Then in order to show what this entailed, I might ask the entire class to act as teachers for one child. After the youngster read his or her piece out loud, I would lead the class to respond to the piece, then to ask questions of the writer, and perhaps also to making tentative suggestions. Afterward, by reviewing what the class had done, I would list the steps involved in peer-conferences.

This mini-lesson, like most, could be repeated many times during the year. Each time, I might add a new point of emphasis. For example, children often ask trivial questions. If a writer's piece is about falling down while roller skating, it would not be unusual for a child to respond, "What color were your roller skates?" Mini-lessons can highlight the need to ask important questions. I might suggest that children think of the single most important question they could ask to respond to a particular draft. Then, instead of having the writer answer those questions, we could record them, reflecting on why some are particularly effective. Or I might confer publicly with a child, asking the class to notice especially the questions that I raise. Later I might talk about the differences between my questions and theirs. Another time, I might give each child a slip of paper and ask everyone to imagine that they were sitting in the author's chair and to write down the question they would most want a friend to ask them.

Children not only have a hard time *asking* important questions, they also have difficulty following a line of questioning. It would not be unusual for a discussion to go like this:

ONE CHILD: Where were you when you caught the fish?
WRITER: Near a lake.
NEXT CHILD: What did the bite feel like on your fishing line?
WRITER: It was a gentle pull. It surprised me because it wasn't a jerk.
NEXT CHILD: What kind of boat do you have?

In a mini-lesson, I might talk about the importance of pursuing a line of thought. "Keep the idea going," I might say, "Keep it going back and forth between you and the writer, just as if you were keeping a ball going across the net." To illustrate, I could take a segment of the class discussion and role play how it could have been done differently:

ONE CHILD: Where were you when you caught the fish?

WRITER: Near a lake.

SECOND CHILD: Can you tell us a little more about where you were, can you set the scene so we can picture it?

WRITER: Well, it was early morning and the mist was still on this lake near my aunt's house. I had planned to fish in the brook but it was so pretty at the lake, I just put my stuff down and sat on a soggy stump near the edge of the water.

FIRST CHILD: Do you think you should add that because when you told me, I could feel like I was there. I think it would make your story much better.

WRITER: Tell all of it? My story would get pretty long!

CLASS: So?

One word of caution: we must avoid turning conferences into recitations of preset questions. Too much attention to conferences can make children overly self-conscious. This is probably less apt to happen if we avoid laying down rules and preaching the "right way" to respond, and instead, use mini-lessons to create a *gestalt,* to show our concern about conferences and gently coach children to become more responsive and more helpful listeners.

Classroom procedures

When I first began telling teachers about writing-process classrooms, I rarely bothered to address issues of classroom management. My job was to translate research into practice, and I was content to leave the more mundane matters in teachers' hands.

There is nothing worse than a reformed sinner, and perhaps this accounts for why I now spend so much time addressing classroom management. I am finally convinced that the single biggest reason why many writing classrooms flounder is that the workshop context requires new sorts of expectations, rules, and rituals. Writing teachers cannot afford to assume, as I did, that belief in children and knowledge of teaching writing will ensure a productive, smoothly-run workshop. Not only will administrators evaluate writing classrooms according to the level of productivity and the amount of order in the room, but also, children need to know what is expected of them. If we are going to have the luxury of responding well to individuals, the class as a whole needs to carry on without us. For this reason, we need a simple, clear, reasonable management system—and we need to teach it to our children.

The simplest mini-lesson on classroom management is one the teacher trainers in our Writing Project sometimes give after we have worked with children (of any age) for about a week. In the mini-lesson, we simply review the predictable structure of the writing workshop. "Children, you may have noticed that we have been writing from ten o'clock to eleven o'clock every morning. You can count on this time. This will be our special time, set aside for writing. And the writing workshop will always begin with us gathering here on the floor for a mini-lesson, as we are doing right now. During the mini-lesson, I may give you a tip about good writing or I may read some fine literature. Every day it will be a little different but you can count on our meeting together. After the mini-lesson you will have the chance, every day, to work on your pieces and share them with each other and with me. Then, for the last ten minutes of writing time, we will meet again for a share meeting. During this meeting, several children will read their work-in-progress and we will talk about it as we did with Miguel and Marissa yesterday."

This mini-lesson paves the way for others. Another day we may want to focus specifically on the procedures for coming to a mini-lesson. This may entail having the children actually practice pushing in their chairs, leaving pencils and paper behind on the desk, and walking quietly to the meeting area. This may sound very mundane, but an extraordinary amount of classroom time is wasted on transitions. If children know how and when to come to the meeting area, it will save time and spare everyone irritation. The mini-lessons will begin on a better footing.

Children also need to learn that they must return the stapler to the writing area and put caps on marker pens. They need to know that once they complete their final drafts, they must staple all the rough drafts together in order and file them in their cumulative folders. All of these expectations can be subjects for mini-lessons. Once, in an effort to engender respect for rough drafts, I brought in an iron from home. After the children had gathered for the mini-lesson, I used the warm iron to smooth a crumpled page from one child's messy writing folder.

Mini-lessons can also convey procedures for peer conferences. If two children arrive at a peer-conference, each determined to read his or her piece right away, it often leads to trouble. Instead of listening well to the other person, children wait impatiently for their friend to be finished so they can have a turn. In Aida Montero's kindergarten class, children learned in a mini-lesson that they must begin a peer-conference by deciding which youngster will be the writer and which will be the listener. Then the writer sits up on a makeshift author's chair (an overturned plastic milk crate) and the listener sits on the floor below. This outward, physical commitment to a role seems to remind Aida Montero's children of their respective jobs.

Response groups, more common in junior high classrooms, raise a number of procedural issues, and these, too, can be the subject for a mini-lesson. In a mini-lesson the teacher might mention her concern over the fact that one or two students dominate many of the response groups. The class could then brainstorm ways to rectify this situation. There are, of course, hundreds of other possible mini-lessons dealing with classroom management. I hope I have given teachers ideas for inventing mini-lessons suited to their own classroom procedures.

Rehearsal and revision strategies

Several years ago I watched a youngster alternate between writing and crumpling her paper. With tremendous intensity, she would lean low over her paper and carefully write her story. Then, taking the page in both hands, she'd scrunch it this way and that. I was astonished and bewildered by what I saw and so I asked the youngster what she was doing. "Revising," she answered, as she proudly patted the well-worn page. "See, it is all loved up."

We laugh at this story, but I have found that this youngster is not as unusual as we might think. Across the country, many children have sensed that their teachers have new agendas. Nowadays, teachers seem to want (oddly enough) messy drafts, and they seem to want the work to drag on forever. Since children are extraordinarily good at giving us what we want, many youngsters are producing one draft after another. They revise up a storm. A closer look shows that these children often do not know what revision is. Often they write successive drafts, none with any connection to the one before it except that they all address the same general topic. Even more often, the drafts are almost identical, one to the next, save for a few insertions, deletions, or corrections.

We need to demythologize revision and help children see what it entails. The first step may be to take a hard look at the component strategies we use (I recommend Murray's book, *Write to Learn,* and Elbow's *Writing With Power* as reference), which might result in a list such as this one:

- Change the piece from one mode to the next (personal narrative to poem, journal entry to published narrative, etc.).
- Rework a confused section—the ending, the title, the lead, etc.
- Reconsider tone or voice. Try a different sort of voice and see if it is preferable.
- Take a long piece and make it shorter.
- Take a short piece and expand it into a longer one.
- Experiment with different leads.
- Select a functional purpose for the piece of writing and then if necessary, reorient the writing so that it accomplishes the task.
- Predict a reader's questions, then revise in order to be sure they are answered, ideally in the order in which they are asked.

- Reread the draft, evaluating what works and what does not work. After selecting what works, write another draft or portion of a draft, building on that strength. Decide whether to delete, repair, or ignore what does not work.
- Read the draft over, listening to how it sounds.
- Put the draft aside and return to it another day.
- Talk with someone about the topic, then rewrite the draft without looking back at the previous versions.
- Take a jumbled piece and rewrite it in sections or chapters.

Each of these—and other—strategies can be the topic for a mini-lesson. Sometimes during the workshop I deliberately encourage one or two children to try a new strategy. Then, what they do becomes the source for a whole-class lesson. For example, Mrs. Howard sensed that many of her fourth graders were restricted to small scale revisions: they inserted clarifying phrases and omitted needless details, but they rarely approached a second draft with a spirit of openness and adventure. In conference with one child, Susie, Mrs. Howard suggested a larger-scale revision. "Susie," she said, "do you notice that all of your stories seem to be about the same length?" It was a wise observation, for Susie seemed to have developed a scheme for writing two-page stories, and each story was similar to the last. In the discussion that ensued, Mrs. Howard suggested the girl challenge herself by taking the two-page draft of "Seeing My Grandparents," and extending it into a much longer draft.

Susie reread the original draft, circling sections of it with her pencil. "These circled parts are places I can spread out with more detail," she explained as she worked. After circling several sections and rewriting them, she added, "I had no idea there were so many parts I could fix up!" Her voice was high with excitement. "I'm discovering more on this draft than I ever did. I never realized I could change so much!"

The next day she told the class about what she had done and, using the overhead projector, she showed them her first and second drafts. The class noticed the similarities and differences between the circled draft and the final one. Here is a portion of what Susie showed the class that day:

DRAFT 1—WITH CIRCLES

I started walking up to the airport from the plane. We had to go through a tunnel. I squeezed my mother's hand. I couldn't wait to see my grandparents.

FINAL DRAFT

My mother and I started to get off the plane. My sister, Jill, was right behind us. I looked at Jill. Her face was red from excitement. She smiled at me. I giggled. I could tell she was just as excited as I was.
By pulling my mother's hand, I hurried her to the entrance of the airport. As we got nearer, I heard the

crowd inside, laughing and talking. I saw a lot of people. They were looking for the person they came to meet. They stretched their necks, searching through the crowd. Everyone was smiling, everyone was happy.

We were almost in the end. I saw my grandparents.

My grandmother's face was tanned. It made her look so healthy. My grandfather looked pretty much the same except he was tanned too. Somebody stepped in front of me. I lost sight of my grandparents. The crowd was moving very slowly so I wiggled past everybody. I ran straight to my grandparents. First I went to my grandmother. I threw my arms around her.

The next day Birger reread the draft of his piece, "The Day My Cat Died," and decided he, too, would make the parts longer, as Susie had done. The mini-lesson had worked: a new revision strategy was in the air, and it was spreading like wildfire.

There are other ways to introduce revision strategies. Sometimes it may be more helpful to survey several options rather than discussing one in detail. I could begin a mini-lesson by saying, "I thought it might help you to hear what I saw yesterday as I went from writer to writer. Let me tell you, specifically, about some of the revision strategies which people in this room are using. Several of you, Mohammed, Allison, and perhaps others, are working on different leads. You are listing alternative ways to start your piece, and trying to select the best beginning. This is exactly what some writers do—they call it experimenting with leads—and I think it is a strategy we could add to our chart, "Revision Strategies." Marigold has invented her own revision strategy. She read her piece over and decided she could hear a song in it, and so she is making a tune up and changing the words to match the mood and beat of her song. Not everyone will want to write songs, but the idea of changing modes is an important strategy; taking a narrative and turning it into a song, taking a letter and making it into a story, and so forth. So let's add that strategy to our list."

Mini-lessons on revision strategies will not always come from what the children are already doing. I might, for example, encourage children to revise for the sound of their language by reading them Katherine Mansfield's description of how she wrote "Miss Brill." "I chose not only the length of each sentence," she said, "but the sound of every sentence. I chose the rise and fall of every paragraph to fit her, to fit her on that day on that very moment. After I'd written it I read it aloud—numbers of times—

just as one would play over a musical composition—trying to get it nearer and nearer to the expression of Miss Brill—until it fitted her.''

I also used my own writing as a source for mini-lessons on revision strategies. For example, I sometimes say, ''Many of you are starting new pieces today and I thought I'd show you how I often go about beginning a piece.'' Then, taking a piece of chalk I go to the board as if I was about to write on it. ''Let's say I am going to write about my brother's wedding,'' I say. Then I pick up my chalk, but I do not actually write words on the chalkboard for that is time-consuming and in this instance, unnecessary. Instead, I pretend to write, saying aloud the intended words as I put squiggles on the board.

ON THE BOARD

ORAL TRANSCRIPT

1 〜〜〜〜〜〜
〜〜〜〜〜〜
〜〜〜〜〜〜
〜〜〜〜〜〜
〜〜〜〜〜〜
〜〜〜.

''Last weekend I went to Baltimore to attend my brother's wedding. It was great fun. We got there just in time for the service to begin. I was excited.''

Then I say to the class, ''After I start writing, I often force myself to stop and look at what I have said so far.'' At this point I reread my words to the class. ''It's a boring beginning, so I draw a line underneath it and write number two. Then I say to myself, 'How else could I begin my piece?' ''

ON THE BOARD

ORAL TRANSCRIPT

2 〜〜〜〜〜〜
〜〜〜〜〜〜
〜〜〜〜〜〜
〜〜〜〜〜〜
〜〜〜〜〜〜
〜〜〜〜〜〜
〜〜〜.

''As we drove nearer to the stone church, the bells began to ring. It was a glorious day, and everywhere people hurried toward the wedding.
'Amazing to think my own brother is getting married,' I thought.''

''Then, after a bit of writing, I stop and see what I've said. I reread it and ask myself, 'Is this a better lead?' '' The consensus of the class is yes. ''I could keep this lead, but I think I'll try a third one first,'' I say. Then I draw another and line and write number three and begin a third lead.

This mini-lesson might end with my suggesting that those children wanting to experiment with different leads stay in the meeting area to help each other with leads or to begin to study the leads authors use in literature books. I would *not* end by suggesting that every child stop what he or she is doing and try three leads. No one revision strategy is right for every child, and certainly no strategy could be right for every child on any one given day. The purpose of the mini-lesson is to suggest options, to add to the class pot, to give children a repertoire of strategies from which they can draw. Another word of caution. It would be a disaster if teachers of five-, six-, and seven-year-olds expected their children to use revision strategies such as lead-writing. Revision for young children consists mostly of adding on, and mini-lessons might illustrate how one child reread her book, realized she'd forgotten certain information, and added it in the empty spaces on her pages, or how children added pages to a pre-existing book. Kindergarten children are not ready to experiment with different leads!

Although this section is titled "Rehearsal and Revision Strategies," I have ignored rehearsal. This is not accidental. My hunch is that adult writers can do a great many things in their mind's eye through rehearsal. I can jot down a few key phrases, and imagine how the entire draft might go. I can anticipate whether a particular angle or perspective will be effective. But this requires a great deal of abstract thinking. It is something I have learned by taking the longer, harder route of actually writing a draft out, then seeing the problems and revising accordingly. It is probably easier for children to wrestle with their writing problems through concrete revisions rather than doing this mentally, in anticipation, through rehearsal. I do not mean to suggest that children will accomplish *nothing* in rehearsal. Certainly second graders can consider possible topics and select the best. Most third graders can see when a topic needs to be divided into subtopics. Through mapping, they can outline chapter headings or brainstorm a variety of focused topics from which they can choose (See Figure 19-1).

Figure 19 – 1

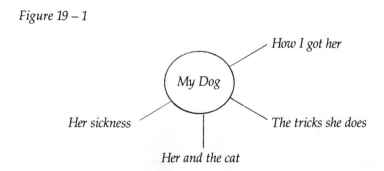

Older children can do much more in rehearsal. My advice for teachers is to think about how they rehearse for writing and then to question whether those strategies seem appropriate for young students. In this way, they can invent mini-lessons on rehearsal that parallel those I have suggested for revision.

Qualities of good writing

"My story is good because it starts exciting, ends exciting, and the excitement keeps on going," eight-year-old Birger told me. Birger often put ten or fifteen exclamation marks on each page of his writing, and he revised even his social studies report on squirrels to add more excitement to it. Birger's understanding of good writing influences everything he does when he writes.

Jen is seven, and she wants very much to be grown-up. She carries a purse now, and envies her friend Melissa for her thin legs. Jen thinks her stories are terrible, "babyish," she calls them. She toils over the shape of each letter and often crumples up her paper in disgust. For Jen as for Birger, a sense of what makes good writing influences everything she does when she writes.

It is only natural, then, that we spend time during mini-lessons helping children deepen their understanding of good writing. During these mini-lessons we will want to tell children about the qualities of good writing that are helpful to us, and we will want to discuss those aspects that seem especially pertinent to the pieces they are writing. But I think that in many of the mini-lessons, we need to give children opportunitites to articulate their sense of what good writing is. For example, we might ask each child to think of the *best* book he or she has ever read, and then to tell a friend what made that book so wonderful. If we were to move among the pairs of children, taking note of what they were saying, we could end the meeting with a brief summary of what we heard and the reminder that these same qualities are important in their own writing. Another day, we might ask children to select the best sentence from the book they are reading and read those sentences to each other. These same mini-lessons could be applied to a particular mode of writing. If the class was working on reports, the children could bring examples of good nonfiction writing to class to read and discuss with a partner. If the class was working on poetry, each child could select the best poem he or she had read recently and then in pairs, children could discuss their selections. Similarly, these mini-lessons could use the children's own writing. Which is *their* best sentence? their best piece? their best poem? Why?

These mini-lessons may sound simple, almost mundane, and yet imagine what fun it would be for us to search for our own favorite poem and then to meet with colleagues to share our choices and discuss what drew us to this poem and not to others. Of course, in these mini-lessons there are no right or wrong answers. Their purpose is to think through with the children their beliefs about the components of good writing, and to consider ways to apply those principles to work-in-progress.

The children's values will differ from ours. Many children place high value on good pictures, action, excitement, and funny topics. We will want to share our criteria for evaluating writing with children, and although each of us will stress the qualities we know and care about, certain characteristics will pertain to most texts. One of these is the inclusion of information. Readers thrive on the concrete and the specific, on the anecdote, statistic, quotation, or example. As Murray points out, "The amateur thinks that the writer has an idea, perhaps a vague thought and a few facts. He doesn't. He has shelves of reports, miles of tape-recorded interviews, notebooks of quotations and facts and ideas and possible constructions. It takes thirty gallons of sap to make a gallon of maple syrup; it takes hundreds of pages of notes to make one *Reader's Digest* article (Murray 1968, 6).

Children may not have miles of tape-recorded interviews, but when they write about topics they know well, they do have a wealth of concrete information. Too often they assume that no one cares about the little details. They are accustomed to adults wanting only cursory answers to their questions. An adult asks, "Did you have a good time at the beach?" and children nod yes. Most children know better than to tell about draping themselves with seaweed and pretending they were brides; they know from past experience that teachers do not want to hear how the sand felt, scratching on their sunburned toes. Yet these are the details that will make their writing powerful, and therefore, as writing teachers, we need to undo the damage and let children know these details are important.

I might show children the importance of detail by telling about one child who rewrote a draft to add detail and improved it significantly. I might read them nine-year-old Susie's two drafts, asking them to notice the wealth of information she added to her second version (Calkins 1983, 2).

DRAFT 1

I was at a beach in Florida. I pressed my toes into the hot sand. I saw my sister jumping out in the waves with my Aunt. She was jumping around as the waves hit her, she was out deep . . . I wanted to go and play in the big waves but I was nervous to.

DRAFT 2

I pressed my toes in the hot sand. I wiggled them around. The gritty sand felt good on my sunburnt toes. I looked out over the ocean. My sister was out deep, jumping over waves with my Aunt. Sometimes the waves got too big and they would knock her over, then my Aunt would pull her up and she'd be dripping wet and

they'd start laughing. My shoulders
were hot from the burning sun. I
would have loved to be out there in
the waves but I was too scared.

Hindy List recently gave a similar mini-lesson. She told a group of fifth graders, "I want to give you a tip about good writing today, so listen closely. I have been going around to classes and often I see pieces like this one:

HAVING FUN AT MY PARTY

I had so much fun at the party. I got a lot of presents and I ate a lot
and the food was delicious.

You know, I have a hard time picturing exactly what the author meant. I would just love it if the author would use more specifics. I would have liked to hear about the T-shirt with a unicorn on it and the giant Unifix cube she was given. And instead of telling us she ate delicious food, I would have liked to see the seven-layered cake and the four glasses of ice-cold coke. So when you are writing, remember to add details. And if you don't add details *during* writing, you can add them afterward, during revision, when you reread your piece. Let me show you how I do this."

Hindy turned to the draft she had written on the chalkboard. With chalk in hand, she continued, "If I had written this story, I might reread it afterward and think, 'Can I tell more?' 'Can I help the reader see?' When I notice that I haven't told specifically about the presents, I put a little asterisk here (and she inserts a star into the appropriate place in her story) and then, turning the paper over, I put the same code on the back, and beside it, I explain the section more specifically. Whenever I get to spots where I could have been more specific, I insert a secret code, and then in a different place I write what belongs there." Hindy ended the mini-lesson by asking, "Do any of you want to reread your pieces today, searching for places where you could be more specific?" Many children nodded, and Hindy told them she would be coming around to help and sent them off to work.

Readers may notice several things. Hindy used a hypothetical draft rather than a real one as her negative example. The only time I would use a child's draft as a negative example is when I want to show how the youngster improved his or her own piece, as in Susie's story. Also, Hindy did not label the component of writing she was trying to teach. She did not write "Telling Details" or "Show not Tell" on the chalkboard and ask the children to recite the phrase. Hindy learned not to do this the hard way. Until several years ago, we told children that writers have a saying: "Show not tell." Then we proceeded to illustrate the motto with a mini-lesson such as Hindy's lesson on details. Now I often visit classrooms and hear children parroting "show not tell," and it is clear to me that *labeling* a quality of good writing creates a cliché. Clichés are too easy. They allow people to recite easy dictums rather than responding honestly and freshly to written work.

Readers may also have noticed that Hindy ended the mini-lesson by talking about how the children might go about adding more specific details to their drafts. Had she not ended the mini-lesson this way, few children would have incorporated the lesson on specifics in their work-in-progress. Almost every mini-lesson ought to end with a specific, concrete discussion of what the children can *do* next with their writing.

There are countless other ways to teach children the importance of revealing details, and there are also many other qualities that make writing good. I find it helpful to talk about honesty in writing; it is easy to say "white snow covered the world," but was the snow really white? It is easy to say "I had a terrific time" but weren't there annoying moments, and feelings that shadowed the happiness? Donald Hall emphasizes that honesty is one of the most important qualities of good writing. "Concentration upon honesty is the only way to exclude the sounds of the bad style that assault us all," he writes, and I would tell children this.

Other mini-lessons could center on focus, order, voice, and point of view. I would also suggest that as teachers of writing, we need to read about good writing. I have learned about good writing from people such as Ken Macrorie, Donald Hall, Donald Murray, John Gardner, Robert Graves, Eudora Welty, and William Zinsser, and their books are available in bookstores and libraries. Find them, and use them as resources. Otherwise we will continue to think that the qualities of good writing are those described in language arts textbooks. From language arts textbooks, I learned that piling adjectives and adverbs into one's sentences creates "colorful language." It was only when I read Zinsser's book, *On Writing Well*, that I realized writers often delete adjectives and adverbs during editing. Strong, precise nouns and verbs are important to a sentence. Often adjectives and adverbs are only used to prop up a weak noun or verb. In the sentence, "I walked softly into the room," the adverb "softly" supports a weak verb. Why not say, "I crept into the room," or "I tiptoed into the room." In the sentence, "The young dog came to greet me," the adjective "young" supports a weak noun. Why not say, "The puppy came to greet me"?

My point in giving this lesson on strong nouns and verbs is that we need to learn what writers have to say about their craft and to use it as a resource for mini-lessons on the qualities of good writing. But my larger point is that teachers of writing need to be students of writing. We need to read the best literature we can find, we need to study what works in our own texts and in those of others. We also need to invite our students to do the same.

20

---

editing: last but not least

The research is conclusive. Teaching formal grammar has no effect on the quality of student writing. After an extensive review of the literature on grammar instruction, Braddock, Lloyd-Jones, and Schoer conclude,

In view of the widespread agreement of research studies based upon many types of students and teachers, the conclusion can be stated in strong and unqualified terms: the teaching of formal grammar has a negligible or, because it usually displaces some instruction and practice in actual composition, even a harmful effect on the improvement of writing (Braddock, Lloyd-Jones, and Schoer 1963).

In 1969, John Mellon, another respected researcher in English education, also did a lengthy review of the literature on teaching grammar and found no evidence of any enabling effect. Around the same time, the well-known linguist Roger Brown wrote:

It is extremely improbable that communication skills should be affected at all by instruction in explicit grammar, whether that grammar be traditional or traditional circa 1958, or transformational circa 1965, or the current transformational frontier. Study of the theory of language is probably competely irrelevant to the development of skill in the use of language (Brown 1968, xi).

Courtney Cazden, a child language expert from Harvard University, puts it this way:

There is no evidence that learning to be aware of one's tacit grammatical knowledge makes any difference in verbal behavior (Cazden 1972, 240).

I could continue. But I know that, whether I quote five or fifty people, many classroom teachers will remain unconvinced. And perhaps rightly so. Being able to write grammatically *does* matter, and this is brought home to me whenever I see student papers log jammed with errors. The content in these papers is difficult to appreciate and the errors are impossible to overlook. What's more, principals, parents, school boards, and even the children themselves not only want to write correctly, they also want old-fashioned teacher-controlled, direct instruction in the so-called "basic skills." I remember that, after I spent an entire year working with students on reader's theater, writing workshop, literature response groups, and editing circles, the students in May were still asking why we never studied "English." They meant grammar, of course, and the workbook.

What are we to do? The language arts teacher is caught in the middle. It is hard to argue against such overwhelmingly clear research evidence, especially because most of us know that, although we teach the preposition in third, fourth, fifth, sixth, seventh, eighth, ninth, tenth, eleventh, and twelfth grades, the kids never seem to "get it." On the other hand, so many people—principals, parents, colleagues, and even the kids—seem convinced that formal grammar is important, and certainly we agree that being able to write and speak correctly matters a great deal. What is the teacher to do?

What I did when I was teaching was to shrug my shoulders and say, "I dunno." I couldn't resolve the issue, so I went through the motions of doing what I was told. I took the path of least resistance. I swept the unresolved issues under the rug.

In the preceding chapter I quoted Peter Elbow: "The mark of the person who can sit down at 8:30 with one set of ideas and stand up at 11:00 with better ideas is a willingness to notice and listen to those inconvenient little details, those annoying loose ends, those embarrassments or puzzles, instead of impatiently sweeping them under the rug." In this chapter, I want to lift up the rug and deal with the troublesome issue of editing. I think it is particularly helpful to do this so that we do not lose sight of the fact that, although some things are confusing in the teaching of language skills, other things are obvious. It is helpful to separate the two, to know what we can be sure of, and to know what remains unclear.

I am not sure, in the face of all the research and all the pressures in a school system, whether I would teach formal grammar and if so, what kind of grammar at what grade level, and using what instructional method. I *do* know I would not teach nouns, verbs, and prepositions in an elementary school classroom. That is a battle I would fight, confident that the research is so clear, I could convince others. Perhaps, however, I *would* recommend a semester of linguistics within the senior high school curriculum. Even then, I am not sure I would teach the grammar that was taught to me. Research suggests that Latin-based grammar is not the ideal way to describe the English language. I would perhaps teach sector-analysis or transformational grammar. In general, these are the unresolved issues for me.

On the other hand, there are many areas in which I am not ambivalent, and I want to address four of them. Then I will turn to classroom applications, discussing editing checklists and peer editors, whether to correct student writing, and how we can work with students with severe writing problems.

Separate transcription from composition

I recently visited my parents. In honor of my visit, my mother invited the local superintendent, a member of the Board of Education, and a journalist who teaches at the nearby university, to dinner. I was particularly looking forward to hearing about the college journalism course. "I can imagine the wonderful projects your students must be doing," I said when the woman arrived, and then I asked her to tell me about them.

The woman sighed deeply. "I had great plans, Lucy," she said. "But do you know something? No one had ever taught those students the difference between *to, too,* and *two.* They didn't even know what a sentence is! Eighteen years of school, and no one has taught them the word *however.*" She sighed again. "All that emphasis on creative writing—no one has taught them the components of writing." Then she said, "No, Lucy, I'm not having them write. I'm teaching them *too, to,* and *two.*"

Despite the fact that she was my mother's friend, I said, "You are wrong. *To, too,* and *two* are all they have been taught. Year after year, teachers have looked at their writing and said, 'They have to learn the basics first.' Those students may never have the chance to write." The infrequency with which students write is a major reason for their problems with mechanics and spelling. Writing is an alien activity for many people. Just as I am awkward and self-conscious when I attempt to roller skate, many students are awkward when they attempt to write; it is an unnatural activity for them. Shaughnessy (1977) suggests, in fact, that the single most important fact about Basic Writers is that, although they have been talking every day for many years, they have written infrequently and only under strained situations.

My first point, then, is that the single most important thing we can do for students' syntax, spelling, penmanship, and use of mechanics is to have them write often and with confidence. Furthermore, students must be encouraged to write without worrying whether they are making errors.

Once they have written a draft they will have time for editing, but during composition, concern about correctness competes with the more timely concern about content, word choice, voice, tone, and rhythm.

Let me be more specific. After my first mini-lesson, just before children head off to work on their drafts, I tell them, "This is just a rough draft. Don't worry about spelling or neatness, there will be time for that later."

"Must we use cursive or can we print?" the children often ask.

"Use whichever is most comfortable for you," I say. "Rough drafts are meant to be rough. There will be a time later for making it beautiful."

"Pen or pencil?" they ask.

I am apt to turn the question around. "What do you think I'll say?"

"Whichever we want."

"Yes, this is just a rough draft."

I find that giving children permission to print and to cross out is not enough. By the time students are in second grade, many of them have been taught that good writers produce neat, correct texts. As I move about the workshop, I watch for the child who writes a letter, scrutinizes it to be certain it is perfectly rounded, then erases it and tries again. "It is important for you to worry less about penmanship," I tell this youngster. "In fact, let's make a rule: no erasing allowed. Just cross it out and keep going." Perhaps, to reassure the child, I show him one of my drafts. "This is what writers do," I say, pointing out my cross-outs, false starts and misspellings. As I move through the workshop I also look for the youngster who composes with a dictionary on the desk. "I want to suggest something," I say. "Instead of interrupting yourself to look up a word every time you are unsure of spelling, would you put the dictionary away and not worry too much about spelling in this draft?" Then, because of course spelling is important eventually, I add, "Later, when the drafts are all done, you and I can look at the spelling and fix it up." Similarly, if a child looks up from a rough draft to ask how a word is spelled, rather than giving the spelling I will say, "Take a guess, OK?" and then add, "Spelling doesn't matter in your rough draft."

"But my children *keep* asking for spelling help," teachers tell me.

"That's because you keep giving it," I respond. If we are clear and consistent, children quickly become independent spellers. But if we intermittently reinforce their dependence by giving correct spellings some of the time and not other times, the children *will* keep asking.

It is essential that we help children separate transcription from composition. If children keep asking for spelling help, it means that during the composing process, they focus too much on editing. In his book, *Writing and the Writer*, Frank Smith explains why this is a problem:

Composition and transcription can interfere with each other. . . .
The problem is basically one of competition for attention. If we are

struggling for ideas, or for particular words or constructions, or if our thoughts are coming too fast, then the quality of our handwriting or typing, spelling or punctuation is likely to decline. If we concentrate on the transcription or appearance of what we write, on the other hand, then composition will be affected (Smith 1982, 21).

Because we are skillful writers, it may seem easy enough to attend to spelling, punctuation, and content at the same time. You and I can do this only because spelling is second-nature to us. The best way to imagine the task our students face is to imagine a teacher telling us to produce a powerful piece of writing about something important—perhaps our relationship with our children—and to insert an exclamation mark after every proper noun, capitalize every *r, v, s,* and *b,* underline every adverbial phrase, star every preposition, and delete every *-ing.* Furthermore, the teacher tells us to follow these rules perfectly from the start. Such an assignment would be an impossible task. Our heads would soon be a swirl of mixed-up rules, and we would certainly not produce our best piece of writing. Yet this is what we ask of students.

As a result, many students have developed ineffective writing strategies. As I mentioned in chapter 3, many unskilled writers interrupt themselves after every few words because of their anxiety about error. They search for words in a dictionary, but it is useless because, as they tell us, it is hard to look up a word when you cannot spell it. They line up behind the teacher and finally are told how to spell the word in question, but by then they have forgotten what they planned to say in the first place.

When students worry about spelling and neatness while composing a draft, their writing becomes so slow it is hard for them to maintain logic and coherence. Smith (1982) points out that we talk, listen, and read at the rate of two hundred to three hundred words a minute, but even the average student writes only twenty-five words a minute, and some students write something closer to six words a minute. While it would be extremely taxing to talk, read, or listen coherently at such a slow pace, it is equally difficult to write slowly.

For a whole variety of reasons, then, I tell students to spell and punctuate "as best you can," and to postpone their worries until the final draft. If I am very clear and consistent about this, the children come to trust me and themselves, and the mechanics of writing begin to improve.

Trust incidental learning

My husband and I are going to buy a car soon. Whenever I drive now, I find myself noticing the differences between Toyotas and Subarus, Pintos and Chevettes. The curious thing is that, all my life I have been surrounded by cars, yet until now I have not taken note of the different makes. Because I now view myself as someone who needs to know about cars, I see them everywhere.

Similarly, when children perceive themselves as insiders in writing language, as members of the club (as Frank Smith says), they will notice the conventions of written language everywhere. Several years ago I did a small study comparing two third-grade classrooms (Calkins 1980a, 86–89). In Mrs. Howard's classroom, the children learned punctuation through writing and editing. Across the hall, Mrs. West taught mechanics through daily drills and workbook exercises. "I start at the very beginning, teaching them simple sentences, periods, capitals," she explained. "Everything that is in the book, I do a whole lesson on it." Mrs. West wrote sentences on the chalkboard and asked her children to insert missing punctuation. She made dittos on question marks and gave pretests and post-tests on periods. Her children rarely wrote.

Both teachers said, "I begin at the very beginning." For Mrs. West, the beginning was the declarative sentence and the rules for using periods. For Mrs. Howard, the beginning was the child's information, the child's desire to be seen and heard. Both teachers believe in basic skills. One taught them in isolation, the other taught them in context (Calkins 1980b, 86).

After observing these classrooms for a year, I met with each child in both rooms. In these meetings, I drew punctuation symbols and asked, "What is this for?" and, "Do you like punctuation?" What I found was that the third grade "writers" who had not had formal instruction in punctuation could define/explain an average of *8.66* kinds of punctuation. The children who had studied punctuation through classwork, drills, and tests, but had rarely written, were able to define/explain only *3.85* kinds of punctuation. The children in the writing classroom liked punctuation. Tracey explained, "Punctuation sounds good. I mean, it doesn't have a sound like a letter has a sound, but it makes all the letters sound better. If writing had no punctuation, it would sound dull" (87).

Chip liked punctuation because his readers needed it. "It lets them know where the sentence ends, so otherwise one minute you'd be sledding down the hill and the next minute you're inside the house, without even stopping."

I can only speculate about the reasons why the children who wrote knew so much more punctuation then the children who studied it every day. My sense is that when children view themselves as writers, they see punctuation everywhere—just as I now see makes of cars everywhere. Even when Mrs. Howard's children had never used a particular kind of punctuation, they were familiar with it. Shawn recognized the colon: "My dad uses them in his writing," he said. "But one thing; I can't read his writing."

Melissa nods at the sight of the ellipsis. "Those three periods; people use them at the end of paragraphs. But I usually just use one period."

Even first grader, Joshua, had seen parentheses. "They are in my math book on a few pages, coming up. I think they mean regrouping."

Across the hall, the mechanics students were baffled and amazed at many of the punctuation marks. "Are those English?" they asked. "I've never seen half of those." They hadn't seen them because they had no use for them.

Young writers learn spelling in the same way. In his article, "Reading Like a Writer" (1983, 558–60), Smith argues that the only way to account for how some children learn hundreds, even thousands, of spellings a year is to recognize that they learn to spell by reading like a writer. When a person reads like a writer, he or she anticipates what the author will say; in Smith's words, "The author is in effect writing on our behalf. . . . Everything the learner would want to spell the author spells. Every nuance of expression, every relevant syntactic device, every turn of phrase, the author and learner write together. Bit by bit, one at a time . . . the learner learns through reading like a writer, to write like a writer" (564).

Smith concludes, as do I, that if we help youngsters perceive themselves as authors, then we can trust the natural learning process. After all, children learn to distinguish cats from dogs without being taught, they learn to run, jump, and skip without our instruction. Learning is what the wide-awake brain does naturally. If we can extend or guide that learning, fine. But we make a tremendous mistake if we fool ourselves into believing that children learn to spell through our weekly spelling drills, or that they will learn punctuation only if we spend class time defining and explaining it. As Emig says, "That students learn and that teachers teach is undeniable. But to believe that students learn because teachers teach is to engage in magical thinking" (Emig 1982).

Respect the intelligence behind errors

The premise that underlies Mina Shaughnessy's brilliant book, *Errors and Expectations,* is that we need to respect the intelligence behind our students' errors. Shaughnessy is addressing especially the needs of basic writers when she writes, "The inexperienced teacher is almost certain to see nothing but a chaos of error when he first encounters their papers. Yet a closer look will reveal very little that is random or 'illogical' in what they have written. And the keys to their development as writers often lie hidden in the very features of their writing that English teachers have been trained to brush aside with . . . a scribbled 'Proofread!' " (Shaughnessy 1977, 5).

Shaughnessy, of course, echoes the earlier work of Piaget who describes errors as "windows to the mind." Whether students are adding or dividing, spelling or punctuating, their errors help us see the logic of their thinking. And generally, there *is* logical thinking behind the errors.

In her story about a make-believe birthday for her teddy bear, five-year-old Sharon used exclamation marks for the very first time. She sprinkled them randomly throughout the story—or so it seemed. But instead of simply correcting her, I asked if she could explain. "I had one of those marks on the invitations to *my* birthday. I remember because there wasn't enough invitations so I copied them to make the right amount, and I copied that mark," she said. "I don't know what they mean. Something about birthdays, so I put them in my story whenever I tell about Teddy's birthday."

Maria, another first grader, put a colon at the end of every page in her homemade book. This puzzled me, but talking with Maria helped me understand. Earlier in the year Maria had written, "There are many kinds of dinosaurs," and her teacher had suggested that if she added a colon before the list of dinosaurs, the reader would know there was more to come. Therefore, Maria figured, it made sense to put the colon at the bottom of each page as a way to signify, "read on, there is more to come!" A closer look showed me that she'd carefully and appropriately omitted the colon from her final page.

There is also logic to children's spellings. Many kindergarten children spell the word *cheese* with an *h* as the initial letter. This makes sense: the letter "haich" (h) sounds more like *ch* than does the letter *c*. Like so many other errors, this misspelling provides a window into the child's thinking. If we study the patterns in children's errors, and if we see the logic behind their errors, we can usually understand and even solve the underlying problem.

When working with college-aged unskilled writers, Shaughnessy found that her students were resistant to using periods. She surmised that they preferred commas or "and thens" because they were afraid that, if they ended a sentence, the piece would no longer hold together. Shaughnessy also found that many errors resulted from fragments of misinformation. Many students believed that "commas go wherever you breathe," or that "commas go before *and* and *that*." No wonder they made errors when they wrote. Then, too, the students were often unfamiliar with the dialect of formal writing. Consequently, many of them tried to effect the style without having mastered it. "The result," Shaughnessy writes, was "an unconscious parody of that style, often a grotesque mixture of rudimentary errors, formal jargon and strained syntax" (Shaughnessy 1977, 33).

Shaughnessy, of course, is not describing the young writer. We do not know if the logic behind our children's errors is the same logic that Shaughnessy describes. We do know that errors are worth careful study, and that if we use errors as a window into our students' minds, we can be more knowledgeable and timely in our teaching.

Teach language as a skill, not a content

"A noun is a person, place, or thing."
"A verb is an action word or a state of being."
"An adjective modifies a noun or pronoun."

I remember writing those definitions into my workbook when I was a kid, studying them and being tested on them. I did the same thing with the sixteen uses of the comma and the nine reasons for capitalizing a word. This, to me, was English.

The curious thing about my study of Pat Howard's third graders and my subsequent study of first graders and their writing, was that, although these young writers could speak eloquently about punctuation and use it wisely, they did not know the correct definitions. Sometimes, they didn't even know the names of the punctuation marks they used. Many marks were entitled "what-ja-ma-call-its." When six-year-old Jennice used quote marks in her story, I asked, "What's that?"

"Um, ah, oh, that thing, you know . . ." was her response.

"Well, when do you use them?" I asked.

Jennice had a ready answer. "When they talk. You know, when they say things."

Exclamation marks were called by all sorts of titles. A first grader called them "happy marks," and many of the third graders called them "explanations." The students' ignorance of the proper titles of these marks did not hinder them from using the symbols to improve their stories. "I like explanations," Diane said. "They change the way people read my words. They read them faster. They are like action words: run! quick!"

The nonwriters rarely gave operational definitions. Instead, they described punctuation by trying to remember the rules they'd been taught. Mrs. West's class knew that periods come at the end of a sentence, but when I asked them how they knew to end a sentence, they didn't know. "You can tell where a sentence ends by the period," was all they could say. One boy had mastered the tricks of the trade. He suggested that you look and see if a capital letter comes next, and if so, insert the period. That boy will do well on the third grade achievement tests, and many of his classmates will as well. But drills on missing punctuation have little carry-over into writing.

Jack, another student in the mechanics classroom, knew that commas were for lists of people—Joe, Frank, Peter. "Anywhere else?" I asked. "Sometimes when you paint," Jack said. "Different colors—purple, green, blue." Then he added, "But nowhere else."

Many of the mechanics students defined commas by referring to one specific use only. "Put them between fruit." "Commas separate states."

The writers, however, didn't refer to rules, but to their writing. Amy explained commas this way:

> *If you have a long sentence and you want to keep it all there, you put a comma in to take a breath. If you were to make a new sentence, you'd change it up. One example is my flying piece of writing. I said, "We got a little lower and over the beach, I saw tiny colored dots."*
>
> *Before and after the commas, they are both parts of the same sentence. Like the first half of the sentence is one paragraph, and the other half is the second paragraph . . . like two edges of the same idea.*

Amy does not know all the proper rules and definitions for language conventions, but she has developed an intuitive sense of the nuances of punctuation.

There is a lesson in what the children showed me. It may not matter whether students can list the sixteen uses of a comma or define a prepositional phrase. What matters far more is that children get a feel for linking sentences and embedding phrases, for using symbols to encode the sounds of their voices. English is a skill to be developed, not content to be taught—and it is best learned through active and purposeful use.

Help students edit

Editing should be kept in its place, yes, but this does not mean it should be banished from the writing room. I do not want to mislead readers into thinking that children learn the conventions of written language through osmosis alone, that neatness, spelling, and correctness are unimportant in the writing workshop, or that correcting children's written work damages their self-concept. Editing has a very real place in the writers craft, and with encouragement and guidance, even kindergarten children can engage in a primitive sort of editing.

Recently I watched Shelley Harwayne as she introduced editing to five-year-olds. This was her third day in this classroom and her goal was first, to avoid a bottleneck of children saying, "I am done, what should I do next?" by clearly telling children what to do when their pieces were finished. Her second goal was to introduce them to a basic, even rudimentary, sort of editing and in doing so, to set up a system for dealing with editing. Shelley began the mini-lesson by saying, "It is nice to see so many authors." She held a stack of folders in her lap, and, turning to the children, she said, "Your papers from yesterday are in beautiful writing folders now. You each have one with your name on it. I am going to hold up your folder and then you can look at your piece of writing and you will have a decision to make. You have to tell me whether you are finished or whether you have more to put in your story. If you are finished, do you know what you will do?" The children, big-eyed and silent, shook their heads. Shelley continued. "When authors finished all the beautiful books in your library, do you know what they did? They started on the *next one!* When you finish one story and it is your best, the very best you can do, then you can start your next one. And so when I show you your piece of writing, you decide if it is your best." Holding up one child's story, Shelley said, "Anthony, what about you? Is this your best?"

"Yes, I'm finished."

"Anthony, I have this big blue box and it says 'Finished Pieces.' You can put your story here, but first do you see what else it says on the box? It says:

1 Name.
2 Date.
3 Page numbers.

Before you put your story in the big blue box, you have to *edit* it. This is the editing list and it tells you to check that you have your name, and the date, and that you have numbered your pages like authors do. What do you need to do before putting your story in the box, Anthony?"

"Page numbers and date," he said, and began to add these as Shelley moved on to the next child.

"Ricardo, is this your best or do you have more to add?" she asked. He was done, and so Shelley reminded him to edit before he put the piece in the big blue box. Soon all the folders had been passed out, and from that day on the children knew what to do when they were done.

The editing chart changes as children become capable of new skills. In this particular classroom, some children were soon adding periods, rereading to be sure the pieces made sense, and capitalizing the first letter in their sentences. They could not define periods or list the uses for capitals, and they did not necessarily edit correctly, but they had learned that editing is a crucial part of the writing cycle. This may be a more important lesson than anything else.

Other teachers have found their own ways to guide their children into editing. In her first-grade classroom, when Mary Ellen Giacobbe went over their finished story with youngsters, she noticed and celebrated the conventions that each child had used independently. These conventions were then added onto a list that was stapled to the front cover of the child's daily writing folder. This was Audrey's list in November:

THINGS AUDREY CAN DO:

1 *Write her name on the book.*
2 *Write the title on the book.*
3 *Write the date on the book.*
4 *Begin each sentence with a capital letter.*
5 *Use quotation marks.*
6 *Use a question mark at the end of a sentence.*
7 *Use a period at the end of a sentence.*

When Audrey completed her next piece, she was expected to reread the list, using it as a guide for editing. In this way, every child had his or her individualized checklist. This is a splendid system, but for crowded New York City classrooms it is too dependent on extensive teacher input, so Shelley devised the notion of a chart, hanging over the "big blue box." Teachers need to be problem-solvers and to find ways to make general concepts work within their own classrooms.

By the time children are in second grade, most of the teachers with whom I work make editing checklists on rexograph sheets so that children can actually check off each item as they deal with it. These editing sheets look something like the one shown in Figure 20-1.

It is important to remember, of course, that the items on the checklist change over the course of the year as children become more and more capable. When most children are using terminal punctuation correctly, this can be deleted from the list and a new item added. The lists should change as the children do, and because there is always a wide range of abilities within a room, it makes sense to have several different checklists, each representing different levels of sophistication.

Children quickly learn that, after they have drafted and revised their piece, they take it to the editing table. There, with the checklist as a guide, they reread and correct their pieces. In mini-lessons and editing conferences, teachers will have shown children how to go about editing. We find it helpful, for example, to ask children to read through their pieces quickly as a reader might, following the content with a critical eye to be sure it makes sense. When checking for spelling, we suggest that children read

---

Figure 20 – 1

Editing Checklist

Author: _____

Title: _____

Date began: _____ Date finished: _____

                                                Editor   Peer Editor

Does it make sense?

Spelling

Punctuation:

   Periods, question marks, commas, exclamation marks, quotation marks

Paragraphs

Capitals

Excess words

Teacher comments:

   Strengths–

   Needs–

with pencil in hand, touching each word and asking, "Is this right?" Some teachers suggest that youngsters begin at the end of a piece and read up the page so that they see words out of context and errors will be obvious. Others disagree, but what matters most is that children read slowly and that they know what to do if a word looks wrong. Generally, we suggest that the child lightly underline the word (circling it destroys the appearance of the draft) and that they then turn the paper over and try spelling the word again another way. Later, they can return to this list and select several words to look up in a dictionary. The key point here is that children, not teachers, are the ones to identify misspelled words. Although spelling correctly is nice, many brilliant people are lousy spellers. The bottom line is that it is important to recognize if a word is misspelled and to have strategies for correcting the spelling.

It is also important that the editing system in our classrooms does not put extraordinary demands on writers who have severe problems. If these children know they must find every single misspelled word in a dictionary, they will write with safe words, choosing *big* when they wanted to say *enormous*.

Readers may have noticed that on the editing checklist, along with obvious items such as periods and capitals, I included "excess words." In a mini-lesson, I will have already shown children what this phrase means, perhaps by demonstrating the amount of cutting and pruning I do during editing. My larger point, however, is to show children that editing involves more than correcting errors. It is a creative act, a time for tightening and linking, for smoothing out one's language, ordering one's thoughts and for listening to the poetry and rhythm of one's sentences. Instead of "excess words" I might have said, "adjust the rhythm of your sentences" or "use paragraph breaks and varied sentence length to direct the reader's attention," or "listen for where the pace falls apart," or "notice and correct places where your readers will stumble."

In some classrooms, the editing checklists contain a column for peer editors. There are obvious advantages to this; children help each other, they talk punctuation and spelling, they use each other's strengths, they need less input from teachers. The disadvantages of peer editing are less obvious until one introduces it in the classroom. Then they become all too apparent. Children love to play teacher. In large scrawly letters, they mark all over a friend's piece. Major warfare often breaks out, especially when the writer protests that the peer editor is wrong (as is often the case). My suggestion, then, is that if children edit each other's papers, they must understand that the writer makes the final decision. One way to emphasize this is to say that peer editors can advise but they cannot write on a draft.

Once a child has edited his or her piece, it is time for the teacher to look it over. Ideally, the child brings the draft and the editing checklist to the teacher, and they have an editing conference. Classrooms are rarely ideal, however, and I find that generally the class size is too large for this to work. Teachers end up spending half their time in editing conferences, and those youngsters waiting for editing conferences become restless, adding to the chaos in the room. The best way we have found to avoid this bottleneck is for children to put the edited work into the teacher's box and while waiting for a conference, to begin a new piece.

Often teachers say, "When you have edited your piece, show it to me, and if it looks as if you have done your best, you can put it in my box." If, as we glance over the work, it seems the child has *not* done his or her best, then we might say, "Is this your very best, Ramon?" If the child answers no, then the piece is returned to him. "What is the point in not doing your best?" we say, as if amazed and baffled at the notion of giving less than one hundred percent to a piece of writing. Children eventually get the message.

This reminds me of a story Donald Murray tells about a senior editor who assigned a project to his team of writers. They turned in the work on the day it was due, and the senior editor took it home, but he did not read it. The next day he called the team together and, returning the paper to them, he barked, "Was this your best?"

The writers shuffled their feet, hemmed and hawed, and began to explain. "You see, sir, we would have done our best but this and that happened. . . ."

The editor cut them off. "Turn it in on Wednesday." Wednesday came and again the editor took the paper home, and again he did not read it. The next day he held it out to the team of writers, and shaking it in the air as he spoke, he said, "Was *this* your best?" Again there were apologies, and the editor said, "Bring it in on Monday."

Monday night, he once again took the paper home and did not read it. Tuesday he dropped it on the table in front of the writers and growled, "Was this your best?"

"God damn it, *yes*," they answered.

"Then I shall read it," he said. I think we would do well to learn from this example.

When reading students' edited work, I find it helpful to read it over quickly first without a pen. This allows me to see the broader picture of what the child has and has not done. But a word of caution. Many times when I read work that students have pronounced done, my temptation is to recycle the piece back into content conferences. The story may be a laundry list of everything the child did all summer, but if I return the piece saying, "What is the one thing you want to focus on?" my message is that the child is not in charge, I am. How much better it would be for me to make a mental note that next time, I need to confer with the youngster earlier, when it is not too late for a focus conference.

When I read the piece in an editing conference then, I am *not* looking for focus, voice, telling detail and so forth. I am looking instead at spelling, punctuation, paragraphs, clarity, sentence length, language, syntax. I always try to look first at what the child *has* done, and especially at the risks the child has taken. I jot notes in the appropriate space on the editing checklist because I know that when the writer and I meet for an editing conference, I will want to begin by celebrating what the child *has* done.

What a difference this makes! When I was a child, editing meant error (bad, wrong, red pen and points off). It is important to reverse this negative learning and to help children be *learners of language conventions*. Children, like adults, learn best in a supportive context. They are more apt to remember kind words about their successes than harsh words about their failures. They will take risks if we reinforce risk-taking. The tendency, instead, is to reinforce correctness. In playing tennis, I do not know how to serve well because I find that simply dropping the ball and then hitting it over the net is safer. The ball doesn't go out that way, and no one laughs at me. But I will never learn to serve unless I take risks. Children will only learn quotation marks and colons and the spelling of long and difficult words if they, too, are risk-takers. There is a space on editing checklists for strengths, and in an editing conference, I begin there.

I also look at errors, but instead of dealing with each one in isolation, one after another, until the students' minds begin to swirl and their eyes get glassy, I try to see patterns in the errors and to simplify the chaos of mistakes into one or two key items. This is essential because we need to show students that they can begin to take control of written language. We need to change their self-perception from ''I can't'' to ''I can.'' In an editing conference, then, I begin by celebrating what the student *has* done, and then I teach one or two items. If I show the student how to add periods to their work, they will probably return to their seats with the draft and add periods to it. Later, we go over it again, perhaps continuing to work on terminal punctuation, perhaps going on to a second issue. By then, I will probably decide that the student has learned enough from this one piece of writing, and so the draft is once again put into my box. This time, I will correct it at home (with blue pen or pencil) and eventually the student will recopy it so that the final draft is perfect (well, almost).

I suspect that I have raised a host of questions and inspired disagreement. There are people who feel that by correcting students' writing, I contradict all that I have said about ownership. I respect this point of view, but I disagree with it. There is a time when published writing leaves the writer's hands and becomes a public document. This book has been edited professionally, and for this I am grateful. I don't want to ''own'' all my errors. Much of my writing will never be published, and I feel differently about this—it needn't be corrected. One option is to suggest that children publish a certain number of pieces only, or a ratio (one out of four stories?). But I also think it is entirely legitimate to suggest that all of the work that has gone through successive drafts deserves to be brought to completion.

The exception, it seems to me, is the writing of primary school youngsters.

I am always sorry when I visit classrooms where the children's invented spellings are kept hidden and only the teacher's spelling is evident. It is so much more exciting and interesting to see the children's own efforts! I recommend, therefore, that kindergarten and first-grade teachers rewrite student writing correctly when and if they decide to do so (after typing or writing it over themselves, they might allow children to make their own final copies) but that they also proudly display the children's own rough drafts. The spellings are not "wrong"—they are spectacular.

Meanwhile, with children of every age I would periodically give mini-lessons on editing. Most of the learning would be incidental, however, and most of my instruction would be one-to-one. Teachers will ask, "Isn't this inefficient—teaching periods to one child at a time?" I could argue by showing how conventions spread throughout the room from child to child, and I could encourage teachers to let children eavesdrop on their one-to-one editing conferences. I could point out that it would be hard to find *any* method of teaching mechanics that is as wasteful of time and joy, or as unsuccessful, as the methods we have been using. But my strongest argument may be to show how children grow when put into classroom contexts such as those described in this book. Figure 20-2 shows an example of Craig's writing in September of third grade, and Figure 20-3 shows an example of his writing in December of that year.

Figure 20 – 2

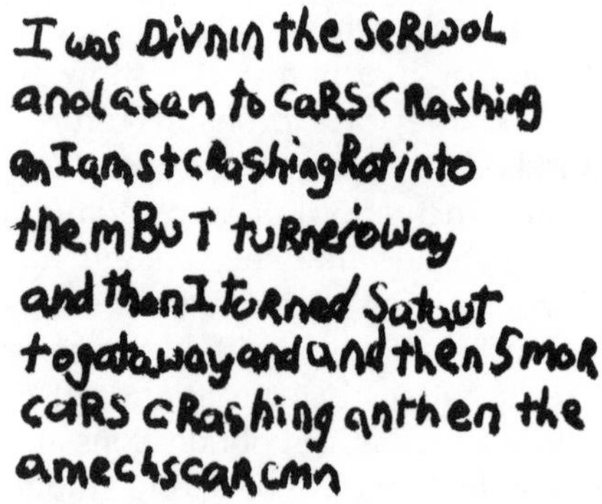
I was Divnin the SeRwoL
andlasan to caRS cRashing
anIamstcRashingRatinto
themBuT tuRneroway
and thenI tuRned Satuut
togataway and and then 5 moR
caRS cRashing anthen the
amechscaRcmn

Craig — September of third grade

Translation:
I was driving the steering wheel and all of a sudden two cars crashed. I almost crashed right into them but I turned away and then I turned straight to get away and then five more cars crashed and then the emergency car came . . . .

Goofy the cowboy   Dec. 18

when goofy was a little boy,
every body teased him. An he
grew up being teased. Goofy has
funny ears and funny nose and
Legs. And he didn't like it a
bit. Then he started to get
Mad Then!! he got some guns
and had fun. And killed a few
People. But he didn't care a bit.
He was Having fun. Then he

was the king of the Village. And
had a blast. NO body would teased
him any more. Then the people
of the village made a law you
couldn't kill any body. And goofy
got mad and disobey and Went
to Jail.

Figure 20 – 3   Craig — December of third grade

21

---

improving the quality of student writing

Our Institute on the Teaching of Writing always ends, as many of these institutes do, with a ceremony in which participants stand and, one by one, read their work aloud to a hushed auditorium. My husband came to the closing ceremony last summer and afterward as we were hiking in the Wind River Range in Wyoming, he told me, "What I noticed most was the sheer quality of what those teachers had written." I was surprised. We Writing-Process-people do not often talk about the quality of written products. We talk drafts and revision; we talk exploration, discovery, nudging, and self-awareness. But we don't talk about the need for excellence, and I think this is a mistake.

Human beings have a primal need to do good work. I love my job because I do it well. If a teacher says she loved our institute, it is not because I gave good speeches, but because she wrote good pieces. We all need to believe in what we do. Our students are no different. Yet we forget this. In fact, popular opinion seems to be that today's students are "getting away with" lousy work . . . as if anyone *wants* to produce poor work! No, we all want desperately to succeed. We all want our writing to be brilliant or funny or full of insight or important. In talking about this human yearning for success, Becker says that what man really fears is not so much extinction but extinction with insignificance, and he speaks of a "burning desire for the creature to count."

I am not arguing that students need compliments and robin stickers, but that they need the chance to do good work. I think we miss the point

213

if we run around giving students "positive reinforcement." An undeserved compliment is hollow; a deserved one, unnecessary. When a piece is well-written, writers know it. Readers will laugh at just the right moments, they will lean closer to the page, and when they look up, their eyes will show that the piece mattered. They'll ask to read more. This is the feedback our students need, and it has the power to make them love writing. The adage, "Nothing succeeds like success," is a wise one.

In a recent workshop, therefore, I asked teachers to jot down ways we can help students improve the quality of their writing. Later when we shared these lists, their ideas were very much like mine:

- In conferences, find important ways to challenge students so that they do more than they thought they could.
- Identify widespread problems in students' writing and give alternate solutions in mini-lessons.
- Teach students to recognize the characteristics of powerful writing.
- Show students ways to make significant revisions rather than simply small additions and deletions.
- Reach more students in our one-to-one conferences.

Readers can add their own items to the collection; our list went on. I think it is important to step back and examine the assumptions behind such a list.

When I looked honestly at my list, what I saw was this: I had figured that the way to improve the quality of student writing was for me to run around the room pulling each person's writing up by its suspenders, tugging, nudging, teaching, showing. This comes precariously close to the traditional view of teaching as pouring information into the passive receptacle of the student. In this chapter I want to suggest another way to think about improving the quality of student writing. It requires us to remember that, although we tend to give only cursory attention to the arrangements which shape our students' activities, these are vastly more influential than the words that come out of our mouths during lectures, conferences, and talks.

We can raise the standards of our students' writing by creating a gracious, beautiful setting conducive to craftsmanship. Two months ago I bought myself a beautiful leather notebook that zips up like a briefcase. I almost didn't buy it; it seemed like such a luxury when a three-ring notebook could work just as easily. Yet that leather notebook has made me a better learner. Because I have it, notes from my reading and data from classroom observations no longer end up crumpled at the bottom of my canvas sack or spread about the office. And because the notes are even legible, I take the time to reread them, incorporating the new information into my thinking and writing. I find that when I treat my work with respect, the quality improves. The same is true for our students.

When I go into classrooms and see writing folders stuffed this way and that into dilapidated cardboard boxes, each folder full of tattered drafts,

I am not surprised that the work itself seems trivial. Why wouldn't it be? If students are writing with dull lead pencils on that yellow composition paper that has a greyish tinge to it, and if their erasers are so filled with lead that they make noticeable smudges all over the page, I'm not surprised that neither teachers nor students are studying drafts with respectful attention.

How different it is in classrooms where teachers have carefully covered the folder boxes with contact paper, or neatly filed hanging folders into plastic milk-carton crates. How different it is when children are taught to label and save each draft, stapling them neatly together. How different it is when there are daffodils on the editing table, and when final drafts are covered with plastic and placed in beautiful hardbound notebooks. These small touches are *not* small because they create a sense of respect. In such a context, shoddy work is out of place.

We also need to examine the issue of noise in the writing workshop. Around the country, the assumption seems to be that good writing work-shops are loud and messy (the polite term is "free"). It is true that in writing workshop students do not sit silently in even rows but instead move about, getting more paper, looking through a file for an old draft, referring to an anthology of poems, sharing a draft with a friend, finding the address for a letter they are writing, speaking with the teacher. When thirty students move and interact in these ways, there will be some noise and commotion. But the teacher of writing needs to know the difference between this sort of purposeful motion and chaos, this workshop hum, and the clatter of unfocused activity. Teachers need to become diagnosticians, studying not only the strengths and weaknesses of each student's writing, but also the points of disruption and tension within the classroom.

Recently Marilyn Grubstein, a first-grade teacher, formed a network of practitioner-researchers in her building, P.S. 321. Each month these fifteen teachers select an issue of concern and collect data on it. Last month they decided to investigate the noise in their classrooms. They agreed that, rather than hurrying to hush each noisy outbreak, they would first attempt to observe and document the situation. They would listen to the nature of the noise and ask "What is really going on here?" If there *was* a problem, they would try to see its underlying cause. Then in weekly network meetings, the teachers use this information to work toward large-scale, enduring ways to circumvent significant problems.

These teachers will probably find that little things matter a great deal. I know when I was teaching, it was important that the workshop began with a sense of quiet industry because this set the tone for the rest of the hour. For that reason, I dismissed children from the mini-lesson system-atically, allowing one tableful at a time to quietly fetch their folders and begin their work. In some instances, it is simply the physical layout of the classroom that creates problems. Sometimes children must walk through the peer conference area in order to get paper, and sometimes chairs are constantly being moved from one place to another. But more often, noise can mean that there is a lack of commitment to writing. Perhaps students are writing on topics they don't care about, perhaps they are not writing for an appreciative audience, perhaps this is their third year of cranking out little personal narratives and they need important new challenges. Sometimes students are perplexed and stymied by their teacher's expectations. The teacher talks about revision, but what is it? The teacher wants them to add on, but they already told everything that happened. The teacher wants them to keep working on this piece, but what else is there to do? Sometimes workshop rules create bottlenecks. If a teacher insists on checking the drafts before students begin editing their pieces, this rule may result in ten restless children who, quite justifiably, say, "I don't have anything to do until you check my paper."

We can improve the quality of student writing, then, by encouraging students to write with their favorite pens on their favorite paper. We can put daffodils on the editing table, provide fine pointed pens for editing, create routines to reduce the commotion during transitions, and work toward that cherished workshop hum. We also raise standards by celebrating good work. When Peter Elbow speaks of the magic in powerful, honest writing, he says, "Magic is catching. It can help enormously to put yourself in the company of people who are succeeding in using their magic. Read their words. Listen to them read their words out loud" (1981, 371). Anyone who has ever attended a writing workshop knows that, when someone reads his or her piece aloud and the whole room is hushed, awed by the power of the author's words, we will look again at our own little pieces and ask ourselves, "Is this *really* my best?" and "Did I just pick this topic because it was safe?" Our students will also catch the magic from each other—if we let them. This means that we must focus at least in part on the very best writers in the room, extending what they can do and celebrating their successes. This is rarely done in schools. Generally we focus on the bottom level, coaxing along those students who won't write, or who have nothing to say, or who merely whip off hasty efforts. But because success *is* contagious, we would do well to focus also on our best writers. They can help us raise the level of everything that is done in the room.

The most magical writing of all is that found in literature. It follows, then, that we improve the quality of our students' writing by surrounding them with great literature. The best writing teachers I know fill their classrooms with books, give students the luxury of time for reading, and weave literature into everything that happens in the writing workshop. These teachers spend evenings searching for examples of good leads, for bits of strong description, for ways writers create suspense in their stories. As important as this is, I cannot help but think that the teachers are having all the fun. Why shouldn't students collect selections, why shouldn't they browse about in libraries in order to glean tips for their writing?

reading-writing connections

22

authorship: when children are insiders, they make connections

Lessons from a Child was published two years ago. I knew approximately when it would be out and for a month in advance I'd rush home to see if it had arrived. Driving home, I'd construct images of the book. In my mind's eye, I'd retrace the cover photograph and recall the carefully worded dedication. I even bought wrapping paper and mailing envelopes, and day after day, I hurried home.

Then one day the book was there. My husband had opened the box. There were dirty coffee cups on the kitchen table and copies of my book strewn this way and that. I stared. They looked so casual, so small, so insignificant. I took one copy into the living room and, looking at it, began to cry. All those years of work . . . it looked so small.

I think I expected that a truck would arrive at the house and three men would stagger in with The Book. Gazing at my monument, I would feel Authorship. All the years of work would culminate in that moment of Authorship.

Now, two years later, I have learned that authorship has little to do with creating a monument and more to do with gaining consciousness. Although I touch, look at, and hold *Lessons from a Child* with affection, the book itself is still relatively inconsequential in my life. It is the experience of writing and of *having written* that has changed everything for me. I knew that composing would be a process more than a product, but I thought once the book was published, the process would be over. Authorship, by definition, would mean having and holding the product. But

I have found that authorship is also a process, and that it has less to do with looking back on a monument than with looking forward with new insight into what I read, finding new layers of meaning in the work of other authors. I have become an insider in reading. My perception of myself has changed, and this affects my entire experience as a reader. I now feel part of the inner circle.

The change is rather like the difference between my first National Council of Teachers of English conference and the ones I now attend. Because I am an insider, everything at the conference now takes on extra significance. Even a lousy session is worth thinking about—Who spoke? Where is he from? With whom does he work? Why did the University of Texas people leave early? Who was that fellow up in the front row, the one who kept nodding? I look for the meaning behind the events; I do the same when I read.

Everything takes on extra significance because I am an insider. Why did the author decide to start it this way? Where did the information come from? How else could the book have been organized? What an unusual chapter heading. What a difference this powerful image makes in the chapter! I read with admiration, with envy, and above all, with an eagerness to learn from my more skillful colleagues.

I also read critically. Because I know, as no one else could, the gaps in my book, the compromises I have made, the goals I haven't met, I view the collection of books and journals on my shelves a little differently. They are less imposing to me, they seem less final and complete. Because I know that behind my own book there is an emperor with no clothes on, the books I read have taken on a more human dimension. I can see writers behind the texts, and I can learn vicariously from their successes and struggles.

I am thirty-three and I've only begun to discover the ways in which being an author changes how I read. Noah has just turned five. His legs don't quite reach the floor when he sits on the little red chairs in his kindergarten, and he doesn't sit for long. But Noah has written a ten-page book, with letters and a picture on each page.

"Would you read it to me?" his teacher asked. Leaning against her, Noah began to read. He told the story of each picture, and then he decoded the words he'd written underneath it. It was a book about his father's cooking and Noah was proud. "There," he said, when he came to the last page. "That's all. The end." He closed the book and looked up expectantly.

But the teacher wasn't looking at Noah. Instead she peered down at the book. Centered on the back cover were four letters:

BP

NM

"What's this?" she said. "You forgot to read this page."

"Naw, that's nuthin," Noah answered and waving his hand, he dismissed the letters.

More curious than ever, his teacher asked again. "What's it say?"

"Oh, it's just sumfin for the library," Noah told her. Pointing to the letters he read:

BP (Big Picturebook)
NM (Noah Mystand)

We can laugh at this story, enjoy it for a moment and dismiss it. Or we can pause and consider its significance. Noah is only five, yet already he views himself as an insider, as a member of the circle of authors. His teacher has not only helped him develop skills, she has also helped him develop a self-concept as an author. She believes that, rather than simply instructing children in a piecemeal fashion in the components of reading and writing, she must also give them a gestalt, a sense that "I am an author." Because her children perceive themselves as authors, they will make connections with the books they read. They'll notice the way a word is spelled, the use of the table of contents, the presence of exclamation marks. For them as for me, reading will provide an opportunity to learn from their more skillful colleagues.

The amazing thing is that even five-year-olds can make these reading-writing connections. They may notice items we think are unimportant, but the fact that they are noticing aspects of their reading and transferring them to their writing is vastly more important than any specific connection they may make. Some kindergarten children will notice the dedications in their reading books and soon their teacher—and the class pet—will have many books written in his or her honor. Other children will notice page numbers, chapter titles, or "about the author," blurbs on the back cover of books.

Recently, several of us watched Noah as he worked on a scary Halloween book. Every time he finished a page, Noah flipped to the back of the book and jotted something onto it. "What are you doing?" we asked, and then Noah showed us what he had written:

gosts	*p.1*
wiches	*p.1*
owls	*p.2*
skeletn	*p.4*

He was making an index for his own book to match the one in the back of his reading book.

Several years ago, a youngster at Atkinson Elementary School entitled her story, "The Three Pigs." It was a curious title because the story had nothing to do with pigs. "How did you happen to name this?" I asked Audrey.

"It's like a book I read," she answered.

Mystified, I pressed further. "What book is it like?"

"The Three Pigs," Audrey said. The scorn in her voice insinuated that I'd just asked a very silly question. I still didn't see the connection, and so I pressed further, asking how her story was like *The Three Pigs.* "Simple," she answered. "They begin the same and they end the same." Indeed they did. They both began "Once upon a time" and they both ended "They lived happily ever after."

My favorite reading-writing story took place in a crowded kindergarten in Brooklyn. As in many writing classrooms, each workshop in this class ended with a share meeting. The children would gather together on the carpet and one or two youngsters would read their work to the others. On this particular day it was Kendra's turn to share (see Figure 22-1).

Figure 22 – 1

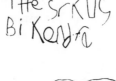

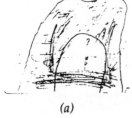

(a)

(b)

Translation:

The Circus
by Kendra

This is a circus.
The man is training the lion.
The man said to the lion,
"You roar."
He did.

When Kendra finished reading, Brad's hand was already up. "Why is the man training the lion?" he asked.

"Because he's gonna work at the zoo, this is a zoo lion."

"So why do you have to train the lion?" Brad wondered.

"So, cause, children will pet him and he has to be trained," Kendra answered, and then she called on Rachel.

"How come you call your book *The Circus* if it is gonna be about the zoo?" The teacher and I exchanged glances, amazed that even these five-year-olds were wrestling with issues of main idea. But Kendra was not stumped by the question. "I'm writing *another* book about the zoo. I'm taking the lion to the zoo in another book."

Harry wasn't pleased with her answer. "No, that's not fair. You can't have two books about the same people and the same animals." For a moment Kendra looked troubled.

Then Hanif got an idea. "Hey, wait. What about Curious George? *Curious George Goes to the Hospital, Curious George Gets a Medal.* That's two books and the same monkey."

Rachel agreed. "My sister reads lots of books and Laura is in every one. Laura and Pa and Mary." Because these children view themselves as authors, they notice and learn from the choices made by the authors of the books they read. Their writing also helps these youngsters to read critically.

Graves tells the story of how a cluster of youngsters in Ellen Blackburn's first-grade classroom sat huddled together on the floor, whispering as they read to each other from one of the Basal Readers in their class library. The story began something like this:

Go Dan Go
Run Dan Run
See Dan Go and Run.

After a few minutes of talking to each other about the book, they approached their teacher with the book in hand. "Who wrote this?" they asked.

For a moment Blackburn was caught off guard. Then she answered, "Well, it wasn't really written by one author. It was written by a committee."

The children looked at each other, shrugged, and started to return to the reading corner. Then they stopped, returned to the teacher and skeptically said, *"Grown-ups* wrote it?"

Of course, the amazing thing is that more children do not marvel about how grown-ups could have produced such a story. In his recent article, "Young Writers as Critical Readers," Newkirk thinks this may be because, in our efforts to teach youngsters to respect books and to read "correctly," we've taken reading out of children's hands (Newkirk 1982, 452). Reading has become less like romping about in one's own backyard and more like those stifled, pained visits to a grandparent's house. Youngsters are taught to be polite guests; they're told not to ask rude questions or to blurt out their uninformed opinions. Young readers are to be seen and not heard. Most reading programs rarely offer opportunities for children to ask questions of a text. Instead, questions are prewritten and are not directed at the text, but at the reader. "Did you read well?" the questions say to children. They also convey other messages:

- The printed word is final and unquestionable.
- If you read well, the text should mean the same thing to you as it does to me.
- Texts are to be respected and remembered. It's your fault if you do not recall or comprehend what was said.
- These texts have been written by very great people. You are just a child and are not in a position to pass judgment on your superiors.

In this article, Newkirk suggests that our reading programs are geared toward teaching deference rather than critical thinking.

Many students at all levels view written language as unassailable, as beyond criticism. Any reading program must acknowledge this potential of written language to intimidate, to bully the reader into submission. . . . Even students who can accomplish the important comprehension tasks such as locating the main idea, summarizing, and drawing inferences are controlled by written language if they must accept the writing on its own terms; if they lack the power to question the integrity of the text before them. Lacking this power, they are only deferentially literate; they are polite readers. Like good guests, they do not ask impertinent questions (Newkirk 1982, 455).

Newkirk goes on to show that writing programs can make texts less imposing to children. When children see their own writing as the result of human choices and when they work on their own unfinished texts, they view their reading material differently.

Seven-year-old Greg is a writer, and he describes reading this way:

Before I ever wrote a book, I used to think there was a big machine and they typed a title and then the machine went until the book was done. Now I look at a book and know a guy wrote it and it's been his project for a long time. After the guy writes it, he probably thinks of questions people will ask him and revises it like I do, and copies it to read to about six editors. Then he fixes it up, like how they say.

If five-, six-, and seven-year-olds can make reading-writing connections such as these, it is no surprise that by the time children are in the sixth grade, their connections are sometimes very sophisticated indeed. Morat, an avid mystery reader, often uses techniques from his reading in his writing. Recently he put "fake clues" into the story he was writing. "I want to fool the reader, give them the wrong ideas so the ending is a surprise." He added, "In the book I'm reading, that's what the guy did." Morat also decided, based on his reading, not to put much description into his story because he figured the kids would just skip it or get bored, like he does during those sections of his reading book. Once Morat looked up from his reading and said, "I'm better at titles than this author is. It is pretty stupid how he calls this book *Mystery of the Silent Friends* when they talk all the time." I could continue at great length discussing the reading-writing connections made by upper-elementary school writers, but many of these connections will be appearing in a future chapter. For now, it is enough to note that the connections young children make between reading and writing are only a beginning. As youngsters grow more skilled in both processes, they make more sophisticated connections.

These reading-writing connections do not happen automatically, nor do they happen simply because children are drafting and revising their writing. In the remaining sections of this chapter, I want to suggest ways we can help youngsters—of any age—experience and learn from authorship.

Help children know they are authors

With the new emphasis on reading-writing connections, more and more school districts are celebrating Authors' Days at the end of the school year. Selected stories are bound into books, and teachers and parents rally to pay tribute to these publications. Public sentiment points to these events as a fine way to support young children and their writing. But at the risk of seeming like Scrooge at Christmas, I want to raise questions about these Young Authors' Conferences. For those who organize these events, the emphasis is on selecting fine stories and binding them to make beautiful publications. In truth, putting shiny covers on stories is not what authorship is all about. The meaning of these Authors' Days depends entirely on what has gone before the hoopla. Too often they are preceded by hasty assignments telling children that stories for Authors' Day are due the day after tomorrow. Even when the Authors' Days are part of ongoing writing workshops, they are often the culminating event of the year and involve selected children only. As such, they have all the problems of the class play at Christmas. Who will be involved? Who will not be? What happens to the ongoing classroom experiences when yet another Big Event dominates the calendar? Even more than all this, implicit in the notion of a single culminating event scheduled near the end of the year, is the notion of authorship as an end point. Publication means that the process is over and children can now gaze at their monuments.

But if you believe, as I do, that authorship is a process and that it involves new ways of relating to reading, then helping children see themselves as authors should be the beginning rather than the end of a writing workshop. "As soon as your workshop is underway," I often tell teachers, "it is time to help children view themselves as authors. Publish the pieces, put out book binding supplies, celebrate their finished work . . . and do it by late September."

"But the papers aren't any good yet," teachers protest. "They haven't done any revisions, their pieces are short and general and voiceless. Shouldn't we wait until they produce some reasonably good work?"

I don't think so. The first step toward improving our student's earliest efforts is, I believe, to attend to them. The first way to improve their initial skills is to give students a sense of authorship.

I like Authors' Days best if they are scheduled frequently and predictably. Many teachers find it helpful to set aside, say, the first Wednesday of every month (for young children) or of every other month (for older children) for such a celebration. Just as the ending and beginning of a semester provides Kira with a chance to clean her looseleaf notebook, to buy new spirals and to make new resolutions, so too, these Authors' Days can become part of the rhythm of a writing classroom. In preparation for Authors' Day, children complete whatever pieces they are working on, make sure their rough drafts are stapled with their final copies, and that their work is either filed into cumulative folders or taken home and published. They may spend some time looking back on what they have done, perhaps ranking their pieces from best to worst and talking about their progress during the interval, since the last Authors' Day. (This, of course, is revision: looking back in order to look forward.) After choosing their best work, children may want to be sure that it *is* the best they can do. Authors' Days provide a natural sort of deadline, an impetus to finish dangling pieces, a chance to look back over what students have done and to learn from it before they move on. Authors' Days provide a chance for new beginnings, for a fresh start with a new resolve.

What actually occurs on these Authors' Days is probably less important than the fact that they occur at all. In one third-grade room, children go into the hallway for "Publishing Conferences." Each time, the ritual is the same. The author lays out on the floor all his or her work and says to the partner, "Guess which one I'm going to publish!" Then the friend must read *all* the pieces, trying to second-guess the author's decision. "Wrong!" the author announced with great glee on the day I observed, and then he proceeded to explain *why* he'd chosen a piece called, "Lice, Fleas, Roaches and Flies." In many upper elementary and junior high classrooms, students bring empty photo albums to school at the beginning of the year, and as they complete a final draft, it is sealed into the plastic-covered pages. Needless to say, no other books are as widely read during reading time! In some upper-grade classrooms, students read their final pieces to youngsters in other classes, or they copy their completed work onto rexograph masters so that duplicates can be made for each class member. Some teachers make the day special by bringing in juice and fruit, or by having children meet in small sharing groups. A ritual I particularly like—one I use often when working with adults—is to have each writer read a short piece of his or her writing aloud. After each reading, there is a moment of silence while listeners jot down their responses on index cards, which are later given to the author. I recently mentioned this strategy at a conference, cautioning that it would only work in the upper grades. Two weeks later a kindergarten teacher proved me wrong! Even when the readers/writers are adults, these index cards are cherished. My brother used to have a quote on his bulletin board: "I can live two months on a good compliment," so I recommend that Authors' Days be scheduled at least every two months!

But a word of caution. Just as a lesson on listening is inconsequential compared to what happens when teachers listen to children and expect them to do the same for each other, so, too, no amount of fuss and trumpeting on Authors' Day will ever substitute for the little, everyday ways in which we show children we regard them as authors. Graves tells a story about Ellen Blackburn. Her children wrote eagerly, published their stories, and frequently read them to each other. They called themselves authors. Yet when they were asked, "Which of these books does your teacher like best?" and shown three kinds of books—a work of literature, a Basal Reader, and their own writing—the youngsters all said their teacher liked the literature best, then the Basal, then their writing. "What makes you say this?" Graves asked, puzzled by their answer.

"When we have reading time on the rug, she reads *this* the most, and this the next most," they told him, pointing to the literature and then to the Basal. Because Ellen Blackburn never read the children's stories during reading time, the youngsters had decided that their own writing wasn't as valuable to their teacher.

Ellen now reads two kinds of books during her literature sharing time— one written by an author from the class, and one by an outside author! In her classroom, as in many others, the writer sits on the author's chair during share meetings. In many classrooms, bulletin boards feature "Author of the Week," with one child's photograph and a collection of his or her work. Some schools have built "Publishing Houses" in their hallways, often manned by parent volunteers. Visiting authors from upper grade classrooms are sometimes interviewed by younger children (and vice versa). During silent reading time, children are encouraged to read each other's work as well as the work of more well-known writers. These are only some of the little everyday ways in which teachers help youngsters view themselves as authors.

The emphasis I place on publication is new for me. At Atkinson Elementary School, only the first- and second-grade teachers stressed the importance of publishing student writing, and for them this emphasis grew largely from the belief that, especially when children's invented spellings were translated into correct spelling, the writing could become the reading. None of the upper-grade teachers stressed publication and none of the children seemed to miss it. Although Mrs. Currier's fourth graders each made a bound book for their final pieces, when the pages began to fall out and the covers curled, the students didn't seem to mind. I began then to believe we'd put too much emphasis on the beginnings and ends of writing, on assigning topics and publishing final work. It is only recently that I've rediscovered the importance of publication.

I still question whether it is a good use of time for teachers to type up their students' writing. In primary grades I recommend having parents or volunteers make book covers and run a class Publishing Center. I also recommend that we find simple, effortless ways to publish children's best work. One of the teacher-trainers in our Writing Project, Georgia Heard, publishes children's final drafts by simply folding a piece of brightly colored binding tape around the outer edges of the page. The result is an eloquent frame—yet the process is so simple! I do not think publishing should occupy a great deal of a teacher's time. If it does, how often will any given child publish his or her writing? More importantly, those of us who work with children must be wary of spending our evening hours typing children's stories. We will be more helpful to youngsters if we spend time on our own reading and writing, on our own projects. None of this disputes the overall importance of publishing.

Since my research at Atkinson Elementary School, I've realized that publishing does not have to involve a heavy investment of our time, and that it is most helpful to children if publishing begins early in the year and occurs often and predictably. I have also realized that the reason we didn't value publishing in our initial research project was that at Atkinson, the children, the teachers, and the researchers made fewer reading-writing connections than we might have made. We knew children were developing reading skills while they wrote, but we paid very little attention to the fact that the reverse could also be true. The children could have developed writing skills while they read if we had helped them approach literature as insiders. The reading-writing connection can be a two-way street. Now that I see this, publishing student writing seems crucial. If our children see themselves as authors, they will read with admiration, marveling at another author's efforts and learning vicariously from another author's successes and struggles.

Helping children see the authors behind their reading

Recently, Eileen Jones, who is another member of the Writer's Project staff but was, at the time, an exceptional writing teacher in District 15, decided to help her youngsters make reading-writing connections. At the end of one reading time, she suggested that her third graders close their books and then she asked, "What did the writer do to get you interested?"

I held my pen poised, ready to scribble down all their ideas. But the class was strangely silent, as if they were perplexed. Several exchanged glances. Near me, I heard one child whisper, "Writers? This isn't writing time."

Then a girl raised her hand and said, "What piece are you talking about?"

Now it was our turn—Eileen's and mine—to exchange glances. Amazing. It had never dawned on these children that their library books were "pieces," that a writer had sat down with pencil and paper and tried to find a way to catch the reader's interest. If children are to make reading-writing connections, they need both to see themselves as authors and to see the authors behind their reading. This is so obvious it is easy to overlook.

I am embarrassed to look back on my own teaching. Except for when I taught secondary school English, I rarely discussed authors. I read *Where the Red Fern Grows* to my children . . . but did I ever read the author's name? We didn't talk about the author; we never wondered how he knew so much about hound dogs or whether he cried when he wrote the book (as we did when we read it). The reading skills I worried about were sequence, main idea, inference, story structure—never authorship.

Oddly enough, it was quite the opposite in the literature courses I have taught in secondary schools and colleges. It was not unusual for these courses to be organized around great authors. The study of literature involved bringing the author's life and times to bear on the text. But little of this occurs in elementary schools, and when Eileen Jones asked, "What did the writer do to get you interested?" her children asked, "What piece are we talking about?" and whispered to each other, "But this isn't writing time." Ever since then, Eileen has made a point to talk about authors as well as books.

There are countless stories about authors. Children will love learning that while E. B. White wrote *Charlotte's Web*, he kept a specimen of a spider in a matchbox on his desk and also spent long hours observing a spider at work in his barn. E. B. White wrote *Trumpeter of the Swan*, however, without ever seeing a trumpeter swan, which is the explanation some critics give for why that book never became a favorite. The gossip about children's authors continues. William Steig's efforts to depict his characters as animals got him into trouble because he portrayed policemen as pigs, inadvertently offending many people. Sendak wrote *In the Night Kitchen* as his goodbye to New York when he moved from the city to his present home in the quiet woods of Connecticut. The bottle of milk is Sendak's transformation of the Empire State Building, and Mickey and his plane are reminiscent of the shooting of King Kong (Cullinan 1981,

129). When children know details such as these about their favorite authors, the names on a book cover take on a more human dimension, allowing them to see that the literature they read is not totally separate from the literature they write.

Even if teachers do not have files of biographical information on authors, they can help children speculate about the author by asking, "I wonder why the author began the story like this?" or "Where did this information come from, anyway?" All of the techniques children use in their own writing can be found in the works of other authors. Almost any writing question has parallel reading questions, and vice versa. These are some of the questions that upper elementary school and secondary school children might ask of their reading and of their writing:

	WRITING	READING
Focus/Main idea	*What is the one thing I am trying to say? Why did I choose this topic—what is the important thing about it?*	*What is the main thing this author is saying? Why did he or she choose to write this, what was the important thing about the topic?*
	How can I let readers know which is my main point and which are the smaller points?	*Is there one big point? How does the author show which is the main point and which are the smaller ones?*
Beginnings	*How could I begin this piece? How else? What difference will this beginning make over that one? How will each possibility affect the reader? Do I usually start pieces in a similar way? How can I improve my beginnings?*	*How did the author begin this piece; a quote, a description, dialogue, an action, a survey of the scenery, an idea . . . ? Where in the sequence of events did the author begin the piece? How else could the author have begun it? Why did the author decide on this way? What expectations are set into motion? Is the lead effective? What can I learn from what this author has done?*
Characters	*Do I have a main character, even if it is myself? How can I bring this character to life? In literature, authors show characters through their*	*Who are the main characters? How (and where in the text) does the author bring them to life? Do some characters seem more alive than others? What*

	dialogues with each other, their responses to events, and through telling details; can I do the same? Are my characters real and human, or flat? Do they change during the story? Have I shown these changes?	*can I learn from this? How do the characters change? How do they interact with events?*
Mood	*What is the tone of this piece? Where in the text can I convey mood? Should it be intensified or altered during the story? Where—and why? How could I create these changes? Am I succeeding in creating and using mood?*	*What is the tone, the mood, of this text? Where do I first sense the mood? Does it change—where? How? How does the author create mood? Why did the author select this mood?*
Point of view	*Who should tell the story? Why? What are the alternative points of view? Where should the camera be located? Which sections should be conveyed through close-ups? During what sections should the camera be moved further away? How can I make these transitions? Are there places in my piece where the point of view gets lost?*	*Who tells the story? Where is the camera located? Does it shift—from close up to farther away, from one person's perspective to another? How does the author make these transitions? Why does the author select the point of view which controls this story?*
Sequence	*How could I sequence my piece? What are the alternatives? Will one sequence work better than another—why? Should I tell the reader my structure or let it be implicit? Will the reader get lost? How else could I do this? Are there sections where the transitions seem bumpy? What can I do about them?*	*How does the author sequence events or ideas? Is the sequence chronological? Cause and effect? Flashback? Main idea to supportive details? Is the overall structure clear? How does the author convey a sense of the structure? Am I ever lost? If so, what happens in the text which causes this confusion? What can I learn about sequencing my own writing?*

A list of reading-writing questions could consume many pages. There could be similar lists for less and more advanced students, and there could be lists that focus on each genre. But lists of questions don't do justice to this topic. The reading-writing connections that matter most belong to the quiet moments when a writer is snuggled up, reading a book. The reading-writing connections that matter most are the small "ah-has" that happen when a youngster sees glimpses of the relatedness between reading and writing. They are the times when youngsters look up from their writing and suddenly recall another author who has struggled with similar issues. They are the moments of connectedness that a child experiences because he or she is an insider in the world of written language.

23

---

teaching the reading process

It is telling, I think, that although this section is titled, "Reading-Writing Connections," my focus at the beginning and end of each chapter is on writing. The teaching of writing provides my frame of reference. I have told about the kinds of reading-writing connections that can develop through the writing workshop. In the next two chapters, I will suggest ways in which the teaching of writing can influence the teaching of reading. Even when the subject of my discussion is reading, my approach is from the perspective of writing.

Most teachers approach the reading-writing connection from an altogether different perspective. The majority of elementary school teachers have their degrees in teaching reading, on which they spend approximately 40 percent of their school day. Because they are trained and confident in reading, they approach the reading-writing connection from this perspective. When pressure mounts for them to pay attention to writing, they insert a bit of it into the reading program. They may use writing as a prereading activity, or as a way to activate students' prior knowledge. Before students read a tall tale, they write one ("quickly now, we have only twelve minutes"). Or they use writing as a way to predict what will happen next in their reading books. When the class reaches page twenty-six of the reader, everyone closes the books and writes an ending to the story ("quickly, we want to finish the story before the bell rings"). During the last half-hour in a reading class, children may be asked to write a response to their reading or to imitate the style of an author they have read.

I suppose I should be glad that some time is being spent on writing, but I cannot help but think that these writing activities—doodads, I call them—fly in the face of what we know about teaching writing. Under the rubric of reading-writing connections, writing is being squeezed, stretched, and distorted to service existing reading programs. Children are being asked to produce quick bits of writing on someone else's topics ("write a new ending for the story"). They are given little time for rehearsal ("close your books and write"), and no time for peer-conferences and revision. Much of the writing has no clear purpose and only one audience: the teacher. In the name of reading-writing connections, writing is being treated as an elaborate ditto.

Then too, it is questionable whether these writing activities make a significant contribution to reading. Granted, it is pretty clear that if we dole out related writing assignments before kids read, halfway through the reading and after they finish, they will score a little better on that day's reading test. But *so what*? So what if they score a little better on the days when we pass out little connection pills. The fact is, although reading scores may (or may not) be rising, our kids don't like to read. We know this in our hearts but even so, the results of the National Assessment for Educational Progress (1981) are staggering. As students grow older, they like reading less. Eighty percent of nine-year-olds say they like to read, but only half that number of seventeen-year-olds like to read. Only 13 percent of youngsters would choose to read rather than watch TV or go to a movie. If students do read, they rarely read for pleasure. "They value reading most for its presentation of information, not for personal growth or pleasure (NAEP 1981). There are sixty million people in our country who cannot read and this includes 47 percent of all black youth (NAEP 1981). Yet these statistics are nothing compared to the number of people who *can* read but choose not to. Many say the most serious problem is not illiteracy but aliteracy. "It is not so much the case that they cannot read, but that they choose not to, especially when given the opportunity to do other things like watch television or go to a movie" (NAEP 1981).

Priscilla Lynch, resident educator at Scholastic Books, claims that our methods for combining reading and writing are not solving the problem. Instead, they are adding to it.

Students are to read up to page 47 and then wait until everyone else catches up to them, and they then answer questions, orally or in writing. There are questions to show if they understand and questions to motivate them to the next bit of reading. For millions of children in the United States, this is reading and they don't want any part of it. It is hard to blame them. None of us, as adults, would do a writing exercise or answer questions before we got into a book, in the middle of it, and at the end of it. Children find it hard to understand that we find anything pleasurable at all in reading. We've made reading

into something our kids don't want any part of—and who can blame
them? (Lynch 1984)

The reading-writing connection may be fashionable, but current applications of it often hurt both disciplines.

Am I, then, against the reading-writing connection? Not at all. But I think putting a little writing into every reading activity amounts to putting on a Band-Aid. Such a solution hides the real problem. We may squeeze, push, and pull the curriculum to connect reading and writing, but the connections which really matter are those the children make, in a natural fashion, in their day-to-day lives as readers and writers. Perhaps we should focus our attention less on making *their* connections for *them* and more on making our own connections. We need to build our own links between methods of teaching writing and reading, and we need to draw on the best we know from both areas so that our children become lifelong writers, readers, and connectors of reading and writing for themselves.

In both fields there has been a growing recognition that we need to teach process as well as content. This shift is based, in part, on the saying: "If you catch someone a fish, they'll eat for a day. If you teach them to fish, they'll eat for a lifetime." But it is also based on the fact that language cannot be poured, ready-made, into children. Language is not content that can be taught so much as skill that can be developed. Most language-learning occurs through self-generated, functional, holistic activities; through approximation and error; through bonded relationships with people who are joyfully literate. This understanding of language-learning challenges traditional images of teaching, learning, and classrooms, while it focuses attention on language learners, and on ways we can nurture, guide, and extend their processes.

Earlier, I discussed the shift from products to processes that has occurred in writing. Rosenblatt describes a parallel shift in reading:

. . . on a darkened stage I see the figures of the author and the reader, with the book between them. The spotlight focuses on one of them so brightly that the others fade into practical invisibility. Throughout the centuries, it becomes apparent, usually either the book or the author has received major illumination. The reader has tended to remain in the shadow . . . usually cast as a passive recipient. Within the past few years, the spotlight has started to move in the direction of the reader (Rosenblatt 1978, 1).

This passage was written in 1978 and serves as the introduction to an important book on the reading process. Since then, more and more people are spotlighting the reading process. Now there is a school of thinking, known as the transactional approach to literature, based on the premise that the reader composes meaning from the text. "Does not the reader, like a director, have to supply the tempo, the gestures, the actions not only of Hamlet but of the whole cast?" Rosenblatt asks. "The text serves as a blueprint, a guide for selecting, rejecting and ordering what is being called forth" (Rosenblatt 1978, 13). Rosenblatt is not alone in her focus on the reader. Educators who are interested in the reading process will also want to read the work of Iser, Bleich, Petrosky, Holland, Tompkins, Fish and others.

For now, I want to share my ideas about what it could mean to teach reading as a process. I will first approach this in a conservative way and show how a traditional literature lesson could incorporate more attention to the reading process. Then I will take a more radical approach and begin, not with what already exists in schools, but with the questions, "What does a good reader do?" and then, "How can we create classrooms that support those behaviors?"

One of my responsibilities at Teachers College is supervision of student teachers in secondary English. In doing this, I see a great many traditional literature lessons. Whether I am visiting urban or suburban schools, fifth grade or twelfth, most of these lessons follow a consistent pattern. On the day I observed Ralph, his lesson exactly fit the pattern, so I want to describe it and then suggest ways the lesson could have incorporated more attention to reading process.

When I entered the room, Ralph was reviewing the short story his students had already read. "Who were the main characters?" he asked, and several students raised their hands. Then there were more questions. "How old was Dave?" "How about Daniel?" "How did the characters get along?" "What happened at the beginning of the story?" "Then what?" and so on.

After the story was retold in this fashion, Ralph read aloud a section about blood oozing from a wound. He wanted students to notice the language: he thought the descriptions were especially well-written. But this point was made almost as an aside, and soon Ralph, returning to the main line of his discussion, raised the key question around which the lesson was to center. When students responded, Ralph sometimes stopped them to ask, "Where did you find that in the text?" As I listened, the group opinion moved closer to Ralph's own answer until, at some point, Ralph took over and supplied his response. By then class was over.

I have watched hundreds of such classes—sometimes there is a motivating activity to kick off the lesson, sometimes there are several key questions, and some classes are better than others—but each has the same pattern. I am convinced that in each of these classes, students learn more about the text than they learn about reading. They do not develop skills which will help them another day on another text.

In writing classrooms, I say, "Our job is to teach the writer, not the writing. If texts get better and the writers learn nothing that will help them another day with another piece, then all we have done is to create better pieces for our bulletin boards." It is no different in reading classrooms. Our job must be to teach the reader, not just the text. If students learn about a short story but do not become more skillful, reflective, and confident readers—then so what? Let me show you what I mean.

By the time students reach high school, they have probably sat through thousands of reading classes that begin, as Ralph's class did, with recall questions. "Who were the characters?" "What happened first?" Amazing as it may sound, most students never learn a general strategy for recalling a text. I think this is because, when the teacher asks, "Who were the characters?" and students try to remember the characters' names, the students see their task as answering the teacher's question. The class is a live version of a worksheet, and students see themselves as dutifully filling in the blanks. They do not see the activity of recalling the story in whole or organic terms. Students do not even realize that they are recalling the text, and they certainly don't realize that this is something good readers do on their own. It probably never occurs to them that, after reading a text, it is helpful to ask recall question of themselves.

Ralph could have changed this. He could have begun class by saying, "Before we probe into the story you read last night, I think it is helpful to recall what actually happened in the story. You will notice we begin every reading class with recall . . . and this is a strategy good readers use often. When they finish reading something, they stop to retrace what has been said so far." Then Ralph could have launched into his battery of questions or, better still, asked the class to compile a list of recall questions. In this way he would help his students internalize recall questions. Eventually Ralph should be able to begin a class by saying, "Before we dig into the text, let's recall what we have read. How should we do that today?"

Before giving students responsibility for initiating a recall activity, teachers may first want to introduce them to a range of recall strategies. One way to recall a text, for example, is to make a timeline of it. Students can jot down a timeline in their reading logs, or pair up to make one with a friend. If they do this often, they will eventually internalize this strategy, and as they read they will make mental timelines. Another recall strategy, better suited to some literature, involves making notes on the characters and how they change. Some nonfiction lends itself to rough outlines, sketchy maps of main points, or summary statements. Again, these strategies can be internalized so they become part of the student's repertoire of reading strategies.

The specifics of how to recall a text do not matter as much as the general issue of involving students in strategies of effective reading. Recall seems to be a strategy many teachers value, so I have begun with it. But just as Ralph's purpose should not be to teach his students the sequence of events in a story but rather, methods for recalling a text, so too, my purpose is not to list strategies for recall but instead, to illustrate ways we can teach the reading process within a traditional literature lesson.

Similar changes could be made throughout Ralph's lesson. Ralph's purpose in reading the paragraph about oozing blood aloud was to help students notice powerful language. But he was the only person in the room that day who had the opportunity to search the text for examples of powerful language. For the students, there was no such process. When the students heard the passage Ralph selected, I imagine they were probably thinking, as I was, about the blood, and not about the process of reading with an eye to words, noticing strong, clear writing. Ralph could have changed this by asking students to scan the text, searching for powerful language and then sharing their selections with a friend. Later, the class could have discussed the process. Did they read differently the second time? Did they immediately tend to choose certain kinds of writing—description? action? feelings? Was it hard to choose their favorite section? Did they learn anything about their own writing from doing this? When they read at home, do they notice the author's choice of words?

I hope I have made my point. If this were a workshop, I would ask participants to anticipate for themselves the ways an awareness of process could be added to the upcoming sections of Ralph's lesson.

Next on Ralph's agenda was the key question. Ralph asked the question, and students answered it. In real life, there are no questions at the end of a chapter. It is up to the readers to do their own probing of a text. Students need to ask as well as to answer key questions. Ralph could have introduced this section of his lesson to his students by emphasizing the importance of asking questions when they read and of rereading in order to answer those questions. Students could have been given time to scan their text and to jot down questions in their logs. Then they could have shared the most important questions from their logs with a small group, and each group could have selected one question as the starting point for discussion. This process would have taken time, but that time would have been an investment. After several days of doing this, students could be asked to come to class with key questions in mind.

Reading involves answering as well as asking questions. As we move through a text, we draft and revise responses to our own questions. On the simplest level, we ask, "What will happen next?" Our tentative solutions change in light of new information. On a more complex level, we ask, "How does this aspect of the text connect with all the others?" and as we read and reread, we form more comprehensive and complex interpretations of the text. Reading, then, is a composing process. The reader drafts and revises meaning.

In Ralph's class, meaning was composed through whole-class discussions. One student suggested an answer to the key question, then another offered a different perspective, and so on. From Ralph's point of view, the class as a whole was doing exactly what good readers do. It developed ideas, elicited new information, raised new considerations, and redeveloped ideas. Or so it must have seemed.

I wonder, however, whether this is a fair description of what went on in each student's mind during those discussions. Robert stated his opinion, Juanita stated hers, and the teacher's sense of what had been said changed in light of each person's addition. But did Robert really revise his ideas or, after making his point, did he just shrug his shoulders when someone raised another idea? Did he tune out of the discussion, glad that he had made a contribution and was therefore off the hook? Or did he listen passively, wondering which of his friends would be lucky enough to guess the right answer? My hunch is that these are fair descriptions of what most of Ralph's students did that day. The class *as a whole* may have drafted and revised responses to the text, but each individual's experience was very different.

My somewhat cynical appraisal of what went on inside each student's head is based, to an extent, on data gathered by a recent National Assessment for Educational Progress (NAEP) study which shows that only 5 to 10 percent of our students have internalized the process of forming, critically judging, and refining their responses to reading.

The most significant finding for this assessment is that while students learn to read a wide range of material, they develop very few skills for examining the nature of the ideas that they take away from their reading. Though most have learned to make simple inferences . . . they cannot return to the passage to explain the interpretations they have made (NAEP 1981).

It is sobering, I think, to realize that whole-class discussions geared toward helping students form, critically judge, revise, and extend responses to a text, comprise the bulk of time in literature classes, yet the NAEP survey suggests that these are the very processes students cannot do on their own! These data suggest to me that, although responses to texts are formed and revised in whole-class discussions, very few students are actively engaged in this entire process, and even those whose are do not see this as part of what it means to read.

If, instead of trying to lead the class toward his interpretation of the text, Ralph had wanted to nurture and extend each student's own ways of responding to the reading, he might have asked students to come to class with a rough draft of a response to the text (or to the key question). In class, the students could have met in small groups to discuss, challenge, and rethink their responses. Later, students might have revised their initial responses in light of the new information and perspectives they had gained from this interpretive community. Finally, Ralph could have explained to the class that this is the kind of process good readers often follow in their minds as they read a difficult text. Of course, this entire approach assumes that classrooms can become workshops; for many teachers, this is hardly a conservative notion. Yet even if teachers want to work with the entire class in teacher-led activities, they can make small changes. For example, when Ralph raised his key question, instead of immediately calling on the one or two students who had instant answers, he could have allowed enough time for every class member to review the text and formulate a response. He might have suggested that students share their responses with a friend. Then, by the time students discussed their ideas within the whole group, each would have a reference point against which to weigh what other classmates said. One problem with most traditional literature lessons is that many students never give serious attention to the issue at hand. If one classmate makes a point, the others listen without any investment in the discussion.

There are other adaptations that could have allowed more attention to looking at reading as a process in Ralph's classroom. Instead of delivering his interpretation as a *fait accompli*, Ralph could have shared the evolution of his interpretation of the text. He could have demonstrated his process of reading the text, saying, for example, "When I read this I moved along easily until I reached page five and then I was stumped by . . . but I figured I'd read on and see if pieces of the puzzle would fit together. By the time I reached page twelve, I had new questions and so I stopped and reread. This time I realized. . . ."

Instead of continually reminding students to cite specific examples from the text, Ralph could have talked with students about the general need to base all interpretations on the text. He could have given the class a few minutes to skim through the text so that whatever they said was grounded in particular references. I hope the gist of my argument will inspire other ideas about incorporating more attention to reading as a process in traditional literature lessons.

Using the traditional literature lesson as the starting point for discussion implies an acceptance of its underlying structure and tone. There are other possible starting points. Nancie Atwell suggests one in her brilliant article, "Writing and Reading from the Inside Out," and in her forthcoming book, *In The Middle*. Atwell begins the article saying that, although writing as a process has become, for her, a way of life, she only recently began to think about reading as a process:

> *We are constantly gathering ideas for writing, planning, writing, conferring and seeing our writing get things done for us in our real worlds. I know these same principles of writing are at work in many schools and classrooms. Occasionally I become really naive and complacent and imagine we're on the cutting edge of a trend sweeping the nation . . . and just as soon as I start feeling smug, something comes along to take the stars out of my eyes. More often than not, the "something" is a realization about my own teaching. . . .*
>
> *A little over a year ago, I began to be aware of the contradiction between my beliefs about written language and my instruction in*

reading. I confronted a situation Tom Newkirk calls "the writing ghetto. . . ." What my students and I do as writers is reflected in writing workshop, but what they and I do as readers has little to do with what went on in the reading course (Atwell 1984).

Atwell is making a crucial point. Much of what we do in the writing workshop comes from what we know about how writers go about writing. We begin with the question, "What do writers naturally do when they write?" and we try to create classroom environments in which our children can do the same. In devising a reading program, we rarely begin with the question, "What do readers naturally do when they read?"

Over the past few years, I have raised that question in various ways in my workshops and courses. From Rosenblatt's book, *The Reader, the Text and the Poem*, I formed the idea of dividing workshop participants into pairs, with one person as the reader and one as the researcher; then I give the readers a quatrain of poetry, such as this one by Robert Frost, and ask them to say everything that comes to mind as they read, reread, and make sense out of the poem.

IT BIDS PRETTY FAIR

The play seems out for an almost infinite run.
Don't mind a little thing like the actors fighting.
The only thing I worry about is the sun.
We'll be all right if nothing goes wrong with the lighting.

A researcher's transcript of how one person went about reading this poem might begin, "She started with the title, 'It Bids Pretty Fair,' and she said, 'I guess they mean all is well. I guess it will be an upbeat poem.' Then she was quiet. 'The next lines mean the play will be on the road for a long time. I don't know if the part about the quarrel being a little thing is sarcastic. Maybe all this is supposed to be symbolic. I hate symbols. Let me keep going.'"

After a few minutes, I interrupt this activity, asking the readers and researchers to go back and study the transcript to see what the reader did in order to make meaning. We then collect a list of reading strategies like this one:

1 Readers paraphrase. They put things into their own words, tentatively, and then check to see if their version makes sense.
2 Readers ask questions and make predictions.
3 They reread time and time again.
4 Readers shift their attention between one part and another, between parts and wholes.
5 Readers monitor their own mental movie to see if it is making any sense and if it isn't, they change strategies.

6   Readers skip over things they don't understand.
7   They relate what they know with what they do not know.
8   They guess.
9   They feel: hope, competence, frustration, pleasure, incompetence . . .

Several years ago, when researchers began to describe the writing process, it was immediately clear to many of us that most children in our classrooms were doing something very different. So, too, when we describe the reading process, it is apparent that many of our children do not read like skilled readers. When our students cannot make sense out of their textbooks, most of them either shrug and give up or reread the texts over and over. I don't think they have any other reading strategies.

Instead of using traditional literature lessons as our starting point, then, we can begin by thinking about what skilled readers do when they read and by creating environments in which our students will use some of these strategies. In designing reading process classrooms, I think we need to look not only at the components of the reading process, but also at our own lives as readers. Sometimes in workshops, I ask teachers to make timelines of their growth in reading. In talking and writing about our experiences, we think about what the turning points have been for us as readers, about the one person who has been most important to us as readers. Sometimes we meet in small groups to talk about the reading we like to do at home, how we choose books, what we like to do after we have read them, and so forth. Always, we ask, "What does this have to say about the teaching of reading?"

What I am finding is that most teachers have never belonged to a community of readers. Most don't know what it is to read favorite passages aloud to a friend or to swap ideas about an author. Most teachers don't have anyone with whom they share books. Across the country, in-service programs on the teaching of writing are based on the premise that, when teachers draft and revise and share writing within a community of writers, they discover a new vision of what to give students. Yet there are very few in-service courses based on the premise that teachers need the chance to read, share, and discuss books. Until programs like these are instituted, we can only imagine what it would be like to belong to a community of readers and do whatever possible to make these fantasies into realities for our children. We can try to create such communities in our classrooms. The next chapter is about one teacher who did just that.

24

---

the writing-reading workshop

Although our summer institute at Teachers College did not focus on reading, Rose Napoli and the other members of the advanced section did recall their favorite reading teacher, make timelines of their growth in reading, brainstorm connections between reading and writing, and hear my ideas on teaching reading. By the end of the institute, Rose had filled two spiral notebooks with ideas for the fall.

She was not alone. There were twenty others in that seminar and all were interesting. Rose especially intrigued me, probably partly because she taught sixth graders in District 15, and I was fascinated by the age level and deeply bonded to the district, and partly because she was particularly enthusiastic, dedicated, and talented. And so when Spencer Foundation agreed to fund my study, "How Teachers Change as Teachers of Writing," I knew immediately that I wanted Rose to be one of our subjects. She didn't fit the design of the project—the plan had been for my research associates and I to follow a teacher-trainer and the teachers with whom she worked, and Rose had long since graduated from that relationship with a trainer—but I figured that, since many researchers had already studied how teachers learn the writing process, through Rose I could tell the sequel to that story. I didn't know at the time that the data on Rose would become a chapter on teaching reading.

By September, Rose had recopied her notebooks from the institute and reread the books. "My head is a swirl, I have so many ideas all whirling around," she told one of my research associates, Marilyn Boutwell, two days before school began. Rose had above all been rethinking her approach to teaching reading. "I want the kids to read books together, in twos and threes, and then to talk about them. I will model reading conferences and confer with students and turn the room into a workshop," she said, and the inflection of her voice showed her enthusiasm. "I want them not only to follow the story line in books, but also to notice the hard work that went into the writing." Since the institute, Rose explained, she had been looking at "literature" from a writer's point of view. She said, "Now when I read Robert Ludlum, I notice his wonderful descriptions and wonder, 'how can he write about places he has never seen?' I want my kids to think about the authors of their books in the same way." As Rose talked, one idea spilled into the next. She wanted her students to become conscious of their reading strategies, to notice writer's techniques. She wanted to schedule reading and writing in back-to-back periods so that one would flow into the other.

I worried about whether Rose's swirl of ideas could easily be translated into practice, but her enthusiasm was contagious. The day before school started I wrote in my field notes, "Rose is beginning where the other teachers I observed left off. I'm glad we will follow her; she is ready to move."

Then school started. How can I convey the bitterness and the clashing expectations? It was as if Rose and the kids all came into Room 413 like humming wheels, but rather than meshing, into a smoothly turning cog, the wheels clanged against each other, their teeth grinding metal against metal, scraping and biting and clattering. Rose's class became a cacophony of noise, of conflict, of smashed hopes.

It started on the first day, when Rose told her students to copy the schedule off the board. Eager to please, the children elaborately took out their papers, put their notebooks away and began drawing careful lines to separate each day of the week. If someone needed an eraser, he or she industriously, quietly, brought out the brand new pencil case, fixed the error, returned the pencil case to the desk, and again, set to work, slowly copying the schedule. "Math, math, math," one child whispered as he copied the label from the board to his paper. Meanwhile, Rose began talking loudly, passionately, about reading. "Whenever . . . whenever you finish your work," she said, speaking slowly, and with exaggerated pauses for emphasis, "I want you . . . to take out . . . your *reading*, to take out your *reading*." The children, working intently on their schedules, were mouthing the words as they transferred them to their papers, while Rose continued, "And so, in this class, you must have a book, at all times. . . ."

That first day was a harbinger of what was to come. A week later Rose introduced the reading process, which she intended to emphasize during the year. Standing at the front of the room, her hands shoved firmly into the pockets of her white denim skirt, she started. "Last week was probably the first time you have ever been allowed to choose your own books," she said. "Diana, how did you go about selecting your book?" As she spoke, Rose leaned close to Diana's face.

Diana drew back. "I just chose it," she said, her voice strained and unsure. What was the teacher asking?

"Thyessa how did you go about selecting your book?"

Thyessa spoke softly but then, with prompting, repeated the answer so it was audible. "Looked at the title. Waited for one to catch my eye."

Rose nodded crisply. In a staccato voice, she asked another question, "*How* did it catch your eye? Did it reach out and grab you?"

I knew Rose was trying to extend Thyessa's first response, but it wasn't working. When Rose repeated the question, her voice louder still, Thyessa was silent. Another child came to the rescue, suggesting that maybe the title caught Thyessa's eye because it was interesting.

"How could you tell it was interesting?" Rose asked, and soon this child had retreated like the others. "What was interesting about it?" Rose didn't wait for a response. Instead she picked up a book from her desk, and shaking it in front of the kids, she asked, "Do you know what is at the beginning?"

"Contents."

"Okay, table of contents, and sometimes I look at the contents and see things I am interested in. But usually books are on the rack so you see the what, class, the what?"

"Title."

"The title," Rose nodded. "Would you like this book if you picked it up?" The students who were still following her discussion shook their heads. "Why not?" Then Rose answered her own question, "The topic doesn't interest you. Choice of books, then, is based on personal preference." Her heels clicked against the floor as she walked to the chalkboard and in large, exaggerated letters, wrote:

P E R S O N A L

"What does this mean?"

"Yourself."

"OK, we have developed personal (and she underlined the word for emphasis) preferences. OK, I have talked too much about myself. I want you to know how you feel. Charles, what is there in a book that tells you if you'll like it?"

"Words."

"WORDS," Rose repeated, her voice towering above the other voices in the room. "What kind of words?"

The children were silent, probably thinking, "What does this lady want from us?"

When Rose didn't get an answer, she walked from one side of the room to the other. Then she spun around toward the class. "Do you know what I want? I want you to choose a book and then, in your reading log, to write all the things you did when you were choosing it. Slow . . . your thinking . . . down. Did you hear that?" Her voice showed her commitment to helping children become aware of their process, but the children did not share or understand that commitment. "I want . . . through your writing . . . to know . . . what is inside of you."

That is how reading went during those first days, except that as time went on, fewer and fewer children spoke out, and Rose became more and more keyed up. When I recovered from the shock of Rose's teaching, I began to recognize that much of what Rose was doing had its origin in my ideas on teaching reading. After the children wrote in their logs, for example, she told them to glance at what they had written. "Just glance at it," she said. The children, totally confused by this directive, glanced at their pages. I sighed bitterly because I knew perfectly well that Rose was trying to show them that writing is a process of focusing in to write and pulling back to read one's writing, and it was sad to see what had happened to my well-intended ideas.

Sometimes I listened as Rose conferred with the children. Joseph, for example, came to her with a story that began with his friends urging him to "take it serious" when he played sports. Joseph went on to write that he couldn't seem to take anything seriously but his job. On weekends, Joe helps his grandfather in the funeral home. They go on calls together and pick up dead people, then Joe has to dress up the corpses. "I take it very serious, about dying," the boy said. When Rose heard this, she bypassed what Joe had shared with her and asked conference questions from her spiral notebook. I was growing more frustrated by the moment. The worst of it was knowing that she was, in some ways, teaching "by the book"—by *my* book, no less.

Rose was frustrated too. After all, she was an experienced and skillful teacher. She knew it wasn't working. At home, she had started a log and each night she poured out her frustration in it. "What is going wrong?" she wrote, "Are the ideas unworkable? How can I salvage things?"

She talked with the research team a little, but my research associates and I mostly listened. In part I wanted to keep my research distance, but at the same time, I didn't know what to say. I was losing faith in Rose. I had to keep reminding myself that she was—or had been—a wonderful teacher, although everything seemed to be turning sour.

Rose retreated to the Reader. She began leading whole-class lessons on vocabulary and on the questions in the book. "The kids need more structure," she told me. "They were too busy minding everyone else's business." Things calmed down and soon everyone was dutifully plodding through the Reader. But for me, Room 413 was a sad place to be. There seemed to be low-level animosity in the room: the kids didn't like Rose and vice versa. "They have no internal drive," Rose told me.

I refrained from saying, "Are you surprised?" While research associates and I still observed the class, our notes became sparse. What was the sense of documenting the lessons on vocabulary words, or the discussions in which the students gave only sullen, one-word answers? Rose was doing more and more of the talking, and we just didn't feel like writing down all that she said. We didn't want to have to look at it. Then, despite the fact that we were supposed to be studying teachers, not children, my research associates and I decided (for lack of anything else to do), to interview each student. We told ourselves this was important baseline data, but in truth, we wanted a legitimate excuse to retreat to the hallway.

Hasun, a very small fellow with very black skin, sat perched on top of a plastic milk crate. My seat was a pile of discarded textbooks. In a singsong voice, Hasun began telling me his story, and I listened spellbound. It was the sort of story I'd never heard before. Hasun had been to nine schools already; the last was in Queens. "I wanted to see how my uncle and everybody was doing and they kept me for a little while," he explained. Now Hasun was back with his parents, but things were different. "I said to my father, 'Why are you home, Daddy?' and then my father told me he got fired," Hasun explained. His father had been working on elevators until they ran short of materials. "Now he's lookin' at jobs but they don't give him none." The conversation turned toward reading.

"Do you like to read?"

"Half and half. When I read a book it is boring and all the time I fall asleep but my father, he says I still have to read it. That's how come I like to come to school. I don't have to read. At home, my mother and father make me read."

Surprised, I asked more about the reading Hasun did at home.

"All the time I read to myself except when this lady comes to my house and I have to read the Bible and she's teachin' me to read aloud but it's not working. Every Sunday she comes from the Jehovah Witness and she has me read and she asks me little questions like 'What is the name of God?'"

Hasun also had writing assignments at home. "Most of the time my parents tell me to write a little bit of a book. Sometimes they tell me to watch TV if it is about animals and that's educational, and then I have to write about it."

I marveled at all this supervision, but Hasun shrugged it off. "I tell them I want to be a doctor and they're helping me, and I am starting to not want to be a doctor because they're making me work real hard. And they tell me I gotta go to a lot of college, about twelve years of college, and I was hopin' to get out of school fast, real fast."

The interview continued for a long while but when Rose met with Marilyn Boutwell and me for lunch the next day, she didn't let us skip over a bit of it. "Who are you going to interview next?" she asked eagerly, suggesting one child after another. Soon my interviews and our lunches had become a daily affair. I was elated; there would be a story in this classroom after all, even if it was gathered in the hallway in stolen moments. The children would be the stars of the tale, that was clear, and knowing this gave us the energy to resume our data collection even when we were not in the hallway. Now we took copious notes, and we took them even when we were in the room. I jotted down the fact that Jung had covered his textbooks with Harvard, Yale, and Princeton book jackets. Later, in the hallway, he was able to put this detail into a broader context. "I want to go to college so I can be a scientist and make my country better, more scientifically," Jung said. He had only recently come from Korea, and he preferred his home country over New York. "In Korea, not much people throw garbage in the street," he told me, and then shrugged, as if to dismiss the difference. "I'm doing like the other kids in school but I want to be better, smarter," he said, poking his gold-rimmed glasses. "When I go home and other kids are playing, I read a book, not a storybook but a nonfiction book, a book about science, a hard book."

There were thirty-four children in Rose's class, and the interviews took longer than we expected. Perhaps it was for this reason that Rose began to do some of the interviewing. Now during our lunches we swapped stories about her children's backgrounds as readers and writers. I told her about Marsha, whose parents spoke only Chinese, and Diana, who described a good reader as someone who discusses the story with another person, as her parents do when they read the Bible together every night. "They do the same part of the Bible together," Diana said, "Sometimes my father reads it out loud and then he tells my mother how it means, and then she tells him how it means to her."

Rose, meanwhile, had interviewed Morat and she read me every word of the transcript. "I had no idea he was so interesting," she said. "This guy is something else. . . ." More and more of the children were turning out to be "something else."

Morat had recently moved from the Soviet Union. "We came because when you turn eighteen they send you to the army, and my mother was afraid of the war," Morat told Rose. It had been hard for him in this country. "Everyone here bothered me, especially this Chinese kid. They called me bad names, like when the Korean airline was shot down." Morat's parents still speak mostly Russian. "They speak English good for the store, like 'how do you do?'; but for me they speak it very poor. They have an accent. When school is off, I teach them language. They tell me to practice Russian but for me it is the worst punishment because I don't need Russian." Like most of the children in Rose's class, Morat's family owned few books, so the library was important to him. "I don't have a library card because I am always late to bring the book back," he told Rose. "I just come to the library and put a little paper in the book and I go there every day if I have a book. I look how many pages there are, divide into how many pages I could read in a day and if my friend come to go outside, I see how many pages I still have to do. If I have a lot, I say 'no.' I like to finish the book on schedule."

The class was filled with fascinating children, and Rose, Marilyn Boutwell, and I felt like proud parents. "I've never had such an interesting group," Rose told us. I knew what she meant: in all my years of teacher-training and research in the New York City schools, I'd never met a class like this one. Of course, the children were not what was different; our interest in them was different. These children were telling us their stories, and without realizing what was happening, the teaching in that classroom changed.

Now, as I look back, I realize what had happened. Our focus on the children helped Rose focus on the children. Our research stance was contagious: she, too, wanted to pull a chair alongside the youngsters and learn about their learning. To do this, Rose realized that she had to free herself from being director, lecturer, choreographer. She had to stop rushing to teach them everything she'd written in her spiral notebooks from the summer institute. She had to slow down enough to let the children lead the way. Without a word to us, she devised a simple, predictable, and brilliant structure for the reading period. She rearranged the children's desks in clusters of four or five and turned each cluster into a reading response group. The first hour of every day became reading workshop. On the first morning, Rose asked one member from each group to select a book for his or her group (there were multiple copies of books on the back bookshelf). When a group finished their book, another group member would take a turn in selecting the book for the group. If a student finished his or her book before the others in the group, that child turned to the back-up book kept in the desks for that reason. When everyone was ready, the group moved on.

Every day the room was quiet for at least thirty minutes of silent reading. Then Rose would say, "Would one person from each group come and get your secret questions?" With a rush of excitement, five or six children would cluster around her and then return to their group holding a tightly folded bit of yellow paper. On the paper there would be a handwritten "secret question." For fifteen minutes, the group talked about the question, and then the entire class discussed it at the back of the room.

It sounds simplistic, but against this clear, consistent background the children began to do complex and amazing things. Rather than teaching the children about the reading process, Rose had created a context in which they became deeply involved not only in reading, but also in reflecting on and extending their strategies as readers. The change in that classroom was nothing less than a miracle.

This is not to say that the class underwent an instant metamorphosis. The changes were gradual. On the first day, these were the secret questions:

Why do you suppose the author started here? Is there flashback? Does the author hook you? How?

In her group, Diana was the one to read the questions aloud. "I don't get it," she said, and read it again, silently. "Mrs. Napoli, what do you mean 'start here'?" she called out. Jung twisted the paper out of her hands, but he was equally perplexed.

Hasun, leaning over the table to see the question, his knitted cap pulled low over his eyes, said, "Simple. Why does the author start here? 'Cause he wants to." The others, a bit startled by the simplicity of the answer, agreed, and they moved to the next question. None of them knew what flashback meant, so they went on to question number three: How did the author hook you?

"The way he says it," Morat suggested, and again everyone nodded. Simple. The discussion had lasted about two-and-a-half minutes and they were finished. They had, of course, treated the questions as if they were part of a fill-in-the-blank worksheet, answering them with a single word. Because the other groups were still talking, Morat, Diana, Hasun, and Jung started chatting about their book. This turned out to be the first probing, flowing academic discussion I heard that fall in Room 413. The four youngsters discussed the clues to their mystery they'd found so far and some of them suggested possible solutions. They also compared "how far they got" in the book, and Morat, who had read the farthest, told the others, "When you get to page twenty-seven, take it real slow." Then he added, "Tell me when you get to page twenty-six."

Meanwhile Jung had returned to his reading. The others chided him to join the conversation. "Come on, Jung, you get so attached to a book," they said. I thought of how my husband says the same thing to me when I stay up far into the night reading. The group's treatment of the secret question had been far from profound, but a comraderie was beginning to develop. Whether they knew it or not, the children were becoming a community of readers.

The next day, the small group discussion was worse yet, but this time when the whole class met, they dealt with the question in so much more depth that I think Hasun, Morat, Diana, and Jung began to see that their job was not only to answer the questions, but also to reflect upon possible answers, critiquing and amplifying them. The secret question that day had been an odd one:

How is your book put together?

The answer was easy. It was put together with glue. Only later, when the entire class gathered at the back of the room to discuss the question, did Hasun, Diana, Jung, and Morat see that there were other possible answers. Robert said that his book was like a collection of pictures, only it was in words, and Daniel claimed his book was divided into categories of magic tricks. The groups reading fiction had a harder time describing the structure of their books. One child said that in fiction, the whole story connected like a train and there were no separate pieces.

No one wanted the discussion to end, so Rose decided that on this one day, the reading discussion could merge with the writing mini-lesson. The discussions on structure in their reading books led into a discussion on the structure of their rough drafts, and soon the children were writing.

The next day the secret question was this:

What would you ask the author if he or she were here right now?

When the whole class met in the back of the room, Rose first suggested that they compile all the questions each group had chosen. When one group began to repeat questions which had been asked by other groups, Rose suggested that the class make a "short list" of the universal questions. These, she pointed out, were questions that could be asked of almost any author, including each member of the class. When the writing workshop began that day, the children spent a few minutes rereading their rough drafts and reconsidering them in light of their universal questions. From then on, the reading discussion always led into the writing workshop. Elements discussed during reading became concerns during writing as the reading-writing connection was worked into the structure of the day.

Some secret questions proved more effective than others. For example, Rose learned that it was more effective to group related questions together so that they encouraged children to be specific, to enlarge their answers, and to consider alternatives:

LESS EFFECTIVE	MORE EFFECTIVE
What questions would you ask if the author were here?	*What questions would you ask if the author were here? Which would be the most important question? How might the author answer it?*
Do you think that the author did a good job with descriptions? What made it into a good job?	*Select sections of the book in which you think the author has done a particularly good job with description. What makes these sections effective? Be specific and refer to the text.*
What was the setting of the story?	*What was the setting? Where did you first begin to learn about it? How did the author convey the information about the setting? If the story had taken place in a very different setting, how would the plot have been similar or different?*

The children had been working in reading response groups for less than a month when Rose first raised the issue of a story's setting in her secret question. The students' responses to the question show the growth that had occurred in that short time. Morat read the secret question aloud to his group:

Where does your story take place? How does the author let you know the setting? How does the place affect the story?

"It took place in a park," Morat answered without a second thought.

But the others weren't content to let that response stand. "Be specific," Diana warned, and so Morat corrected himself, suggesting that it took place in Prospect Park. The other children weren't sure and so for a few minutes the group was silent as they all leafed through their books.

"Page forty-nine," Jung called out. "Central Park." Then they wondered if every city had a Central Park and finally agreed Central Park had to mean the story took place in New York City. Jung figured that the author chose Central Park for just that reason. "He names a famous park in New York, so he won't have to say New York," Jung suggested. The group nodded and only then were they ready for the second question. . . .

Day by day, week by week, the class discussions became more perceptive and more entertaining. I was spending more time than I had planned in this room, but it was hard to miss a day. One time the secret question (I looked forward to them as much as the kids did!) dealt with the reader's sense of anticipation:

What do you expect will happen next? What clues does the author give you?

It was a wonderful question for many of the response groups, but the group I knew best was reading an anthology of ghost stories and, as Jung pointed out, "the question doesn't match our book."

"Why not?" Diana asked.

"Our book is not one story. It is a whole book of little stories. We cannot guess the next one."

"Well, we know it'll be about more and more sickening stuff," Diana said, her displeasure with the book clearly showing. "There will be ghosts, more ghosts, more ghosts."

"I want to know if there will be *facts* about ghosts," Jung said, "They tell only a little bit of facts."

"There are never going to be facts about ghosts, stupid," Diana retorted. "All you can expect is what ghosts did, stories."

Hasun, who had been listening all the while, interrupted, "Do you believe in ghosts?" he asked.

Jung shook his head. "No, I believe in God." Soon the two boys were deep into a discussion of death, ghosts, God—and reading.

Before long, the children were talking about books before school, on the way to lunch, during the writing workshop and, in whispers, during silent reading. The youngsters who owned books at home brought them in and, if their friends were lucky, they were able to borrow them. Everywhere in the classroom, books and magazines were being shared, discussed, fought over and enjoyed. One morning before school began, I watched Diana going through her satchel, taking out whatever she would need that day. Jung sat nearby, magazine in hand, intent on his reading. Then Jung let out a long, low whistle. "I wonder how Indians eat piranhas," he said, addressing neither of us in particular.

Diana went and stood behind Jung, looking over his page. She wrinkled her nose, "I wouldn't eat them."

"They cook it," Jung said, then turned to me. "If everyone told you to taste a piranha, would you?"

"I'm not sure," I said, uncertain of what Jung was getting at.

"I wouldn't 'cause piranhas eat people so it would be like you were eating people too. I would not like that. But Indians don't think like that." Jung pointed to the picture, and grimaced. "See that man eating it, he likes it." Diana left to get her book and returned with a page open, ready to show Jung something equally amazing she had learned.

Some of these little, informal discussions dealt more with the author's style than with his or her subject. For example, when Morat encountered this paragraph in his reading, he said, "Something is the matter with this paragraph." And he showed it to Hasun:

At that, he turned and hurried down to her. "Janny," he said, over the rail of the cellar steps, "tas the truth when Henfrey sez. 'E's not in uz room, 'e ent. And the front door's unbolted."

"I don't know what it means," Morat complained. They spell it wrong. That 'e ent is weird." Then he said, "Maybe it is a weird kind of an accent."

Diana, overhearing Morat's comment, said, "Sometimes I see weird things in my books too. Like when they put two *hads* together."

For about six weeks, the format of Rose's writing workshop remained the same. One child from each group selected a book, and then each child read a copy of it at his or her own pace. After a half hour of silent reading, the children met in response groups. Then the whole class gathered on the floor at the back of the room for a reading/writing discussion that led into the writing workshop. Once these routines were in place, the children began assuming increasingly active roles in the workshops. They tried to predict what the secret question would be, and sometimes suggested questions to Rose. Many groups developed systems for dealing with the little problems they encountered. One group set up a rotation to ensure that each person had an equal number of chances to "hold the question." Another group decided that each discussion would begin with every member stating his or her response to the question, that way allowing everyone a chance to contribute ideas.

Once the structure of the workshop was well established and the children had a sense of responsibility and control over what went on in it, Rose began making a few changes. First she added reading logs. After children completed a book—whether they read it within the group or outside it—they were asked to enter their response in a spiral notebook. At first these responses were sparse, but once Rose began writing back to the children, they quickly invested more energy in their logs.

Next, Rose began to look for ways to use her own time more wisely. She didn't know what to do during silent reading, and she felt she should be doing something. Eventually, she began using that time for responding to student logs and for conferring with youngsters on their reading.

The biggest change came in early December, and it was prompted by the scarcity of books in the school, especially of multiple copies of books. By December, children were choosing from a very limited number of books. With great reluctance, boys were even choosing "girls" books such as *One Hundred Dresses*. Clearly, more books were needed. Since there was no money for them, Rose developed another plan.

First she gave the groups a deadline for finishing whatever they were reading, and then she began spending time in the school library. The children weren't sure what she was doing there until one morning Rose told them that from then on, rather than reading multiple copies of the same book, each youngster could now select his or her own book, but that the entire class all would read from within the same genre. The first genre would be mysteries. The next day, Rose brought out seventy-five mystery books and set them on the bookshelf.

A loud cheer went up and soon the suspense in Room 413 was tangible. The structure of the reading workshops remained the same. Children still met in response groups, and Rose still provided secret questions. One day, the question was this:

What do you think is the most important clue in your story? How does the author signal that this clue is important?

Another day, this was the question:

How does the lead in a mystery differ from the lead in any other kind of book—or doesn't it? Be specific, and refer not only to the book you are reading now but also to previous books.

Rose also asked this question:

You have now read mysteries by several different authors. Try to find

*a way to describe how these authors' styles are different from each
other. Do you think one is most effective? How would you describe
your style?*

Once the children adapted to the design of Rose's class, her teaching
again receded from their attention, providing a backdrop against which
the children lived their lives as readers and writers. For me, perhaps the
most wonderful thing about Room 413 was that it was for real. Children
weren't just going through motions. In no sense was the classroom an
alien place, cut off from the children's lives, feelings, and relationships.
Instead, the classroom was a literate environment, and in it, the children
laughed, gossiped, exclaimed, joked, and even, sometimes, cried. They
experienced the full gamut of emotions, they did what people do when
they are fully present in their lives, and all of this living was done in
relationship to books.

Diana sometimes brought in paperbacks from home. "My mother gets
them at work, at the shoe factory, and she lets me hold them," she
explained. Sometimes Diana let the boys in her response group borrow
the books, if they were good. I watched Morat race through *The Secret of
Terror Castle*, and knew that he wanted Diana to lend him her Wells book
when she finished it. But on the day Morat finished *The Secret of Terror
Castle*, he found Hasun with his nose buried in Diana's book. Hasun
wouldn't relinquish the book until he finished it, and so Morat turned
away from the group and, his clenched fists hiding his face, started to
cry. Seeing this, Diana and Hasun looked at each other. Hasun shrugged.
"You can have it," he said, his voice slightly belligerent. Morat shook his
head: it was too late, he didn't want the stupid book anyhow. With that,
he got up and slowly, as in a daze, went back to the bookshelf, returning
with *Apple Dumpling Gang*. Sighing deeply, he made a limp effort to read
the new book. Finally he put it aside and laid his head on the desk.

Hasun took the Wells book home that night and came to school the
next day saying he was finished (I don't believe Hasun had ever before
read an entire book in one night). That day was more peaceful, although
during the response group, Morat was quieter than usual. Diana read the
question:

*How are mysteries similar or different from other kinds of writing?
Do you read mysteries differently than you read other things?*

Hasun had an immediate response. "It is different because in a mystery
they tell things that are exciting, in a regular book they mostly describe
people."

Thyessa, Hasun's sister, had joined the group for the day. She shook
her head vehemently. "I disagree," she said, and this time it didn't seem

to be sibling rivalry. "In a regular book there can be mystery. A lady puts her pocketbook on the table and it is missing; it's like a little mystery inside your whole book of fiction."

Morat nodded. "But in a regular book, the mystery is only a small part of it."

Diana returned to the question. "For me," she said, "I think I read mysteries differently. They give me clues and I solve it. When I get clues, I try to put things together, and then keep reading to see if I'm right or wrong. In a mystery, I have to solve something; in a regular book, they solve it for you."

"It is like doing the mystery yourself," Jung added, confirming what Diana had said.

Although Morat had been quiet throughout the discussion, the next day he made up for it by dominating the discussion. Rose had asked the youngsters to compare two different mystery authors. Thyessa began. "Sometimes in books there are two mysteries going on at once to make it complex, and that is how it is in this Hardy book." But her answer wasn't a comparison, as Rose had asked, and the others were quick to point this out.

Jung knew of differences between the Hardy Boys and Alfred Hitchcock. "In the Hitchcock book, those three investigators think they are tough. The Hardy boys ain't. But if the crime is scary, the Hardy boys go through it. The investigators from the Hitchcock book take the easy way and so they don't have so many adventures."

At this point, Morat stepped in. "Wells is different, because in the Hitchcock book the author is kind of *in* the mystery and it is a little bit of a comedy because Alfred Hitchcock is in the book. But Wells makes his stories scary. He doesn't put in any comedy, and he just blurs it all around. One time we'll be in the hotel and the next minute, we are in the forest. How? All they say is he got away. It is blurry, you see?" The other children weren't sure they knew what Morat meant, so he began reading sections from one book and then from another, pointing out the differences.

By this time, of course, many of the children were working on mysteries of their own during the writing workshop. Everything they learned in the reading workshop became fuel for thought as they worked on their own pieces. Hasun, for example, looked up from the mystery he was writing and said, "I am going to begin it by saying that Joseph and I had a fight. You know how in the beginning of mysteries, they tell who is going to be in the book and what they are doing? That's the part I'm writing now."

Jung made a different sort of connection. One day during the reading workshop, he and Robert spent some time exclaiming over Alfred Hitchcock's logo on his books. The logo was a silhouette of a man. "He's ugly and bald," Jung said, but obviously he was quite taken with the idea of a logo because the next day a similar drawing appeared at the top of his story.

Hasun and Morat noticed it at the same time. "Hey, what's that?" Morat asked.

"Alfred Hitchcock," Jung answered. "He has the same thing on all his mysteries."

"Why is it on your mystery then?"

"Because I'm writing a mystery too."

"That's stealing, Jung," Hasun whispered. "That belongs to Alfred Hitchcock's books, not yours."

"I know, but . . ."

"Look, we can fix it," Hasun said and proceeded to work on the logo for a minute, and then handed it back. "Now the guy has your glasses and hair. It's not stealing now."

Jung looked at the silhouette of the little man with the butch cut, then tore it off. My research associate, Marilyn Boutwell, asked him why he did that. "It was OK, but I looked ugly."

Now when the children worked on their own mysteries, revision was a great deal easier. They didn't have to grope about for ways to improve their writing. They had a clearer sense of their options. They also had standards for measurement, a repertoire of techniques, and a vocabulary for talking and therefore, for thinking, about their writing. Jung described the reading workshop, in fact, as part of the writing workshop. "The people like Alfred Hitchcock are famous and we are just beginners, we're not famous. So we're learning things from the good authors so we will be better authors." Jung glanced around the room.

"Everybody's authors are different. When we have writing conferences, we teach each other what we learn from our authors." He added, "I pick a book that has a famous author because if you read famous books, not goofies, you learn to be a better author. In an excellent book like Alfred Hitchcock, I pick out things to put in my story, to make my story more better. My writing got better because I started reading more better books and it was like talking with other authors, when I read their books."

When Rose, Marilyn Boutwell, and I had lunch that day, Rose heard everything Jung had said, and she laughed until she cried when she learned about his logo. "What wonderful kids," she said. I think we all knew that those children were wonderful because Rose stopped teaching her spiral notebooks and started teaching her children. She had gotten out of their way and let them learn, and she had followed their lead admiring, enjoying, and extending their thoughts and feelings. She had realized that the greatest gift she could give them was each other . . . and themselves.

VI

modes of writing

25

---

writing across the curriculum: the potential power of learning logs

When readers look at my chapter heading and see "writing across the curriculum," I wonder what expectations are set into motion. Do you figure I'll list thirty neat ideas for using writing in other disciplines? I could easily come up with such a list. Brainstorming an array of activities is the easy part of teaching; deciding which ones ultimately matter is more difficult. It is no different in art. A painter can easily find blues, oranges, and greens to add to a canvas. Knowing where, when, how, and why to add is the challenge. The hard part is to have an organizing vision.

My challenge in each of the next chapters will not be to list activities that encourage students to write poetry, fiction, or reports, but to capture the essentials of each mode. And although it would be easy to list writing-across-the-curriculum activities, my goal instead is to discover and to write about what I believe ultimately matters in this area.

It is no easy challenge. I avoided my desk this morning, occupying myself instead with small life-tasks. My step-daughter Kira has a school vacation soon, so we got out the map and calendar, jotting down tentative plans for a tour of colleges. Then the nursery man came, wanting to know where to leave the ground cover plants I had ordered. I sketched where they might go, and scribbled notes about his response. Then there were phone calls: Nancie Atwell and I tentatively outlined a joint talk; Tom Newkirk critiqued my chapter for a book on composition research and I made notes of his suggestions; and I scheduled an appointment with the vet. Finally there was nothing more on my agenda and I returned to my desk, to the question, "What is essential about writing across the curriculum?"

The answer was clear. All morning I had been writing across the curriculum. I had been writing to schedule, rank, plan, map, inquire, record, recall, organize, evaluate, assign, remember . . . I'd been writing to learn.

I think with pencil in hand. Writing gives me awareness and control of my thoughts, it allows me to hold onto ideas long enough to scrutinize them, to think about my thinking. When a student comes to my office to talk with me, I often say, "Wait, let me get a pencil." The pencil allows me to listen, to structure what I hear. My fingers itch for that pencil. I carry pencils in my car, and when I plan speeches or rehearse chapters, I sometimes jot a word or two down on nearby scraps of paper. I do not care about neatness or word choice; I am not writing to produce but, instead, to think. Fulwiler, one of the influential scholars on this topic, points out that only in peculiar circumstances, such as the English classroom, is the precision, shape, and correctness of the writing act viewed as more important than the thought engendered by the act. He writes, "Scientists, artists, mathematicians, lawyers, and engineers all 'think' with pen on paper, chalk on blackboard, hands on terminal keys" (1982, 19). Like these people, I think by writing and I want students to do likewise.

Let me be clear: the task is not to insert more writing into subject area classrooms. Students already spend 44 percent of their classroom time writing (Applebee, Lehr, and Auten 1981). But they spend only 3 percent of their time on actual composing; the rest is devoted to filling in the blanks and so forth. The writing that commonly occurs in the content areas can be divided into mechanical writing (notetaking, copying from the board, short answers, etc.), formal compositions (book reports, research papers, etc.), and essay exams. In each of these instances, the purpose is not to learn but, instead, to reveal to teachers what the student knows and does not know.

When I write to learn, when I think with pencil in hand, the resulting text would not convince anyone of what I know. This is true for most writing across the curriculum; it has very little place in our classrooms.

Recently, one of my student teachers tried to change the status quo. Ellen began her literature class by passing out dittoed copies of a poem and asking her eighth-grade students to reread it several times. "Do me a favor and jot down in the margins what the poem means to you," she said. In the subsequent whole-class discussion, one student after another pitched in, and the class as a whole reconstructed the poem. "Let's look at another poem," Ellen then said, and this time it was in the anthology. "On a piece of paper, jot down your ideas for me." Later students discussed the poem, two lines at a time.

This *was* writing to learn, but something wasn't right about it. What I am suggesting is that the *context* for this writing-to-learn event made it seem like just another teacher-led exercise. "What I want you to do . . ."

Ellen had said, and later, "Jot down your ideas for me . . ." The writing was done in the margins of a ditto and on a scrap of paper. If Ellen had begun the poetry unit by telling students that they would be reading and writing about poems in order to develop and refine strategies for interpreting poetry, her students might have sensed that there was a cumulative purpose to their readings, that with each new poem, their interpretations should be more skillful. They would have felt this even more if, during the whole-class discussion, Ellen had allowed selected students the opportunity to present their interpretation in full to the larger community, later coming to see the strengths and weaknesses of their individual reading. Instead, the writing led immediately into a whole-class discussion in which each student's view was amalgamated into one conglomerate interpretation. Then, too, just the fact that the students did their writing on an odd assortment of papers that were later lost in the shuffle meant that each individual's thinking was treated casually.

Tools have a way of shaping behavior. Although writing-to-learn should be first-draft writing, full of sketches, lists, and fragments of ideas, this writing needs to be taken seriously if students are to see it as an important vehicle for learning. If each of Ellen's eighth graders had written their notes in their own learning log, the writing would have seemed less like a series of exercises for the teacher and more like a vehicle for developing and recording their ideas. Perhaps with foresight, Ellen might have Xeroxed each poem and punched holes in the right margin of each page, thus allowing students to keep a double-entry ledger, with poems on one side and jottings on the other (see Figure 25-1).

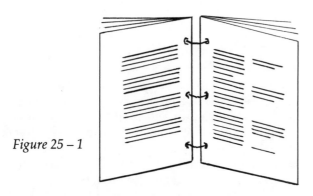

Figure 25 – 1

In this diagram, the right page of the ledger contains two columns, one reserved for notes prior to discussion, and the other, for later revisions of this first interpretation.

My point is not to equate writing-across-the-curriculum with this particular form of literature log, but instead, to show that we can gain a great deal by having a forum for writing to learn. I also believe that as teachers, we tend to focus on what we will say and on what students will say and write, and pay less attention to the arrangements that structure those events. For example, deciding whether a discussion will be conducted with the whole class or in small groups is vastly more important in a lesson plan than determining the content of the short talk preceding that discussion. Yet we are apt to focus on the words we will say rather than on the ways our students will work. Likewise, the decisions about whether the writing-to-learn will be done in a spiral or a looseleaf notebook, and whether the logs will be graded for effort or not graded at all are vastly more important than the words a teacher says to introduce writing-to-learn activities.

I cannot make many universal recommendations about how logs should be used; use will depend on purpose. A science log will probably contain detailed sketches and observations, with sections set aside for recording patterns and for listing new research questions. Math logs will contain calculations, notes on numbers, pasted in computer sheets, sketches. Writing logs will contain alternative leads, maps of possible sequences, clippings from newspapers, titles, endings, lists, and more lists. Sometimes logs will be in looseleaf notebooks, sometimes in spirals, sometimes they will consist of a collection of letters to the teacher, or of files on a subject. The form *does* matter, but there is no one, supreme form.

Despite this diversity, there is also continuity. No matter what the subject area is, learning logs provide a forum and an occasion for learning. Learning consists of similar activities in any subject: asking questions, stating hypotheses, organizing information, assimilating and accommodating and so forth.

Asking questions

A little while ago, my husband John and I were watching a television show in which people were making a movie. When the cameras were focused, an actress took out a fake gun and pretended to shoot a guy. He fell down, pretending to be dead. The camera people called, "Retake," and again the actress took out a fake gun, pretended to shoot the guy, and again he fell down, pretending to be dead. This continued until the actress interrupted filming to say, "I have to fix my face."

As she walked off to the dressing rooms, my husband muttered, "She's going to switch guns." I glanced sideways at him, perturbed by his morbid notions. The actress returned, filming resumed, and all was well. Once again she took out her fake gun and pretended to shoot the guy, and once again he pretended to be dead . . . only this time, he didn't get up.

Startled, I turned to my husband. "Did you see this before?" I asked. "How did you know? There wasn't any bad music. . . ."

My husband shook his head. "Lucy," he said, "it was obvious." Then, after a long pause, John asked, "When you watch television, Lucy, what are you doing?"

"I'm watching television," I answered, and the sarcasm in my voice showed that I thought it was an obvious answer. But in retrospect, I realize that John does something quite different than I when he watches television. He is asking questions, searching for answers, asking new questions, building hypothetical answers, looking for confirmation. Meanwhile, I wait for things to happen.

My husband's predilections about the actress and her fake gun illustrate a crucial difference between us. John is a problem-finder, a question-asker, and I am not. In his book, *The Informed Vision*, Hawkins (1974) notes that few people are problem-finders. Hawkins suggests that this is particularly true when it comes to dealing with the scientific, technological world in which we now live. We spend two minutes admiring scientific products—airplanes, mirrors, computers, engines—and then we quickly pass from excitement to boredom. Hawkins's comment hits home for me. If I ask for a window seat on an airplane, it's because I can sleep more easily leaning against the window. I don't wonder at the interactions of wing and atmosphere. I don't look out the window and speculate about whether space is a kind of fullness or emptiness. I don't marvel at vapor trails. I live much of my life as I watch TV . . . and I suspect most of our students do the same.

It often seems that students watch our classes as I watch television. With glazed eyes, they wait for information to come to them. We see their glazed eyes and think, "I've got to be more stimulating." Our lessons become more animated, more varied, anything for a flicker of interest. Of course, we've fooled ourselves. We've bought into the notion that we can "learn them." This is not only bad grammar, it is impossible. Learning isn't something we can do for or to our students. Learning requires an act of initiative on their part. We can only create conditions in which learning can happen.

Learning logs can help create those conditions by encouraging students to ask questions just as my husband asks questions. It is hard to stress enough the importance of problem-finding, of question-asking. Certainly the ability to ask appropriate and probing questions is a crucial part of comprehension, and this is true whether comprehension involves a book, film, lecture, math problem, or life situation. Yet we do not teach question-asking in schools. Often, we do not even allow for it. In most classrooms, students rarely ask questions, they only answer them. Over the course of twelve classes, for example, Bellack (1963) found only nine instances of pupil-initiated sequences of thought. Discussions were all led by teacher initiative. Yet asking questions is often the most challenging and important part of thinking. As Wertheimer writes, "Often in great discoveries the most important thing is that a certain question is found. Envisaging the productive question is often more important then the solution of a set question."

Logs can provide students with a forum for asking questions. Before showing a film on the Civil War, for example, we could ask students to record the questions they have about the war. Or, if we were showing the film as an introduction to a particular topic—perhaps the causes of the Civil War—we might ask for questions relating to that topic. Similarly, we might begin a lesson on long division or a reading assignment on clouds, with students jotting down the questions they have. After the film, lesson, or reading assignment, students could look back at their list of questions, checking off those that had been answered, crossing out those which now seemed irrelevant, and adding the new questions which emerged from the activity. But asking questions is one thing, and learning to ask more probing and more appropriate questions is another. We might go a step further and ask students to think about their questions: Which were their best? What makes one question more effective than another? They might meet in groups to compare their questions and to select a single important question that could then become the basis for class discussion.

Making guesses

Not long ago I observed a science resource teacher working with a group of third graders. "What do all living things need in order to survive?" She asked the children. The youngsters were silent, then a hand shot up. "Skin?" Tracey suggested. "If you don't have skin then your heart will pump and it will go all over the place." The class enjoyed Tracey's guess but the resource teacher did not. She sighed loudly and looked for a better response. Hesitantly, Noah asked, "Is it mothers?" No, the science teacher told him, it began with *F*. "Fathers?" The expert turned and on the board she wrote: Food, air, water.

What that expert forgot is that in science, guessing is called forming hypotheses. In reading, it is prediction. In either case, guessing—like asking questions—is a crucial part of learning. Yet often, like the resource teacher, we inadvertently dismiss children's guesses. "You're guessing," has come to be a negative expression, meaning, "Don't guess." Logs can help undo the damage we've done.

Before students watch the Civil War movie, we could ask them to jot down what they imagine might have caused the Civil War. "Pretend to be an expert on the topic and make up some causes for the war," we could tell them. Elbow calls this an instant version:

Simply deny the need for research, thinking, planning and turn out
an instant version. . . . Pretend you know things you don't know,
act as though you have made up your mind where you're uncertain,
make up facts and ideas . . . and you will be able to get much more
out of any reading and research you (eventually) do (Elbow 1981, 64).

Such an "instant version" will catapult students into a position of initiative and control. They'll watch a movie differently because they've made an investment in the topic. "I guessed right!" they'll say, or "I didn't think of that."

Halfway through, before all the causes of the Civil War are revealed, students could go back and revise their instant version in light of what they have already learned. Or the film could be shown straight through, with time reserved afterward for reflection on the strategy of making guesses. Some students will have based their instant versions on a remembered story, the words of an old song, or their knowledge of other wars. Others will not have thought to make connections, to search through their minds for clues, but will instead have made "wild guesses."

Logs can be used similarly with reading, and once again there could be time for students to reflect on their guesses, on their predictions. Were they wild guesses, or did students base their expectations on clues provided by the author? What clues did the text provide? Good guessing is a skill and students can use logs to develop that skill.

Organizing information

Yesterday a doctoral student brought me a long draft of the "Review of Literature" for her dissertation. In the paper, she summarized the studies she had read. I looked over the draft, and asked, "What are you trying to say in this?" She seemed startled by the question and mumbled something about reporting on various studies. I tried again, this time asking what she had discovered from her research. She couldn't answer that question either. She hadn't considered *her* views on the material, she'd simply read and reported on what others had to say. I sent her home with the suggestion that she reread her notes and begin free-writing, diagramming, sorting, organizing, talking about, and digesting her topic.

I thought about that doctoral student afterward, and about others like her. Why is it that so many doctoral students seem unable to bring their own thinking to bear on new information? My request was really a simple one: I wanted that doctoral student *to think,* to wrestle with her information, to see patterns in her facts, to build an idea out of her data. It seems like a small request—yet the sad truth is, it is not. In many public schools and even in some colleges, when students write reports, they are given the subheadings for those reports, and often these are the same headings found in the encyclopedia. Students rarely have to sort, order, or digest information; they need only report on it. Even when students answer questions at the end of the text, they can be sure that if a question reads, "What are the three reasons . . . ," somewhere in the chapter there will be an orderly list of the three reasons. Students are given very little opportunity in our schools to organize information on their own, and yet this is a crucial part of both writing and learning.

In *Reading Without Nonsense*, Frank Smith highlights the connection between learning and organizing. He tells of an experiment in which fifty picture cards were given to members of two groups. The first group was told to memorize the items on the cards, since they would be tested on them in ten minutes. Members of the second group, unaware of these instructions, were told to organize their picture cards into categories. After ten minutes, both groups were tested to see how well they could recall the contents of the cards. The second group remembered far more than the first group (Smith 1978). Smith reports on this experiment in order to stress that we learn through organizing, through building categories. How often do our youngsters build, critique, rebuild, and defend systems of organization? Teachers commonly complain that students of all ages have difficulty producing well-organized compositions. I wonder whether this is a writing problem—or a thinking problem. Logs can be used to urge children to build systems of organization. Here are a few ways they can do this:

- After they watch a film, listen to a lesson, or read a text, children can create maps depicting the structure of the information. For example, a map of this chapter might look like this:

  Story about TV show Lucy watched.

  Main point: Logs can turn students into active learners.

  Three components of learning and how logs could create occasions for each.

  Review and advice.

  Another map of this chapter might look like this:

  Introduction   Learning   Areas of the
                      logs   curriculum

The point would be for children to think about the structure of a text instead of producing the "correct" map.

- Children could jot down details about any subject matter—whether it is long division, clouds, or the Civil War—and then they could come up with various ways to categorize that information. For example, their information on long division could be divided into these or other categories:
  - Ways long division is similar and different from short division.
  - Steps involved in solving a long division problem.
  - Problems to avoid when solving long division.
  - The meanings of terms used in division and multiplication problems.
- After gathering information on a topic, students could be encouraged to rethink and reread the information, shaping it into categories, or searching for a line of argument or an organizing vision. Then, in their learning logs, they could take notes on the patterns they create.

There are other things we do in order to learn, and I invite my readers to find your own ways to use learning logs both as a forum for turning students into active learners, and as a tool for teaching them habits of thought. Teachers may, for example, want to help students realize that learning does not just involve taking in new blocks of information. Each of the new items must either be stored in one's own existing mental files or lead toward the creation of a new file. In order to accomplish either process—assimilation or accommodation—learners must think about new knowledge in terms of pre-existing knowledge. Logs can help them to "activate prior knowledge," which is a reasonable way to begin any form of learning. A lesson on aspirin can begin by having students ask themselves, "What do I already believe about how aspirin works?" and then, after taking in new knowledge, they can look back and say, "How does this new information fit with what I already knew?" and, "What surprised me? What *didn't* fit? What do I make of the misfit?"

If a teacher asks students to use logs in this way during a lesson on aspirin, it is important that the next week, when the lesson is on another pharmaceutical product, the logs be used in a similar way. Ideally, students could be writing what they already know and then integrating new information into that schema not only in science but also in math or reading. This runs contrary to what generally happens in schools. Our natural instinct is to maintain variety by using logs differently every day. The problem with this, however, is that students never have the opportunity to draft and revise their *learning strategies* over a sequence of days. They cannot work out ways to refine any particular learning strategy because they are always shifting from one to another. Then, too, if students perform new operations in every log entry, they probably will consider assimilating new information, or asking questions, or making guesses as tasks that are somehow particular to the subject matter at hand, rather than seeing these operations as habits of thought that are part of any good learner's repertoire. In their logs, I want students to externalize forms of thinking that they will later internalize. Just as revision strategies that are first done concretely, systematically, and in a plodding sort of way, later become internalized and almost effortless, so too, learning operations can be internalized. Our purpose in using learning logs is not only to nudge students to think, but also to teach them habits of thought. For this reason, it is important to use logs in predictable, well-labeled ways and to emphasize that what is done through writing in the logs can also be done through talking and through thinking.

It is important to remember that, by doing these operations in writing, learners acquire an extra amount of consciousness of and control over their thinking. I began the chapter by saying, "Writing gives me awareness and control of my thoughts, it allows me to hold onto ideas long enough to scrutinize them, to think about my thinking." *Rereading* one's writing, turning back on the traces of one's thought, is essential. Sartre gave up writing when he lost his eyesight because he needed to visualize his thought in order to manipulate and develop it, in order to compose his meaning (Sartre 1975).

A word of caution. Our instinct might be to ask students to reread their logs in order to correct or complete them, particularly after they have received more input from the class discussion, the film, or the text. If students listed their questions prior to watching a film, our instinct might be to say, "For homework tonight, go back and *answer* your questions." There is no harm in this (except that we teach students to ask short-answer questions), but I think it would be far more valuable to ask students, as I suggested earlier, to reread and reconsider their questions and their thinking strategies in the light of new information. Which were their most effective questions? What makes for good questions? Donaldson writes, "Human children can learn to be conscious of the powers of their own minds and decide when and how they will use them. However, they cannot do without our help." When children become aware of their thinking strategies, they can become more strategic, deliberate thinkers. At home, as a child snuggles down with a novel, he or she can say, "I'm going to guess what it will be about," and then proceed to collect the clues which will confirm or challenge that guess. In the town library, as the child researches go-carts, he or she can say, "Let me see how all this fits together" and begin organizing major and minor categories of information. This leads to the subject of our next chapter, report writing.

26

reports: enfranchise students as teachers and they will become learners

Each year at Teachers College, I supervise a new group of student teachers. Since we spend a great deal of time talking about their children's needs and little time talking about their own, I began a recent meeting with a simple, but unexpected, question: "How do you like teaching?"

I expected my student teachers to talk about their roles in school and their relationships with students and colleagues, but they wanted to tell about the effect of teaching on the rest of their lives. "I think about teaching all the time," one said, and the others agreed. "Even at the theater, I find myself drawing connections to whatever I'm teaching." Another added, "Whenever I read the newspaper, I keep cutting things out to share with the kids." For my student teachers, teaching is a lens that changes the way they see everything.

And isn't—or wasn't—it that way for all of us? Have we begun to take for granted the transforming power of teaching? Listening to those student teachers, I felt as if they were articulating something I'd long forgotten. On the topics I teach, I am a magnet; any related information sticks to me. When I know I will be teaching a class on a topic, I become a powerful learner. Everywhere, I see related anecdotes, ideas, and quotations. Because I teach, I learn. "We are the teaching species," Erik Erikson has written. "Not only do the young need adults, but adults also need the young." He adds, "Human beings need to teach not only for the sake of those who need to be taught but for the fulfillment of our identities and because facts are kept alive by being shared, truths by being professed."

Erikson is right. I need to teach because my ideas are kept alive by being shared. And I am not alone—we are the teaching species.

What we sometimes forget is that our students are also part of the teaching species. They, too, need to keep ideas alive by teaching them to others. Perhaps the most powerful thing about nonfiction writing within the writing workshop is that it allows students to become teachers, claiming, developing, and sharing what they know. Our students know so much. In report-writing workshops, students have taught me how to bathe teddy bears and to catch grasshoppers; I have learned about anorexia from a child with an anorectic sister; I have learned about Yugoslavian weddings, the Russian language, cockroaches, and dirt bikes.

In learning what our students know, we give our students faces, voices. I recently attended a large conference in a field other than my own. Sitting among that crowd of people, exchanging pleasantries with those around me, I had a faceless feeling. No one knew who I was, what I do, where I am going. They didn't know my family, my work, my life-stories. If I'd been able to teach others what I know, I would have felt more present. Many students spend years in classrooms without ever being able to teach others what they know. I understand, therefore, why Don Graves has suggested that a competency test for writing teachers might involve asking teachers to list their students' names, and beside each name, to write five or six areas in which that student is an expert. The bottom line in teaching writing is that we must know what it is that our students know. Earlier I quoted Harold Rosen, who has said, "Every child has a story to tell. The question is, will they tell it to us?" I think we can also say, "Every child has lessons to teach. The question is, will they teach them to us?"

Perhaps, by now, my readers are impatiently scanning ahead, wondering whether I plan to address my professed topic: report-writing. Rest assured, I have not forgotten the topic. If I am not meeting the expectations readers have brought to this chapter, it is not by accident. I believe the whole notion of "report-writing," accepted so implicitly in schools, is a bizarre one. For example, this book is a research report on teaching writing, but I did not do that research by going to a library, pulling out the *W* volume of an encyclopedia, and proceeding to "make a report" based on what I found there. Instead, I began with what I had experienced and with what I knew. Then I sought out life experiences and relationships that would help me learn more. I explored questions, experimented with ideas, and pursued interests. This exploration has involved extensive reading, certainly, but equally important have been observations, interviews, experiences, discussions, arguments, fantasies, free-writing, photography, and so forth. And although I have now written a long treatise on my topic, I have spent eleven years writing shorter pieces: notes to myself, letters to friends, workshop plans, speeches, research memos, articles. . . . The irony is that in a field where everyone is saying, "We need to see how real writers go about composing, and to let our students participate in these processes," few people are suggesting that we also need to study how real researchers go about their work, and to use this as the basis for units on report-writing. In the last ten or fifteen years, we have come a long way toward demythologizing the writing process. Students no longer believe good writing flows magically from the writer's plumed pen. My purpose in this chapter is to go another step further and begin demythologizing the process of writing content-area research.

Our students do not know what is expected of them when we assign a report. Nine-year-old Debbie explained to me, "When my teacher told us to write a report, I got goosebumps and butterflies in my stomach and everything. I knew this time would come because all the kids write real reports in fourth grade, but when it was here I didn't know what to do. I was so scared. On Saturday I went to the library like my sister used to do, and I got the encyclopedia and put down the facts: people, places, dates, Indians, wars. Then I wrote it up."

Debbie is only in fourth grade, but the sad thing is that when students reach junior high, or even college, their processes are often very similar. Margaret Queenan asked her seventh graders to turn in their index cards before they started their reports. When Margaret began going through the cards, she wrote "Put in Your Own Words" when necessary. Soon she abbreviated her message to "PYOW," and then, to "OW." "There were hundreds of OW's," she said, "hundreds."

I told this story to my typist, and he was not surprised. "Just yesterday, a student from West Connecticut College called to ask if I could type a ten-page report," he told me. The student arrived twenty minutes later with a musty old book in hand. "Just take ten pages from the book," the student said. "But do me a favor, when you come to big words, change them to small ones." As he turned to leave, the student added, "Don't worry, the book is out of print now so they'll never know."

Something is dreadfully amiss—and the seeds of the problem are in fourth grade when Debbie, with the best of intentions, goes to the library on a Saturday morning to copy down the facts. We need not only to *assign* reports but also to demonstrate report-writing, to coach and guide students, and to observe their processes. We need to bring all we know about teaching writing to this important genre.

In the first section of this book, I stressed that the writing process is not a linear sequence of steps. Just as a class of students cannot move uniformly along in rehearsal, drafting, revision, editing, and publication, so too, they cannot proceed uniformly through a sequence of research-steps. One student may spend ten minutes selecting or narrowing a research topic, while another will spend several days, or will return to this issue midway through his or her work. This should not be surprising to the teacher of writing, nor should it present difficulties so long as report-writing takes place within the structure, mores, and expectations of the writing workshop. The writing workshop can still begin with a mini-lesson, only now the writing tips tend to include finding resource material, strategies for taking notes, examples of good nonfiction writing and the like. Children can still use their folders, only now they contain notes as well as drafts, and the front cover may provide a space for a bibliography. Writing time can still contain a mix of activities, only now these include library work, note-taking, map-reading. I trust that by this point in the book, readers have a feel for the range of activities that can occur simultaneously in a writing workshop. I will risk describing in a linear fashion, some of the operations involved in research-writing. These include, only vaguely in this order, these processes:

- Choosing a research area and beginning to focus on a specific topic for writing.
- Becoming an expert on the topic.
- More focusing of one's topic, early analysis of incoming information.
- More research.
- Readiness for writing: reading, studying models, rehearsing for writing.
- Drafts, conferences, drafts, conferences, editing, publishing.
- Cycling back for more research with a new focus.

Choosing a research area

In the real world, people write neither "reports" nor five-paragraph essays. People write news stories, speeches, research memos, feature articles, briefs, books . . . and all of this writing is grounded in areas of expertise. The writers begin with what they know, they learn more about the topic, and they teach their content to readers. What this means is that the first step in a research report should not be to decide on a "report topic" but, instead, to target an area for investigation. The goal at this point is powerful learning in an area of interest, not the report with margins and bibliography. Powerful learning is not possible within the confines of most research-report assignments.

I remember my introduction to report-writing. The New York State report was a tradition in our seventh grade, part of the rites of passage into junior high school. My teacher, Mrs. Harris, gave us a dittoed outline listing the topics we were to cover. We were to write about New York's history, government, geography, main products, politics, industry, famous people, cities, state bird, and state flower, and the report was to be twelve pages long. Handily, the subtopics on the outline matched the boldprint subheadings in our *World Book,* so for me the report mostly involved transposing information from the encyclopedia to my paper. In seventh grade, my process of report writing was not unlike the process I used in third grade when I copied the abalone-shell report from the chalkboard, only in junior high, I copied instead from the encyclopedia. The New York State report included more than copying; we were also told to make a map. My father "helped" me outline New York onto an enormous slab of plywood, and then we dangled milk cartons and pieces of rock to locate the dairy farms and mineral deposits on the map. The map was unusual, but neither the report, nor the assignment to write it, were out of the ordinary.

In a recent survey of American secondary schools, Applebee found that teachers often assign topics that could be the subject of a book, a series of books, or an entire library—topics on which students would need a lifetime of research before they developed a sense of expertise. It is not unusual, Applebee says, for teachers to ask for a two-page report on topics such as twentieth-century American architecture, or the diesel engine (Applebee 1981). These topics have always puzzled me: Why would anyone assign such huge subjects? I recently asked this of a social studies teacher at Scarsdale Junior High. The man looked at me keenly, and with great seriousness told me, "We want to cover the curriculum while also teaching report-writing. We want to kill two birds with one stone."

"You are succeeding," I said to him. He *is* killing two birds with one stone. Such assignments successfully "cover" the curriculum. As David Hawkins (1974) says, we would do well to *un*cover the curriculum rather than to cover it, inviting students to probe deeply into topics. To do this, school people need to decide that listing and learning vital statistics about New York State is best accomplished through flash cards or dittos (if it is done at all), and that report-writing should serve an entirely different function. They have to decide that it is more important for students to develop areas of expertise, to synthesize and organize information, and to teach others what they know and think, than it is for them to find and report on the "facts" such as those Debbie found that Saturday morning in the encyclopedia.

It wasn't until I participated in a graduate level nonfiction writing seminar led by Don Murray that I realized the first goal in research-writing: to develop an area of expertise on a topic of interest to me. Murray began the semester by suggesting we list what we knew and cared about, and then, focusing on one item, begin researching what we didn't know about what we knew. Hearing this, teachers may wonder if there is a place for whole-class assigned topics. Of course there is. The problem with the New York State report was not that a topic had been assigned, but that the topic was too large for me to develop a sense of expertise. Sometimes the problem with topics (whether assigned or chosen) is that they are too complex and abstract. Phyllis Malone, a second grade teacher in District 15, has found that after her children select topics on which they'd like to become expert, she needs to check over those topics in order to give the children a safety net against failure. She steers children toward topics on which they will find a wide range of resource materials, and she encourages them to work together on areas of shared concern. Phyllis finds that for her young writers, concrete topics such as dinosaurs, box turtles, ballet, and racing cars are more accessible than abstract themes such as evolution or technology. The topics her children write about may seem simplistic—

but I have found students' processes can be more complex and their ideas more insightful, if the subject matter is straightforward and manageable. Some of our best nonfiction writers address similar topics. Loren Eisley has written about the octopus; Lewis Thomas about warts; Edward Hoagland, turtles; Charles Darwin, worms; John McPhee, oranges; E. B. White, the hen; and Virginia Woolf, the moth. The children are in good company!

Then, too, I know that, when Murray asked us to research and write about what we didn't know about what we knew, this was the most challenging writing assignment I had ever been given. An unfamiliar topic—dragonflies, for example—would have been much easier. As it was, I needed to constantly integrate new information with old, book information with life experiences, the ideas of others with my own ideas, abstract notions with concrete facts, and then, because I cared so much about the topic, I needed also to make my truth beautiful. Dragonflies would have been much easier!

Whether students begin with an assigned research area or with a self-chosen topic, they will need to focus and organize their research efforts. Focus, of course, means something very different depending on the age of the child. While a five-year-old may write very successfully on a topic such as "dogs," a second or third grader may find it easier either to divide such a topic into chapters (selecting a dog, when you first get your dog, feeding your dog, etc.) or to limit the topic, perhaps to one kind of dog or to obedience training. Junior high students may be able to select a thematic focus, addressing a particular issue within the broad topic. They may look at whether large or small dogs have more uses in our society, or at why poodles are perceived differently now than they once were.

One way for students to begin developing a focus is for them to write early during the process of research. This writing should fall into Britton's category of expressive writing, and it could be contained within the pages of a project log. If students have used learning logs in their content-area classrooms, they will already have strategies for learning about a topic. In their project logs, students may want to jot down what they already know about a topic so that they can later assimilate some of the incoming information into their pre-existing mental files. Students may want to use their skills as question-askers in order to gather together a list of key questions, and tentatively to select one or two particularly important questions. The important thing is that this sort of writing can *precede* and influence the research process.

Becoming an expert

The goal during this phase of research is not to fill index cards with quotations, or to pore through a big pile of books, or to gather an impressive number of quotations and statistics. The goal instead is for students to be powerful learners. Teachers need to help this happen.

One way to begin is to think back on our own lives as students, and to identify the times when we were powerful learners. For me, one such time was the year I spent observing and teaching in a primary school in Oxfordshire, England. Another time was my first year away from classroom teaching, when I was given the chance to study several children closely in order to document their growth in writing. The third time is right now, but that is another story. What was it about these three instances that made them into powerful learning times? For me, learning needs to be interpersonal. Usually there has been a mentor, and always, colleagues. Then, too, the learning has been *incredibly slow.* I didn't learn about the British Primary Schools through a two-week visit, or about children's growth as writers through pre- and post-observations. Finally, the information has come in through all my pores. My "studies" haven't fit into the hours between seven and ten P.M., nor have they occurred only in the library.

I usually gather the information that adds life and texture to my writing and leads to my own theories through field work and through life experiences. This book is based largely on observations, personal experiences, and interviews. Zinsser seems to suggest that this is true for most nonfiction writing. He says, for example,

> Whatever the form of nonfiction you will write, it will come alive in proportion to the number of quotes that you can weave into it naturally as you go along. Often, in fact, you will find yourself embarking on an article so apparently lifeless—the history of some institution, or some local issue such as storm sewers—that you quail at the prospect of keeping your readers, or even yourself, awake.
>
> Take heart. You will find the solution if you look for the human element. Somewhere in every drab institution are men and women who have a fierce attachment to what they are doing and are rich repositories of lore (Zinsser 1976, 75–76).

Even very young children can learn from interviewing experts. After children in Mrs. Flayton's first grade selected their areas of investigation, they hung a sign alongside the teachers' mailboxes:

Dear Teachers,
  We are becoming experts on a lot of different topics. We have put a list of our topics under this letter. If you have any books or pictures on the topics, or if you know who we can interview, please tell us.

Within a few days, the children received responses. A fourth-grade teacher wrote Emil to say her sister studied karate, and why didn't he phone her

(Emil proudly announced to his friends that he was going to phone an older woman). The reading teacher's father was a vet and children could interview him about animals. Mr. Giordano, the principal, had a new granddaughter and would gladly tell Mellisa about caring for newborn babies. A sixth-grade teacher brought the first graders' list of topics to her classroom and soon sixth graders were sharing resource materials and posing as experts for the younger children.

The book shown in Figure 26-1, written by first graders from Marilyn Grubstein's classroom, illustrates the way in which even very young children can integrate information (and misinformation) from their lives with what they read in books.

It is, of course, easier for teachers to provide rich sources of learning if the whole class is researching the same topic. In Mrs. Seltzer's kindergarten, children have several class projects, and each project results in many small bits of content-area writing. Last fall when the group studied dinosaurs, they took notes on what they read and heard from books. During a visit to the National History Museum, they each estimated the length of the dinosaurs there, and then children lay on the floor alongside the huge creatures, checking their estimations by measuring them in child-lengths. Later the children had a make-believe dig in their

Figure 26 – 1

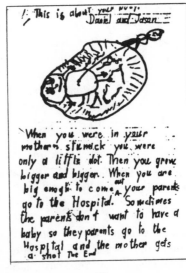

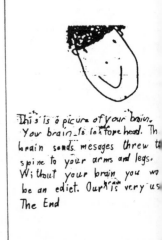

(a) (b) (c)

classroom. Mrs. Selzer hid paper bones of three different dinosaurs around the room and her thirty-four young paleontologists searched for them, then sorted the bones into the three dinosaurs. Each dinosaur became the project of a different group of children. In their groups, the youngsters tried to put the bones into place to re-create the skeleton. Then they studied the skeleton in an effort to find clues about the dinosaur's life habits. Some children wrote about what they learned, as this five-year-old has done in the report shown in Figure 26-2 (p. 280).

Janet Dresser not only wanted to provide her students with rich learning opportunities on a chosen topic, but also to help them learn the skills of note-taking and research-writing. For this reason, she asked her third graders to select an area of shared interest. The children chose space, and then for several weeks they learned about space in every imaginable way. They traveled to a planetarium, spoke with an older student who had won Boy Scout badges in astronomy, and read fiction and nonfiction books dealing with space. Throughout all of this, each child continually added index cards of information to four large orange crates, each representing a different subtopic.

When it came time to write the reports, the class worked together with the contents of one crate, reading, discussing and sorting the index cards;

This is your blood. It comes
out when you get a bad cut.
Our blood has waist products.
Our heart pumps all our blood into
our vains. Without blood we would
be almost usless.
The End of your body.

(d)

There are three parts of the
tung. the sour a sweet and bitter.
Our tung helps us taste. The buds
in our tung are taste buds. But
sometimes we can't control our
tung and we stick it at people.
Our tung is sticky so we can
seal envilopes. The End

(e)

connecting the new information to any previous information; and reflecting on their main ideas and insights about the topic. The class mapped possible sequences for a report, toyed with alternate leads, and eventually collaborated on a draft. Soon the class had divided into small groups. Each group was following a similar procedure as the children worked with the contents of their own crate.

One exciting aspect of this is that children received help with the processes of reading-for-information and note-taking. This help can, of course, be given in the five-minute mini-lessons that precede the writing workshop. In one such mini-lesson, a fourth-grade teacher asked children to pretend that they were researching bird migration. Then she led the class through the steps of selecting appropriate resource material and taking notes. Mrs. Currier had collected books on the topic, including both a primary level book and an encyclopedia. "Which would you read first?" she asked. In the discussion which ensued, children learned to read simpler books first to gain a grasp of their subject before they tackled denser texts. Then Mrs. Currier suggested that students begin by skimming through a book to become familiar with the topic. They did this together with the simplest book on bird migration. After that, the class brainstormed questions they hoped to answer, and filled the blackboard. From this collection, each student and the teacher selected a few key questions. While the teacher wrote her questions on top of sections of the blackboard, the students put theirs on top of sheets of yellow paper. "The next thing we do is we read until our heads are full," Mrs. Currier told the class. In this instance,

---

Figure 26 – 2

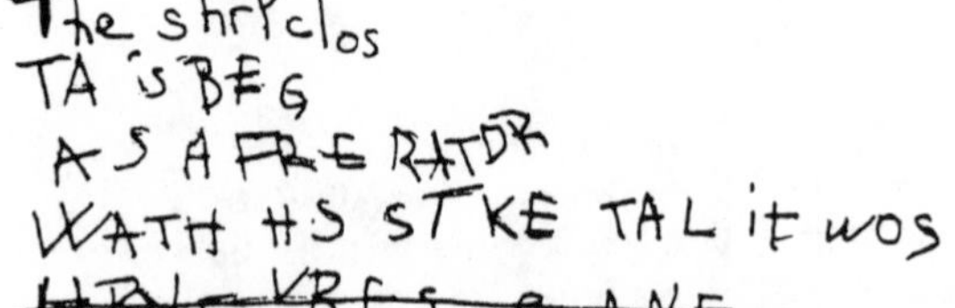

Translation:
They have sharp claws. They is big as a refriger-
ator. With his spiked tail. It was ~~herbivorous and~~
carnivorous and ate meat.

she read the book aloud. After a few minutes, she stopped, and the class recounted what they had learned and then jotted down relevant bits of information under the appropriate question headings on their papers.

This is not the only viable method for note-taking. My message is not that we must teach all students to file their notes on pages with subheadings but that we should not assume that students have effective strategies for taking notes. In my doctoral research seminar, I often ask people to share their strategies for taking notes. I find even doctoral students benefit from hearing each other's methods. Some people take notes as they proceed through a source book, perhaps indexing essential topics by writing key words in their left-hand margin. Other people prefer to use index cards, which they later sort into categories. Still others jot down page numbers and summaries of what was said on each page. The important thing is to help students realize note-taking should be more than the clerical task of copying a text. In *The Modern Researcher* (1957), Barzun and Graff emphasize that it is far more valuable to paraphrase and summarize information than to simply copy it (3). The imprint of a researcher's thinking should be evident in the notes.

Focusing one's research: early analysis of incoming information

We have all had the experience of going to the library intending to gather notes on one small topic and of finding that boundaries around that topic soon disintegrate. One topic relates to another, it encompasses yet others, and before long, we are copying down a library rather than gathering the raw materials for a research report. Barzun and Graff warn that even when people consciously try to target their research to one main point, this is not easily done. Vaguely connected information clings to a topic:

A subject does not let itself be carved away from neighboring subjects the way a butcher carves off one chop from the next. A subject is always trying to merge itself again into the great mass of associated facts and ideas (1957).

It helps researchers, therefore, to continually step back, asking, "What is it I am really learning about?" Sometimes it helps to ask, "What have I learned that is not central to my investigation?" and even to chart the answer to that question (Figure 26-3, p. 282). Sometimes it is helpful for students to stop midway in their research and attempt to put in a single sentence what it is they are studying. A word of caution: the goal must not be to maintain one's initial focus; the purpose of writing is to learn. A teacher should be far more concerned

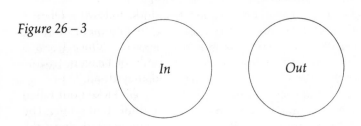

Figure 26 – 3

if students do maintain their initial direction than if they change their course in the midst of research. Nor is the goal, at this point, to be lining oneself up to write a tight, orderly, final draft. Instead, the goal now is learning. We learn by creating hierarchies, by seeing main ideas and subordinate ones, and by probing deeply into one area rather than just skirting the surface of many areas.

The problem is that if students are used to a cover-the-curriculum mentality in their classes, they will try to cover-the-topic in their research. If they are used to merely feeding back the text of the lecture in their classrooms, they will see their goal as recording rather than thinking. When students merely paraphrase or copy the resource books, we raise our eyebrows—not realizing that during the school years, students are *taught* that learning means making copies of someone else's information. Our challenge is to reverse the damage, and it is a big one.

It will help if we remember our own times of powerful learning, and allow our students' learning to be full of the interactions that have been so important to us. Is it really a surprise that children's reports sound like the resource book? Usually these writers have never *spoken* about their topic. No wonder the reports are voiceless! Realizing this, Carolyn Currier from Atkinson Elementary School asked her children to shuttle between studying their topic and teaching others what they were learning. After spending an hour in the library, youngsters found peer-conference partners and began telling them curious or important things about their topics. In these conferences, children developed personal relationships with their information. In one such conference, nine-year-old Susie heard that her friend had learned about beavers. "Imagine how you'd feel if you were a beaver," Susie said to her friend.

"I'd feel wet!" Diane answered, "and muddy. They carry mud on their tails, their strong tails scoop up mud and then splash it on the dam." Seeing Susie's interest, Diane continued, "On the side of the river there is soft mud. And they start digging and digging and sometimes water starts splurting in and their lodge overflows." Diane talked quickly, no longer needing Susie to prompt her with questions.

Susie, meanwhile, was leaning forward at her desk, following Diane's every word, nodding in affirmation. It was as if, at that moment, nothing in the world was more interesting to her than beavers. "Once I saw a thing about beavers and it was sad because a family of beavers froze," she said, and added, "We have warm houses and they don't."

"The growing up of beavers is sad, too. The babies get kicked out when they begin to grow up and it's crowded. I don't think that's fair. The adults should get kicked out," Diane said. Then Diane looked about the room, making sure no one was listening. She lowered her voice. "The mating seasons are yucky. Boy and girl beavers go into the lodge. I can't say what happens." She paused, significantly, then continued in a stage whisper. "They mate, and the female lays down and the male stands up. But beavers don't usually stand up because their head hits the top of the lodge. And the water starts to come in and the female has to move. But she's kind of heavy (if you know what I mean)." The girls giggled at this reference to the weight of pregnancy.

Susie redirected Diane's attention to the empty page. "Before you started to talk, you weren't much interested, and now you are talking and talking!" she said.

"But if I put this all down, it'll be five pages."

"Is that bad?" Susie answered, and both girls returned to their work.

Another time Wendy told Susie that she'd found a book that said raccoons don't wash their food in the water, they simply like to play in water, and this leads people to think they are washing their food. "I thought the book was wrong," she confided.

"You like the idea that they washed their food, and you had to get it into your head that they didn't," Susie said. Wendy nodded, confirming Susie's guess. Susie switched to a question. "Wen, how come raccoons hunt at night?"

"So they won't get captured by their enemies," Wendy answered, "All the raccoon has is his hands. Beavers have their teeth and their tails but raccoons don't have any weapons. In the night they don't get into fights because the other animals are sleeping."

What is happening in each of these conferences is that children are taking kernels of book information and making it their own. Barnes stresses the importance of this in his book, *From Communication to Curriculum*, in which he says, "The journey from being able to parrot a phrase from a teacher or book . . . to being able to use the idea or process to solve new problems in new areas is a long one" (Barnes 1976, 84).

The other thing that happens when children teach each other what they are learning is that this informal opportunity for data analysis provides young researchers with new directions. It directs them as they continue to gather more information. This happened, for example, when nine-year-old Birger was given the chance to tell the class about his topic. Standing in front of the class during the share meeting, Birger spoke about the grey squirrel's diet, mating habits, appearance, enemies, and so forth. The class was particularly interested, however, in a curious statement he made about how squirrels squeak when they are cold and how this saves their lives.

Diane raised her hand, "Does the squirrel squeak even if he's sleeping?"

Birger nodded, adding, "Only if his body temperature goes below forty degrees and the squeak saves his life."

"You mean he automatically squeaks?"

Birger nodded, and then Brad asked, "How does the squeak make its body temperature go up? Is it like a thermostat?"

Birger wasn't sure, and so the meeting ended with Birger promising to do more research and to report back his findings. The process, then, is one of collecting, connecting, and then collecting again; of shifting between learning, teaching, and learning. It is in this way that students develop the expertise from which they will write.

Readiness for writing

Good writing, Murray says, comes from an abundance of information. "The writer needs an inventory of facts, observations, details, images, quotations, statistics," and out of the patterns, contradictions, and relationships among these specifics, writers make ideas. Particularly when writing on topics outside their own life-experiences, our students need the time and the resources to gather this abundance of information.

Virginia Woolf describes it this way, "As for my next book, I am going to hold myself from writing it till I have it impending in me: grown heavy in my mind like a ripe pear; pendant, gravid, asking to be cut or it will fall." Our students need to postpone writing until their information begins to coalesce into ideas, and until they feel a sense of authority. Then they need to write.

We can help students become ready for writing by showing them that their task is to develop only a single aspect of their topic, to write about one corner of their information and to write for a particular audience. The notion that a report should reflect *all* that a student knows about a topic has led to a great deal of bad writing. In *any* piece of writing, the author says one thing. Kurt Vonnegut, Jr. has said, "Don't put anything in a story that does not advance the action," and the same can be said for nonfiction writing. Every line, every quotation, every reference, every piece of information builds up toward one organizing vision.

This does not mean that students must find an umbrella-idea large enough to contain all their ideas, or that they should artfully link each bit of information with the next. They must view their knowledge base as a quarry from which to mine a whole range of small, focused pieces. Eight-year-old Shanti knows a great deal about butterflies, for example, but in this particular piece her purpose is mostly to help people learn how to differentiate moths from butterflies.

SHANTI'S INSECT REPORT
BUTTERFLIES

My subject is butterflies. Ask me, I'm an expert. Those creatures we all know and love are also an important part of the blooming process. For example, bees and butterflies pollonate many various types of flowers and plants. In this way they bring more joy into our life while also nourishing their bodies.

The structure of a butterfly is very similar to a moth's, so it's very hard to distinguish whether a butterfly is a moth or whether a moth is a butterfly. But don't worry or fear. If you go out looking for a well known monarch and end up catching a luna moth, don't say I didn't tell you these tips. Listen up, because here they come!

1   *Don't believe everything people say about butterflies and moths. (But you can believe me because this is fact, if you want to get anyplace with me you have to trust me.)*

2   *Butterflies drink nectar with their wings pointing directly up while moths' wings are flat.*

3   *Butterflies have slimmer bodies than a moth's so never in your whole life will you see a fat butterfly (unless butterflies become modern!)*

4   *Butterflies don't have feathery antennae like moths do.*

When I first began writing for publication, I planned to start with a giant piece which summed up all that I knew on the topic of children and their writing. Murray suggested that instead, I break that topic into twenty possible articles and select just one. Ten-year-old Margaret did the same thing when she began writing her report on bears, except that each of Margaret's subtopics became chapter headings. She wrote ten chapters on bears—telling how to escape if a bear chases you, explaining which sorts of bears one is most likely to find in this country and so forth—and then she ended her book with two chapters on one particular "brand" of bear, the teddy bear. This is one of her chapters:

TEDDY BEARS

Treat your Teddy Bear like a real person and with care. You can take him to the park. Swing him on a swing, just don't let him fall off. Slide him down a slide. Anything you want. Just don't let him sit on a shelf. Play house. He is lovable and keeps you secure.

When you buy the bear, ask the dealer to take off his clothes. Some people bought a bear with clothes on and when they took off the clothes at home, they saw only the paws and feet had fur. This just goes to show you, you should buy the clothes after the bear.

Sometimes, especially when we don't confer with children early in their writing, they will come to us with drafts that are a hodgepodge of subtopics, as is this piece by eleven-year-old Carolyn. I find it helpful to read these pieces with an eye toward helping the writer list the subtopics.

SINGING

Eileen Quinn, who was in the role of "Annie", was well known from singing in schools and so on. Singing is my hobby, I really enjoy it. A singer is a person or a bird that sings. There are many very popular singers in the world. One excellent opera singer who is very well known from our school is Ms. Karen Williams. She sings in specials in my school. I also sing in specials: songs from Fame *and* Eye of the Tiger. *A singer has to go to a special school before they get famous. You have to be good in all subjects and you have to have special talent. My grades would have to improve and so I think if I can't be a singer I will be a nurse. Last year I met Eileen Quinn's mother and she said I have a beautiful voice. There are four different voices: Soprano, alto, tenor, and bass. Say you want to go to singing school and you can't sing for beans, you could be there for a hundred years and you still wouldn't sing well.*

After Carolyn and I reread the draft several times, we jotted down the topics she mentioned in the order she dealt with them. The list helped Carolyn see that her information could have been grouped into several chunks, and she set out to do this in a second draft. Later, she will probably think more about the structure of her piece before she begins a first draft.

Another focusing strategy, suggested by Barzun and Graff, involves writing expanded titles. As I mentioned earlier, most people begin a research report with a general topic in mind, so their titles are just labels: karate, the American presidency, fish. By lengthening the titles, writers target the direction of their reports. While "The American Presidency" allows for myriad possible directions, "The American Presidency: a Study in Personal Power" does not (Barzun and Graff 1957).

Can students consider alternative directions for their writing by listing various titles? For most ten-year-olds, will a list of possible titles represent a list of possible directions for a piece? This would require a fair amount of abstract thinking. Recently a fifth-grade teacher suggested that her students consider different titles. One of her youngsters stopped me in the hall that day to ask which title I preferred for his volcano report: "The Rolling Stones" or "The Earth Boogies Down." I laughed and left the decision in his hands. By combining the two titles, the boy produced a solution: "When the Earth Boogies Down it Turns into the Rolling Stones." I celebrated his success—but had he focused his piece or simply found a better title?

An easier strategy for focusing may be for children to draw diagrams showing what information does—and does not—relate to their topic. It is often hard for children to conceive that something they know about volcanoes does not belong in their volcano paper, but this is an important lesson.

Some children make flow charts of their research area, as Ivan has done (see Figure 26-4), and in this way they visually lay out the subtopics within their general area. Whereas primary children often make each subtopic into a chapter title, older children soon realize that even the subtopics may need to be narrowed down.

Figure 26 – 4

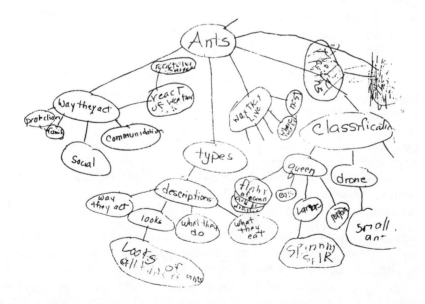

In many instances, it helps to think about point of view. Students can ask themselves, "How close up to the topic will I be? How distant from it?" For example, Douglas is writing about dog shows. He needs to ask, "Am I going to discuss dog shows in general, or am I going to focus in close and portray one dog show, or even, one dog trainer?" Point of view is one aspect of focus, and upper-elementary school children can consciously select their perspective.

Perhaps the most important way in which we can wean students from the notion that reports contain a hodgepodge of everything the author knows on a topic is to encourage them to study examples of fine nonfiction writing. For too many youngsters, the only models are the reports written by their big brothers and sisters, and the encyclopedias and textbooks upon which those reports were based. How important it is, therefore, to show them other models! Students may begin to understand that an author must select his or her point of view, when they read, for example, F. N. Monjo's *Me and Willie and Pa,* which presents a child's eye view of Lincoln as if told by his son Tad. Another book that might illustrate the author's options regarding point of view is Patricia Clapp's book, *Constance: A Story of Early Plymouth.* This book is written in a diary format and tells the story of the early settlers through the eyes of a young girl. Similarly, Jean Fritz's book, *Who's That Stepping on Plymouth Rock?,* illustrates point of view—only in this book, the story is, in effect, the biography of a rock.

The focus and design of a piece of nonfiction writing comes not only from the point of view but also from the genre. Too often, students don't see any genre options; they think they must convey their information in one long report. It may help them to see that Longfellow's information about Paul Revere is contained in a poem and that McCoy's information about the whooping crane is woven into a natural history detective story. In the same way, students can use a whole range of genres as they write about their information.

Drafts, conferences, drafts, conferences, editing, publishing

This section need not be long and detailed because my message is simply this: students must learn to use the same drafting and revision process for their nonfiction writing that they use when working in any other genre. Often, intimidated by the amount of new information, writers retreat to voiceless prose. Writing becomes little more than linking together index cards, stitching together other people's information and language.

Graves tells the story of how *he* agonized over the first draft of his Ford

Foundation report, *Balance the Basics*. "I had reams and reams of data, and the data made me feel like I had to write in a sterile, objective tone. I was suffering from an acute phase of "Dissertation Donny," he says. Then, as the story goes, Graves finally went to Murray for help, bringing with him the two overworked pages he'd managed to produce.

Murray looked at them, sighed, and said, "Wait a moment." Several minutes later he returned from the cellar with a cardboard box, some black paper, tape, and scissors. He proceeded to work for fifteen minutes, and then he handed Graves a black box with one small hole in it. "What you're to do," he said, "is to go home and put aside every single note. Then begin writing as if you were telling folks what you've learned. After each page is written, slide it through the hole, and when the paper is done, we'll open the box."

Not everyone needs a black box, but all of us and all of our students *do* need to learn how to write with voice and energy even when we work on a nonfiction text. For many students, it will help if teachers suggest, as Murray did, that first drafts need to be written without notes. The goal is fluency, voice, and an organizing image. Later the authors can reread their drafts, correcting facts, and inserting statistics and quotes. Many students will find it helpful to draft several leads before proceeding to the body of their reports. These are some of the leads which fourth graders wrote:

A beam of sunlight shone through the crack in the red foxes den. The fox opened his eyes just a slit and looked around his den. It was a cozy stump . . .

Amy

In the stillness of the dark, a 170–200 pound St. Bernard lay on its side, curled to fit on the mat. Looking at him, I wondered if he was dreaming about long winters of rescuing lost travelers. Just that year he'd dug some out with his huge paws, licking their face afterwards to keep them warm.

Hope

The boat started with a sputter as I, Celia Thaxter, and my family left for the Isles of Shoals . . . I couldn't wait to see the island we would live on. Nearer and nearer we came until . . .

Melissa

Eric's lead led him to write his book with a particular slant. Rather than reporting on all he knew (or thought he knew) about health, he decided he would model his writing after other texts he'd seen on the topic. This is the result:

HEALTH TIPS
by Eric (age 7)

1 *Introduction*

You have just seen the title on the cover of Eric Chen's first book. If healthy bodies are important to you, then this book could have value to you. This new book defines what a health tip is and tells the basic health tips people must know in order to be in great shape. After all, a healthy body makes you have a longer life. So if you were already convinced health is great, you must be convinced that this book is very good!

2 *What is a Health Tip?*

"Welcome to the World of Health!"

A health tip is a statement that helps you live. It helps you have a slim, healthy body. And it makes you grow.

Health tips usually come in books, magazines, and even in newspapers. If you see a title called, "Ms. Honey Hart's way to Be Slim," or "The Book of Life," you will find a health tip.

Health tips can serve you. But be careful. And you had better use them correctly. So always use health tips right. Health is great. Make it better with health tips!

3 *Every Health Tip I Can Give You.*

A. When going to a restaurant, get something you like. Check it out. See if it is good for you. Is the food healthy? It should be natural, not have too much sugar, nor have too much food coloring. Otherwise, leave the restaurant and buy foods at a supermarket.

B. Are you taking a shower and washing your hair with shampoo and conditioner? You're doing some for health! Cleaning your hair and washing daily has been healthy as told in a report made by government health experts. It is good to protect your hair and help it grow. Washing your hair? Keep it up!

4 *About the Author.*

Eric Chen is an 8-year-old boy. He is a native of New York City. He loves to write because it is his flair. Mister Chen and his friend, Basil, had just published the Dumont weekly newspaper. Mr. Chen has a whole collection of comic books like SuperDog or the X-Men. His favorite title is the Mighty Avengers. All other things, he says, are personal.

While Eric's report involved writing only one draft, some children spend a great deal of time drafting and revising their reports. In *Lessons from a Child* I tell about how Susie, for example, went from very rough work such as the sample shown on Figure 26-5 (which was abandoned midway) to the draft that follows it (Figure 26-6, pp. 292–293).

Figure 26 – 5

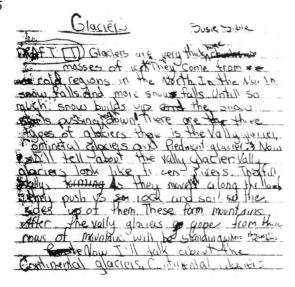

Figure 26 – 6

Susie Sille
The Beginning Of A Glacier

In the cold northern regions, snow falls. More and more snow falls. After many, many years, something amazing starts to form. So much snow fell and turned to ice, the ice got so heavy and big the great weight of it began pushing itself along. This huge ice chunk starts creeping into a valley. That is probably how this glacier got its name. Other glaciers are the Continental and the Piedmont glaciers. But this glacier's name is the Valley glacier.

Making Mountains

As the Valley glacier moves along it pushes dirt and rock out from the sides of it. These huge mounds of dirt and rock form mountains. It would take a long time to make mountains because glaciers travel only about seven hundred to a thousand feet a year. Thats not even a mile!

Melting Away

The melting of a glacier is done at the end of a glacier not at the beginning. The beginning of a glacier is where the glacier was formed in the north. In the north it is mostly cold. Thats why it melts at the end. In the middle of a glacier it will melt. How much it melts all depends on the weather of that year. If it was a mild, and warm lots of melting will take place. But if it was cold and stormy not as much melting will happen in the middle. When glaciers cover a spot then melt away a lake or river might be where the glacier was. The river or lake is water that melted from the glacier.

<u>What Glaciers Left Behind</u>

Do you know how the Great Lakes were made? They were made by glaciers. Probably when the glaciers started melting they left huge pools of water behind them. I really never knew how big lakes such as the Great Lakes were made. Did you?

27

poetry

"Think of an image, Lucy. Let a powerful image come to mind."

I thought very hard, my face scrunched, my mind grasping for something which would qualify as a powerful image. "Nothing, Georgia. I don't think in images, I'm lousy at description. See, I told you I can't write poetry."

"You can, you've just decided that you can't."

"Okay, I'll try again," I said, and this time I thought, "An image? of what? our house? my dog?" Then, remembering a poem I'd written long ago at a workshop, I seized upon that image. "I've got one, Georgia," and I told her about how I rode a motorcycle when I taught in England.

"Okay, make a picture in your mind and tell me what you see."

I cleared my throat and began. "Down the road / I go. / Greyness around me. / The air, lushness melting into greys. . . ."

Georgia was quiet for a moment. "Lucy," she said, "Can I ask you a question. How come you say it so, so funny-like. 'Down the road / I go . . .' Why don't you say it in a more regular way?"

I was stunned. "But then what would make it into poetry?" We talked for four hours that evening, and although I still had not written a poem when we left the restaurant late that night, I had made one of the wisest decisions I was to make all year. Somehow, I would find a way for Georgia Heard to join the team of researchers, teachers, and teacher-trainers who were working with me. A few weeks later, the Spencer Foundation funded me to study how teachers learn, and immediately I phoned Georgia with an invitation to join our team.

A tall, slender woman, Georgia wears full blouses, vests, and loose cotton trousers. I met her when she was a student in Columbia's Masters of Fine Arts in poetry program and a poet-in-residence in schools. For eight months, Georgia helped Marilyn Boutwell and me in our study of how teachers develop as teachers of writing. The three of us observed Shelley Harwayne as she worked with teachers and, because we wanted to study teacher-training from the perspective of the recipients, we gathered case-study data on the teachers with whom she worked. We tried to crawl inside the teachers' skins, to know what it was like to have someone coaching them on their teaching. We didn't intend to study the teaching of poetry. It was one of those things which evolved unexpectedly.

Although Georgia had worked as a resident poet in classrooms throughout the Northeast, she had never seen anything like the writing process classrooms throughout New York City. "The children are writing exactly the way I write," she said. "Their insights on writing are unbelievable." As a live-in researcher in these classrooms, Georgia learned not only *about* the teachers, she also learned *from* them. She noticed everything, commenting on the way Shelley used her hands to quiet children, and how she drew the class in to listen to what she was saying. Once Georgia mentioned that Shelley spoke the same way I do. "Neither of you chatters. Every word counts for you and your tone commands attention. It says 'listen carefully, this is important.' "

Of course, as a poet, every word had always counted for Georgia. People listened to her. When she noted that few children in our classrooms were writing poetry, and worse, few were using imagery in their prose, I listened carefully. "They are comfortable writing about events sequenced in time and about information," Georgia said to me, "but they are less comfortable writing about images and associations. The poetic aspects of their writing haven't been developed." Georgia felt strongly that there should be more poetry in the classrooms, even for the sake of the prose.

I knew why it wasn't there. Without meaning to do so, I'd created classrooms in my own image. Georgia was right, of course, so once most of our data on teaching teachers had been gathered, I encouraged Georgia to take a detour from the research and to bring poetry into some of our best writing classrooms. I watched—and marveled at what I saw.

Because her ultimate purpose was to teach teachers rather than children, Georgia began by spending an hour with a cluster of interested teachers from P. S. 230. The meeting started slowly. Georgia first listed four characteristics of poetry:

1 Poetry uses condensed language. Every word is important.
2 Usually the language of poetry is figurative. It contains simile, metaphor, and imagery.
3 Poetry is rhythmical.

4 Just as the units of organization in prose are the sentence and paragraph, the units of organization for poetry are the line and the stanza.

The list had many limitations, so Georgia balanced this first definition of poetry with a second, more poetic one:

If I read a book and it makes my whole body so cold no fire can ever warm me, I know that is poetry.

Emily Dickinson

Out of a quarrel with others we make rhetoric, out of a quarrel with ourselves we make poetry.

Yeats

Poetry is the spontaneous overflow of powerful feelings recollected in tranquillity.

Wordsworth

Although she had spent fifteen minutes on defining poetry, Georgia had not yet mentioned the terms many of us most associate with poems: rhyme, haiku, sonnet, ballad. Georgia explained that in poetry there are two camps, the formalists, who teach and write poetry in terms of fixed forms, and the free verse poets, who find their forms in the rhythm and content of what they are saying. Georgia belongs to the latter camp, and she believes it is easier for children to begin with free verse. "If the fixed forms were to come first," she said, "it would be like, in September, teaching children that their narratives must contain two paragraphs, with nine sentences in each one, and that six of the sentences must begin with an article, and two with a proper noun. Think what that would do to the writing." She continued, "Children would spend their time trying to remember and to follow the rules, and they'd lose the urgency of what they had to say. They would get the wrong idea of what it means to write."

Georgia's point, I noticed, was not that form is unimportant, nor that fixed forms don't belong in the elementary grades. She was only saying that an early emphasis on fixed forms can distort what it means to write poetry. It was a convincing argument, but I wondered if the children would have better luck with free verse than I had had.

My question was soon answered, not so much by the rest of the workshop as by what Georgia did the next day when she launched Rose Napoli's class. Although most of Rose's children had begun the year reading well below grade level, they had become enthusiastic readers and writers. They did not, however, have positive feelings toward poetry, so Georgia decided to address this issue head-on. She told the children that she'd recently gone into a classroom and introduced herself as a poet, only to find the children sticking out their tongues at her and rolling their eyes. "I didn't think it was me," she said, "and so I figured it was poetry they didn't like." Then Georgia asked these children whether they felt the same way. About a third of the class, the students who had written silly nonsense poetry that year, said poetry was OK, it was easy. The others hated it. "It's boring," they told Georgia. "It's for girls." "It is too hard to understand."

"Poetry is for rich people, it's for snobs," Vanessa said and then explained, "They are talking above us and about us. They don't want us to understand."

Georgia's quiet attention during all this seemed to dissipate the negative views on poetry. The children were warming toward Georgia, if not toward her subject. Some even moved visibly closer as she began quietly telling them about her poetry. "For me, poems have to be about something that is *so* important to me, I need to have a physical feeling of that topic inside me." Then she explained, "You know how when you are scared, really scared, you can feel it in your body, or when you are so, so happy, and your body sings? Well, when I have a physical feeling like that about my topic, I know I have a poem."

No one giggled and no one rolled their eyes. Instead, the thirty-six adolescents, most of them boys, listened spellbound. Georgia continued speaking in her honest, serious way, commanding their attention by giving them hers. "Feelings are the source of a poem, but you can't just write the feelings onto paper," she said. "Instead of trying to tell the reader my feelings, I go back in my mind's eye and locate the feeling in specific, concrete things that we see and hear. I get a picture in my mind and then re-create that picture so the reader can feel what I felt."

Listening to Georgia, I was reminded of a description of poetry that dates back to the eleventh century:

Poetry presents the thing in order to convey the feeling. It should be precise about the thing and reticent about the feeling, for as soon as the mind connects with the thing the feeling shows in the words; this is how poetry enters deeply into us.

Author unknown

Georgia had brought the drafts of her poem, "Oldfields," and she told the children that the poem began when she was sitting at work, and she had an image of how, as a little girl, she'd gone into woods with a spoon to dig up an Indian grave her grandfather had shown her. "I kept the picture in my mind until I got home and then, concentrating on the image, I wrote and wrote and wrote, just trying to get the image and the feeling onto paper, not worrying if it was good." Then, after Georgia had put away the draft, other images came to mind, somehow connected to the first. "I put them down too, the images of my grandfather walking around in his now empty house, and of the clocks he always loved, ticking in that empty house." She added, "I didn't interpret or explain how the images were connected. I never explain in my poems, I just present the images and trust the subtle connections will be there."

I was sure Georgia was talking over the children's heads, but the children didn't seem to think so. Their attention was, if anything, growing stronger. I have since come to suspect that part of Georgia's power was her implicit belief that the children could understand poetry, in all its subtlety. They may not have followed everything she said, but they did feel it's magic, and they sensed the seriousness and authenticity of it. It made them feel important, and it made them take poetry seriously. "Read your poem to us," they said. Georgia read her second draft, in which three images were combined and the lines were divided so they looked like poetry:

OLDFIELDS

1

I went out to see the Indian grave
my grandfather told me about
at the edge of the woods
near the burning field.

I picked off the leaves and stones
that covered the mound
and dug all afternoon
until the woods grew dark
and the kitchen light of the house
behind me came on.

I expected to find jewels,
pots and arrows
or an Indian headdress
with feathers on it.

Except for the dirt
that filtered through my hands,
the grave was empty.

2

I am standing near the wall
at the edge of the burning field.
I see my grandfather
walk around the rooms
of the empty summer house.
He has been dead for years.
Hunched over, thin as air
he walks a path from the kitchen
through the dining room.

3

Years ago,
up the front staircase
in my bedroom in the summer house
I lay in bed awake
listening for the clock
downstairs to strike midnight.
I saw the spirits fly out of the clock
like black smoke going up a fan.

4

In the living room
the grandfather clock
is still ticking.

Any hour now,
it will break into chime.

When Georgia finished reading, there was a silence. Then the children had questions. "Did you use particular writing strategies," Michelle asked and Georgia answered that concentrating on the image was a strategy, as was free writing, and that there were other strategies she'd tell them about in future mini-lessons. One youngster commented that "Oldfields" was like a story, and when Georgia explained it was a narrative poem, the boy wanted to know how narrative poems were different from stories. This led into a discussion of the characteristics of poetry. When Diana asked whether Georgia had used set rhythms, Georgia told the children, as she had told the teachers, about formalist and free verse poets. "I am a free verse poet," she said. "I know I have rhythm in my voice and often, after my first draft, I go back and find that rhythm. Usually, for me, one line has three beats but this rhythm is set from inside of me. If you write a lot of poetry, you'll find your own rhythm."

By then, it was time to write. Georgia reminded the children where poetry comes from and urged them not to censor their first drafts. Soon the room was filled with a workshop hum.

In her conferences that day, Georgia helped children put their images onto paper. "Between their mental image and the writing, something often happens," she explained to me. "I think it has to do with their conception of poetry." Some of the children were using the same "funny language" that I had used in my poem. Hasun's draft was filled with "thee" and "thou," and he used the verb "wept" rather than "cried." Georgia asked him to close his eyes, and when Hasun told her what he saw, she wrote it down. Then she showed him there was poetry in his natural voice.

That strategy didn't work for every child. Jeffrey, for example, described his mental picture by saying, "One day last summer I went fishing and

I was with my Dad and went in a tiny boat. . . ." His voice lacked the urgency and immediacy of poetic language; there was a once-removed quality to it.

Georgia said, "Jeffrey, I want to try something with you that I often do with myself when I want to write a poem. Would you pretend that I'm your best friend and you've just come rushing into the room, and you are telling me, quickly, about the fishing . . . blurt it out to me, what you would say."

This time Jeffrey's beginning was more immediate and it had the makings of a poem. "We went fishing, Dad and me, in this tiny boat. Thousands of fish were splashing around. . . ." Georgia later helped Jeffrey break his sentences into lines and stanzas, and soon he had a draft of a poem:

We went fishing,
Dad and me, in a tiny boat.
Thousands of fish were splashing . . .

Tara's first draft seemed contrived, as if her concept of poetry was getting in her way:

Riding my bike down the hill,
I saw headstones
and a beautiful sky.

In their conference, Georgia asked Tara to bring to mind the picture and then to talk about it. As Tara talked, Georgia interrupted once or twice, softly asking questions that elicited more details. Tara's next draft had more natural language and she had added the image of a gate and the smell of freshly cut grass:

TARA—DRAFT 2

I ride down the hill
I look across
I see a black gate
and lots of headstones.
The freshly cut grass fills my nose
I see a beautiful sky
of pink
blue
and white

I stop. . . .

Am I looking at the sky
or is the sky looking at me?

Georgia took the papers home that night and read through them, looking especially to see whether the children were writing on topics that they took seriously. She found that Rose's class was off to a good start, but that many of the fifth graders in the "talented and gifted" class across the hall were still writing about unicorns and rainbows. Many of them were avoiding important topics, and some were writing quick, silly poems such as Devon's poem, "Lunch."

These peas are fit for a dog!
The stew is swamped in a fog!
Oh no! I reached for the chicken in the back
and the ugly lady gave me a smack.
I swear, in the spaghetti I saw a rat.
That ain't soup I'm looking at.

Georgia spent her second day in this classroom emphasizing the need for important topics. She read poetry to the children and discussed the problem she found in many of their papers. Many of the children agreed that their concern for rhyme sometimes made them forget what they wanted to say. As one child put it, "You lose your mind, all you think about is rhyming the words."

Rose Napoli's children were, for the most part, taking poetry very seriously, so during her second day with them, Georgia talked about revision. She again began the mini-lesson with her own poem, this time telling the children that after she got down the three images, she read through the poem and knew it wasn't finished. "The feeling didn't seem to come across," she said. "Poetry has to hit a person right in the heart or it won't work." The children once again listened with great care to what she said. "If some of your poems don't work, then you have to ask whether you are committed enough to your topic. If you are, what I do is close my eyes again, get the image, and then free write, only this time my first draft has given me a headstart." Georgia ended the meeting by reading Philip Levine's poem, "Starlight," aloud to the class, letting it cast a spell over the room. Georgia read the poem twice, and when she finished, she sent the children off to their own writing. She spoke in whispers and the children did too, as if none of them wanted to break the mood. Georgia's first conference was with Ying.

"This poem I wrote, this doesn't have that much feeling in it," Ying said, her voice so soft I could hardly hear it. "There is another feeling I get but I can't put it into words. It is when I get home from school and I am changing my clothes. I don't know what it is, but it is in my stomach. I can't put it into words."

"You can say just that, Ying," Georgia replied, touching the child's arm as she spoke. "You can say, 'I can't put it into words, this feeling that is in my stomach,' and then you can explore the feeling."

Later that day, Ying came to us with a poem in hand saying, "I want to know if you get a feeling when you hear it." Figure 27-1 is what we heard.

"I got the feeling, Ying, it was a very strong feeling. It was a feeling of anxiety."

Ying nodded. She started to leave us, then stopped and hesitantly said, "I get the same feeling when my brother and father fight, and when my grandfather died." By the time Ying left the conference, she had learned that, just as Georgia put several images into "Oldfields," she could combine the images of her father and brother fighting, and of her grandfather's death, with the feeling she had after school. Back at her desk, Ying began to write, adding lines onto her initial draft:

I see my mother trying to separate my father and brother
It feels like dying, to have a terrible family.
I ask the holy heaven for help
But I get no answer
I'm falling . . .

Inna had written only four lines (Figure 27-2) and she didn't know what else to write.

Instead of conferring with Inna, Georgia asked Tara if she would help.

Figure 27 – 1

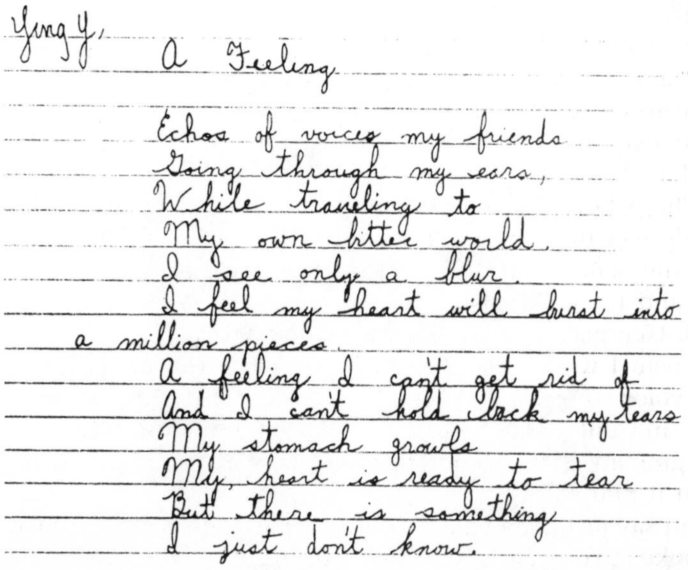

By now, many of the children had picked up the pattern in Georgia's conferences. "Make a picture with your mind," Tara said to her friend. "What do you see?" Figure 27-3 shows the draft that resulted.

Figure 27 – 2

A raspberry bush   Inna

As I looke out the window
I saw a bird on a raspberry bush
As bright as a rainbow
She sang like a grasshoper plays

Figure 27 – 3

Raspberry Eyes

As I looked out,
the window,
I saw a bird,
stare at me.

In the background
there was a fence
standing around
a raspberry bush.

The bird's eyes were,
bright red.
With a brownish dot,
in the center
of the eye.

All of a sudden
I compared.
The bird's eyes
With the raspberry bush

I came closer

to see it better
The bird perished.
Far away in the sky

All I remember,
is the raspberry
eyes.

I was looking for it
Days and Day's

But there was,
only one thing
left to do

To forget it

by Inna

A few children had a difficult time finding topics and getting started. When we reached Robert, he was sitting with his face in his hands, staring at the blank page. "Spelling and poetry are my worst subjects," he said, and when we asked why poetry was hard, Robert explained, "In a poem, you don't have facts or dialogue or setting. All you have is description and I can't write adjectives." Georgia asked him to wait, then she returned with her Norton anthology. Leafing through it, she found a Frost poem. It was almost entirely dialogue, and it had setting and characters. The conference ended with Robert realizing he might write a poem that was different from everyone else's in the room, perhaps one filled with dialogue, and that he could then help the others learn about new kinds of poetry. A day later Robert proudly brought his poem to us. I asked whether poetry and spelling were still his worst subjects and Robert shook his head. "No, just spelling is."

When children gathered for the share meeting at the end of that day, Georgia suggested that they listen for three things:

1   The overall image—was it clear?
2   Did they get a strong feeling? What was it?
3   What strategies did the author use in writing the poem?

Margaret, a youngster who reads several years below her grade level, was the first to share. Her poem (Figure 27-4) prompted Rose Napoli to

---

Figure 27 – 4

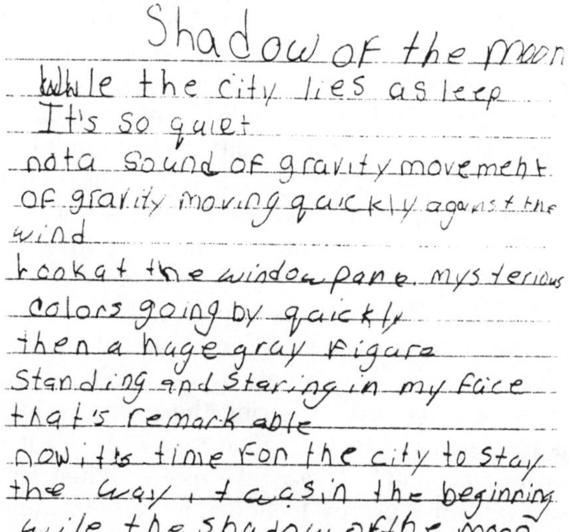

Shadow of the moon

While the city lies asleep
It's so quiet
not a sound of gravity movement
of gravity moving quickly against the wind
Look at the window pane. mysterious
colors going by quickly
then a huge gray figure
Standing and staring in my face
that's remarkable
now it's time for the city to stay
the way it was in the beginning
wile the shadow of the moon
Falls upon the earth

- Margaret

comment later, "Poetry is a great equalizer: all of the children can excel at it." Listening to Margaret, I couldn't help but agree.

But it was Chi Fai's poem which impressed me most of all. Chi Fai had come to this country from Hong Kong just a few months before the school year began, and at the beginning of the year he wrote English with some difficulty. Although his command of the language had improved immensely over the year, he had never seemed comfortable with writing—until now. This was the poem he read that day:

WONDERS OF SLEEP

When I close my restful eye to sleep
I feel like I am in an adventure world
that man has never seen before.
When I am in deep sleep, I feel like
Black Magic has been cast over me.
The next morning it fades into thin air
and the Black Magic
Passes onto the family.
And I hope there is going to be another time
for this wonderful adventure.

Chi Fai was pleased with the poem. "Last night I read it, and it sounded right, and it makes me want to write more. I want to be a poem-maker," he said. "When I read it last night I heard a laughing sound, it made me cover my blanket over my head. After that I felt numb."

I asked Chi Fai whether poetry was easier for him than the writing he'd been doing all year and he nodded. "In my regular writing, I don't do so good. I can't describe it, I can't write it. I just don't have the feelings to write it." Then Chi Fai tried to explain. "I could never get a lot of details in my regular writing. It is like the writing is just a noun: a person, place, or thing. The poetry, I can understand. It is different, it is not like a TV program."

I nodded and said, "The poetry is important to you, isn't it?" Chi Fai said, "I gotta write, I gotta express. I can't see it all at once. In the back of my head, you have the words and if you don't get them down fast they'll disappear." He paused, fingering the poem he had just written. "This poem is fragile. I got to take good care of it, I got to express it." Touching the draft, he said, "This is like tissue. When I write it out too hard, it breaks up, and then my feelings just fade away." I wasn't sure what Chi Fai was telling me, but I was moved . . . and impressed.

Georgia decided the children were ready to take another step. The next day she introduced the concept of form. "There are two aspects to a poem:

the content, which we've talked about, and the structure. After I have written a draft and sometimes during the drafting, I think about the structure of my poem. Just like buildings have architecture—some are tall and thin, some are short and wide—poems also have to be built according to a design which works."

Georgia began with the issue of line breaks. She told the children that her first drafts often look prose-like but that afterward, she rereads the drafts aloud, adding slashes at the places where her voice naturally pauses. "Then I type it up and see how it looks and hear how it sounds," she said. Usually it isn't right and so I do it again and again, making the lines longer and smoother, or shorter, more punctuated."

Georgia, wanting the children to understand that the form can reinforce the content, gave the words of "The Red Wheelbarrow" to the children and asked them to divide the poem into lines. Some divided it like this:

so much depends upon
a red wheelbarrow
glazed with rain water
beside the white chickens.

Others had different ideas, but none of them spread the poem out as the author had done.

THE RED WHEELBARROW

so much depends
upon

a red wheel
barrow

glazed with rain
water

beside the white
chickens.

   William Carlos Williams

In talking about Williams's decision, the children could see that the line breaks reinforced the author's message. They then looked at two ways Whitman could have divided lines in "Song of Myself," and tried to guess which he had chosen. Most of the children were able to see—and hear—that the second version was a more joyful one, and that it was more appropriate for Whitman's message:

SONG OF MYSELF

1

I celebrate
myself,

and sing
myself,

and what I
assume

you shall assume.

SONG OF MYSELF

1

I celebrate myself, and sing myself,
and what I assume you shall assume,
For every atom belonging to me as good belongs to you.

Walt Whitman

Then the children looked at other poems and began to sense the different visual effects an author could create, and to see that creating a structure is part of creating a poem.

Georgia's first conference that day was with Kim. "I don't like my poem," Kim announced, pushing the paper toward her.

"Why don't you like it?"

"There are too many 'frees.'" Kim read a stanza aloud to illustrate the problem. Each line began with "Free . . ." and this repetition held the poem together.

Instead of responding individually to Kim, Georgia asked the class if they would put down their pencils, and then she told the whole group about Kim's dilemma, explaining, "It doesn't have to be a problem because in some poems, and even in some prose, repetition is an important part of the text's structure." She told the children that using the same word in every line was a technique called parallelism, that it started with the Bible and the Psalms. After a few minutes of discussion, she let the class return to their work.

Kim understood, she said, but she still thought the poem sounded funny with so many "frees." Georgia accepted her judgment, and we moved on. Joseph was writing about Mars and had decided that instead of repeating a word he would repeat the first four lines. "They are the most important lines," he said. "If I tell them at the beginning and at the end, they will stay in people's minds."

Next we listened as Michelle discussed the poem she had just finished with Thyessa. "I've worked on it for four days, and that's about fifteen minutes a word," Michelle said. "I like it, but it goes by too fast. Nobody will notice my words." The girls wanted us to solve their problem, but we assured them they could find a solution, and they did, as is evident in the difference between Michelle's third draft and her final one (Figure 27-5).

The energy in the classroom that day was tangible. Several children were frenetically copying and recopying their poems, trying them first in quatrains, then in couplets. Some banged away at the old typewriter Rose had brought from home. A few children had thesauruses on their desks, and they searched through them for the best possible words. Others looked through anthologies of poetry, comparing their own work with the poems in the book. Many children wrote silently, earnestly. Still others listened to a friend's poem. Everyone was talking poetry, writing poetry, and listening to poetry.

Hasun asked if I'd listen to his poem, and when I said yes, he surprised me by walking several feet away from me and, standing very straight, he read the poem just as Georgia had read hers. I thought the poem was worthy of this ceremony (see Figure 27-6).

In the share meeting that day, Morat asked the class for help. "I don't have enough description," he said, and read through his first draft (Figure 27-7).

Figure 27 – 5

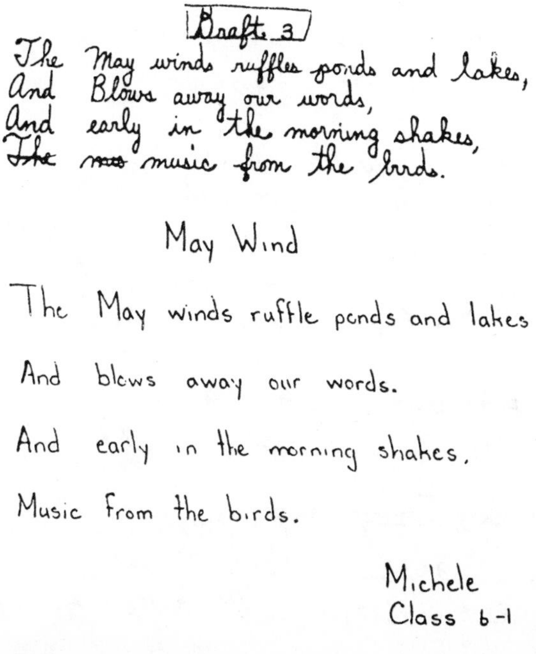

Draft 3

The May winds ruffles ponds and lakes,
And Blows away our words,
And early in the morning shakes,
The music from the birds.

May Wind

The May winds ruffle ponds and lakes

And blews away our words.

And early in the morning shakes,

Music from the birds.

Michele
Class 6-1

Figure 27 – 6

The Victory Bread.

Three blue birds.
Weres at my window
Fighting for a piece of bread.

I ran to the kitchen
got fat two pieces of bread
I went two the window

Two were dead
And one lied on the bread
The two had dead in a fight

For a old piece of stale bread
The winner died there
Closed eye and bare

On The Victory Bread!

Figure 27 – 7

In the sky I see a Bird
it's coming down

what should I do
no time to think

I got to get her
I got you little fellow

why did you Fall
to Be ~~~~~~ with me

~~~~~~~~~~~~
I gess I'll never know
But know I'll take Home

Tara raised her hand. "I think it was good, I could see it. I saw an eagle and a mountain, and the eagle was flying over the mountain."

Robert interrupted. "No, I see you walking in the woods."

Morat held his head, as if dizzy from his classmates' comments. "Whoa, hold it. It wasn't in the wood or the mountains, it was in a grassy plain. It wasn't an eagle, it was a bluebird."

"Why didn't you say that?"

"I didn't know until now." The next day, Morat produced another draft, and this one made the image clearer (see Figure 27-8).

Georgia was pleased with what she had begun in Room 413, and she felt confident that with a little help, Rose could now take over the poetry workshop. That afternoon, Rose and Georgia spent a few hours thinking about possible mini-lessons. The next day it was Rose who gathered the children together.

Rose had decided that for a few days, her mini-lessons would be very simple ones. The children were already juggling a huge amount of new information, and she didn't want them to focus more on technique than on their content. For her first mini-lesson, Rose read Stafford's poem, "Traveling Through the Dark." The poem is a sad one, and Rose read it well. It seemed to me that some of the children were teary-eyed when Rose finished reading it. The children began talking, first about the subject of the poetry and then about the author's choice of words. One youngster noticed how Stafford used tiny details such as "By the glow of the taillight"

Figure 27 – 8

Shkandin

I'm lying on the grass plains.
I see a Bird!
It's circaling above me.
it's a beautiful Bird
It's Blue Like the sky
it's hard to see her in the sun
"oh no"
It's Falling
I got to get it
I got you little Fellow
your safe
"I wonder why you Fell
could it Be Because of me"
"it no matter as longest ve are together
don't Be scared I won't leave you
we will Be together little Fellow.

to convey the general information that they were driving behind another car. Then Rose gave each child his or her own copy of the poem, and suggested they scatter around the room and take turns reading it aloud to each other. All through the room, clusters of children pored over the poem. Some read it quickly, others slowly. They compared their pauses and wrestled with meaning. In retrospect, Georgia, Rose, and I realize that poetry, like the score of a musical piece, is meant to be presented. We could have done a great deal more with having children read aloud their favorite poems. The children could have organized choral readings of poetry—their own, or someone else's—and the unit could have ended with a poetry reading. There will be other opportunities.

Later the children would tell me how much Stafford's poem "Traveling Through the Dark," had influenced them. When Morat wrote, "I wish I had a friend / who cared for me / Who loved to spend some time with me / Who stuck up for me in a shyish way," he told me that the sad, touching feelings in his poem came from Stafford's poem. Jung told me that "Traveling Through the Dark" taught him about poetry. "I learned that in a poem, you can get all these feelings out in a little bit of words, like you have mystery in one word."

Another day Rose began the workshop by asking her young writers to tell the others about their writing process: what they had been doing and what they planned to do next. Some children reported that they were turning their poems into songs. Others were on their second or third poem. Several had left poetry and were working on fiction or personal narratives. Most, however, were still deeply immersed in their first poem: drafting, re-visioning, sharing with friends, rewriting, refining.

The next mini-lesson was particularly effective. Rose read Gwendolyn Brooks' poem, "We Real Cool" to the class, and as she read it the children laughed . . . until she reached the last line.

THE POOL PLAYERS.
SEVEN AT THE GOLDEN SHOVEL.

We real cool. We
Left school. We

Lurk late. We
Strike straight. We

Sing sin. We
Thin gin. We

Jazz June. We
Die soon.

There was a hush over the room.

"At first it seemed like a funny poem, but the ending makes it sad," Hasun said.

"Yeah, the last line changes everything," the others agreed.

Marsha quietly said, "That's how a poem is, everything has to fit like a puzzle, all the pieces fitting together, and if you change one thing the whole poem is changed."

The children began thinking a great deal about endings, and their focus on endings helped them grasp the notion of form. "When I write my poems," Michelle said, "every line has a meaning in it and then at the end, the closing lines tie in with all the meanings of the other lines. See, poems have to have something to cover the whole thing with, something has to hold it all together."

I think the most powerful lesson about endings—and indirectly, about form—came not during the mini-lesson but during the share time when Omope and Gregory read their poems aloud (see Figures 27-9 and 27-10), and the children saw the power of their endings. After this, Rose was careful to include the children's own pieces in mini-lessons as well as in share meetings.

<u>C</u>lowns

When I see clowns they make me
feel like I'm a giggling hyena
because they make
me laugh so much
As I see them I think
I'm in another world
A world that is full
of clowns
And clowns spinning in my head
Saying "Be one,
be a clown." But my mouth
says, no
No No No No
I don't want to be a
Clown.

Figure 27 – 9

by Omope

Figure 27 – 10

as I strold through the
open alleway lonking at the
Stars above that gleam happily
I stare down at debris
below me in disgust
Knowing that some day
I will reach the stars

Gregory

When Cindy finished her poem, "The Mirror," that day's mini-lesson focused on the poem. Cindy is tall for her age, and presents herself as tough and cynical, although she is actually quite the opposite. Her poem is reproduced as Figure 27-11.

The Mirror

I stare at the face,

I see mean eyes, tight look.

Whose face is it?

I turn my head   *Figure 27 – 11*

and realize the face is mine.

Cindy

The class was stunned by what Cindy had written, and for a long while they responded to the content of it. Then, with an overhead projector, Rose displayed the poem and asked the class to think about Cindy's use of the white space. The spaces make the reader pause, and this nudges a reader to *do*, in our mind's eye, what Cindy has said. "I stare at my face," she writes, and in our minds we stare at a face. "I see mean eyes . . ." and we picture those eyes. "I turn my head . . ." and in the pause provided by the white space, we turn our heads, "and realize the face is mine." It would have been an entirely different poem had Cindy written it like this:

THE MIRROR

I stare at the face,
I see mean eyes, tight look.
Whose face is it?
I turn my head and realize the face is mine.

My last day in the poetry workshop was June 13. It was a hot, sticky day. The children had all worn shorts and T-shirts, and their clothes stuck to their damp skin. We all felt sweaty, yet somehow this added to the mood. Everywhere writers toiled over their drafts. The classroom felt, sounded, smelled like a newsroom. Many of the children were still working on their poetry. Six or eight were compiling a book of poems to give to the principal, several others were typing up final drafts, and still others were into new poems. When Morat saw me, he motioned for me to come over when I had a chance. When I got to him, Morat handed me a little scrap of paper. "It's a poem in Russian," he whispered, not wanting to distract the others.

At the end of that workshop, Rose told the class that Morat had brought something special for the share meeting. Morat sat in the author's chair, looking very shy and embarrassed, and in Russian, he read a poem he'd brought with him when he moved to America. He read it several times, and the class marveled at the sound of the poem. "It's so beautiful it hardly matters that we don't know the meaning," they said. Again and again the class listened to it, admiring its sounds. Watching all of this, I thought of how embarrassed Morat had been, at the start of the year, about the Russian language. "It's the worst punishment in the world when my parents make me practice my Russian," he had told me, and now, here he was, reciting this beautiful Russian poem to all his friends, and sharing their pleasure over the sound of his language. Later, Morat would translate the poem into English, struggling with the issues any translator knows. Before the year ended, other children would bring in poems from their countries. Watching all of this and thinking back to it now, I have an unbelievably strong response to the entire poetry workshop.

The feeling is a physical one. In my stomach, I have such a feeling of pride and warmth, such a sense of "God, is this ever important," that I almost feel ready to write a poem.

28

teaching fiction and learning the essentials of our craft

"Fiction is easy. You just get an idea and write it out. It doesn't matter what you put because it's not real."

"I think up a crazy title like *Mystery of the Blue Popcorn* and then I make up a weird story to go with it. I put down the opposite of the truth. I tell a lie in the story."

These third graders—Carmella and Jerome— are members of a very fine writing classroom. For several years now they have drafted and revised their writing, conferring with each other and with themselves. Yet their concept of fiction seems distorted and their pieces of fiction echo that distortion. This is Carmella's story:

> *It was a dark, cool night.*
> *"Come on, Theresa. Move those legs of yours," I said.*
> *"I'm coming, don't rush me," she said. She was about four feet and five inches tall and had shiny brown hair.*
> *"If you don't hurry, my fist is going to be in your mouth," I yelled. We had to go to the store to play the Lotto before it closed.*
> *It was 10:10 pm at night. Me and Theresa were watching the Lottery. We looked at the cards and by the numbers of them, I saw that we won. "Oh my God!" I yelled. "We won the lottery!"*
> *We ran home. "The first thing I'm going to buy is two mink coats," Theresa said. The end.*

I read the story twice, shrugged, and then read another. Jerome's piece was equally problematic—and equally typical:

One day I was coming out of MacDonalds and I saw a car crash into a lady. The blood was gushing everywhere. Bullets zoomed past me. Screams filled the air. I dropped my hamburger, I was so scared. Then I saw the criminal. I ran and ran and ran after him until he was caught for good.

THE END

When Carmella and Jerome's teacher, Mrs. Cohen, asked me what she could say in a conference that would improve these drafts, I didn't have an answer. I suggested instead she think about how to give the children a whole new concept of what it means to write fiction, and I asked if we could work together on it.

It had taken some arm-twisting for Georgia Heard to convince me that poetry should be one of our research priorities, but I never questioned the need to study children's fiction. Critics have asked why the children at Atkinson Elementary School, where Don Graves, Susan Sowers, and I did our initial research, did not write more fiction, and I think their implied criticism is well taken. Fiction is what children read, and it should be part of what they write. Particularly as children get older, it is not easy to give them successful experiences with fiction-writing. Many upper-elementary and middle-school teachers have come to me, as Mrs. Cohen did, asking how they can respond to rough drafts of fiction-writing. They tell me the stories go on and on, an interminable string of incidents. Often the stories seem like rehashed television programs, told with endless detail or with no detail at all. Sometimes teachers have claimed that when children write fiction, the writing workshop grinds to a halt: conferences last forever because the pieces are so long; revision and editing become less and less feasible. Then too, the quality of writing often goes down. "The children forget about focus, detail, pace, and drama. They only want to cover ground, to tell what happened. Their stories are awful," teachers tell me.

Because I felt sure that the quality of the pieces and the tone of the classrooms would improve once the teachers and children learned more about fiction, I loaded Mrs. Cohen down with books and articles on fiction. After school one day, we brainstormed mini-lessons and talked about fiction. We talked about plot, characterization, setting, and theme. I encouraged Mrs. Cohen to steer the children away from writing on grandiose topics such as murder, train robberies, winning the lottery, and suicide, about which they knew nothing. I emphasized that stories consist of character as well as plot: it means little to us when we hear about a flood or a murder on the news because we do not know the people involved, yet we cry over fictional events when we know and care about the characters. Mrs. Cohen and I also talked about how writers of fiction must create a world that, within its own frame of reference, is logical and believable. Mrs. Cohen wrote all my suggestions in her spiral notebook, and she found other ideas in the books on fiction. She was excited and ready to begin.

In the classroom, my research associate and I watched wonderful mini-lessons on the components of good fiction, and we heard Mrs. Cohen respond well to the children's rough drafts. We also saw changes in the writing itself. Perhaps because many of the mini-lessons dealt with characterization, some of the children began their pieces with descriptive details about their characters. Some of the children wrote about real-life events, and their stories became more logical and sometimes even believable. They tended to be longer, more dramatic, more detailed. But the writing still seemed inconsequential.

Nothing went wrong . . . yet neither did it go right. Although some of the stories improved a little, something was missing. I couldn't help but think that the children still did not have a clear idea of what fiction-writing is all about. They were still doing something else entirely: writing "weird stories" to go with a crazy title or telling the opposite of the truth.

Sarah was one of the more skillful writers in Mrs. Cohen's classroom. Her strength as a writer is evident in this story, yet the tale leaves me feeling hollow. When I finished reading it, I shrugged and thought, "So what?"

Nancy was a regular little girl with long brown hair and beautiful green eyes. Nancy's mother was a tall slim woman that has blonde hair and does not look anything like Nancy.

Nancy's desk drawer was the messiest you've ever seen. She does not like to clean up. "Nancy, clean up that drawer!" Nancy's mother said. "Your Uncle Alex is coming over."

"Oh, alright," Nancy shouted. She ran up from the table to her room and dumped the drawer all over the floor. On one side of the drawer there was paper clips and a whole bunch of scrunched up bubble gum, and on the other side there was a bunch of spilled wet paint. "Dumb drawer," Nancy shouted.

The next morning Nancy's uncle came. "Ding dong." Nancy's uncle came in and slapped her on the back. He pulled open the drawer. "Well Nancy, what a clean drawer." Nancy was very proud. The End.

In Jennifer's story, as in Sarah's, I can also see the influence of Mrs. Cohen's mini-lessons. Jennifer tried to portray real characters, and her story has a dramatic, lively pace. Once again, when I finished reading it, I shrugged and thought, "So what?" Something was also missing in her story:

> Grandma Skipper came to Rosea's birthday party. When it was time to open the presents, Rosea saw something black. "I hope it is a beautiful doll with a black dress," she thought. "Grandma Skipper, what's that black thing?"
>
> "Oh, it's my black hat," Grandma Skipper said. Rosea looked like she was going to cry. But then Grandma Skipper put the black thing in a box and slowly Rosea opened the box.
>
> "It's furry," said Rosea.
>
> "Take it out of the box."
>
> Rosea did, and it was a black unicorn. "But Grandma, what will I do with a black unicorn?"
>
> "It's special." said Grandma. "You'll see."
>
> The first night Rosea looked in the box there was no unicorn there. Instead there was a cat. It hissed at Rosea. The next night there was a black rabbit in the box and it had pants on. Then the rabbit disappeared. The next day Grandma Skipper came to visit and Rosea told her she hated the unicorn. "It is stupid," she said.
>
> "It's very special," Grandma Skipper said.
>
> "What do you mean?"
>
> "Whatever you think of, the unicorn will turn into it," Grandma Skipper said.
>
> Rosea said "This is the best, best birthday I ever had."

THE END

I read several hundred stories prior to writing this chapter, and in most of them, I felt that something essential was missing. Although Jennifer, Sarah, and their classmates carefully included the elements Mrs. Cohen had discussed in mini-lessons, their stories did not seem compelling; they lacked personal force. I found myself saying, again and again, "So what?" Their stories did not hook me or make me pay attention. My first instinct was to wonder what the children were doing wrong. Then I realized that the more constructive thing would be to wonder at what we had done wrong.

Mrs. Cohen and I had fallen into the same traps in fiction-writing that I warn teachers of when they begin the writing workshop. Despite all my talk that teaching is not pouring information into passive vessels, Mrs. Cohen and I acted as if the most important question in planning for the unit on fiction was, "What will we say about fiction?" Our sole focus was the information we would bestow on the students. We carefully planned our mini-lessons, but we never even thought about how the students' activities might change because of the new mode. We forgot that teaching is characterized, not by the words out of our mouths, but by the arrangements we establish.

Despite all my talk about teaching processes and focusing on writing strategies rather than simply on written products, Mrs. Cohen and I never asked ourselves, "What does the process of writing fiction entail?" We just grabbed onto the handy labels—setting, characterization, plot, dialogue—and taught these to the children. But these are the terms of literary criticism, not fiction writing. The story writer does not think, "First I need a bit of setting, then a dash of dialogue." These elements merge in the writer's mind. In her book, *The Realities of Fiction* (1961), Nancy Hale warns against the misconception that a story is composed of separate elements. She tells the story of a charming man who raised his hand after one of her lectures and asked, "Do you simply write the basic story first, and then put the symbolism in?" (115) Interestingly enough, if one looks at the stories written by Sarah and Jennifer, it almost seems that these children wrote their basic stories and then added the description and the setting. No wonder. We had not demonstrated the life-cycle of writing fiction; instead, we had discussed the component parts of short stories as if each was a mineral that could be put into a labeled tin box and brought out as needed.

Finally, when Mrs. Cohen and I gathered together as many ideas about writing fiction as we could find and piled them onto the kids, we forgot that good teaching is an art. It is not the *amount* of materials that turns something into art but the organizing vision, the sense of design, grace, and meaning. Mrs. Cohen and I were right to read about fiction, to brainstorm ideas, to fill our spiral notebooks with new strategies and plans. But instead of rushing into the class and enthusiastically dumping all of this onto the students, we needed to think long and hard. We needed to wonder, "What is essential here?" and "What is at the heart of writing fiction?" We needed, perhaps, to have our own experiences with fiction-writing so we could answer those questions with heart and soul. Good teaching, like good writing, has voice. Good teaching is empowered by the teacher's deep and personal investment in the essentials of the subject. Georgia's teaching of poetry differed from our teaching of fiction because Georgia had consciously created an integrated whole that was vitally important to her. Her teaching was a work of art. Mrs. Cohen's—and mine—was a hodgepodge of techniques.

In this chapter, then, I want to take a belated step backward. I want to try to shape my teaching ideas into something integrated and graceful. But these ideas will also be faceless and voiceless, since I have yet to teach fiction-writing well in the upper-elementary and middle-school grades. I hope the chapter serves as an invitation to readers to use and rewrite my ideas, and to animate them with the faces and voices of children.

In teaching a unit on fiction another time, I would begin by helping children see that the fiction writer, like all writers, must take his or her subject seriously. Good fiction must be about something that matters to the writer. It becomes trivialized when we think of it as a lie or as "made up." I want to be clear: I am not saying that fiction must stay within the confines of real experience; the sequence of events in a story need never have happened. The story need not tell about one's own hometown, one's own baby brother, or a real soccer match. But the story itself should mean something, reveal something that matters. This meaning does not come in the form of a moral stuck onto the end of it. It is not something shown or told directly. Only when the story matters to the writer will it matter to the reader.

All good writers of fiction have something important to say, to show, to allow their readers to experience. Faulkner's "A Rose for Emily" is the story of an eccentric old recluse, but it is also the story of pride in the postbellum South. Similarly, Paul Zindel says when he writes he is addressing kids, "trying to tell them to examine self-hate and any feelings of inadequacy and to act to stop the process. I'm telling the kids that I love the underdog and sympathize with his struggle because that's what I was and am in many ways still. I want my kids to feel worthy, to search for hope against all odds . . . I tell them in my novels to take good care of themselves" (1978, 182).

In her acceptance speech for the 1977 National Book Award, Katherine Patterson said, "I have crossed the river and tangled with a few giants but I want to go back and say to those who are hesitating, 'Don't be afraid to cross over. The promised land is worth possessing and we are not alone.' I want to be a spy for hope."

In none of these instances is the meaning an abstraction, pasted onto the story; rather, it is the writer's truth, a truth the writer discovers through the process of writing. Gardner describes this search when he says, "Fiction seeks out truth . . . the writer's joy in the fictional process is his pleasure in discovering, by means he can trust, what he believes and can affirm for all time" (Gardner 1984, 81).

This may sound elevated and beyond the grasp of our children, but it is really very simple. All of us have several seminal issues in our lives: jealousy over a sister, the fear of not doing well, a sense of being overlooked, the desire for a room of our own, the yearning for a best friend. We also have values that imbue everything with significance: a sense of kinship with animals, a trust that hard times will turn out to be for the best, a feeling that we never really outgrow our childhoods. These can provide starting points for fiction. In *Mostly About Writing* (1983), Nancy Martin claims that when children transform the events and feeling of their lives into a story, it makes those elements of their lives more knowable and more distant. "The stories that children make," she argues, "are not whimsical inventions but a kind of fable about things that concern them, but reshaped, so that events are more as the author would have them be." Martin is a British educator. I would argue that, at least in this country, our children's fictions are not usually fables about things that concern them. I wish they were. It would be stretching matters to suppose that Sarah, Jennifer, Carmella, and Jerome were writing fables about things which concern them deeply. Yet when children *do* write fiction out of their own concerns and feelings, it empowers their stories.

Six years ago, just after my husband and I had announced our engagement, his nine-year-old daughter Kira surprised us by spending the entire afternoon banging away at an old typewriter her father had given her. She produced a story called "Daddy-Stealer," and then protested it had nothing to do with the upcoming marriage. It was, Kira insisted, "just a story."

> *Lee was in the car when my Dad came to get me for the weekend. I thought to myself, "How come she is here?" We stopped at a restaurant on the way to my Dad's house, and when we were sitting at a nice table my Dad said to me, "Katie, Lee and I are going to get married. Are you happy?"*
>
> *I didn't say anything. "What will I call you?" I asked Lee but now I had tears in my eyes so I ran to the bathroom. I was wiping the tears off my face and thinking how all the kids in school will make fun of me when Lee came into the bathroom and put her arm around my shoulder. I asked, "You won't take my Dad away, will you?"*
>
> *"Of course not," she said. "What do you think I am, a Daddy-stealer?" She started to laugh but I felt like saying "yes."*
>
> *When we got back to the table I didn't want to eat. My Dad asked if I was okay and I told him I wasn't hungry. The weekend went by too fast and when it was over I thought to myself, "All we did was get ready for the wedding."*
>
> *When I got to my Mom's house she asked me how the weekend had been and I told her it stunk. But it was even worse when the next weekend came and I heard Dad couldn't have me, he was busy. I ran to my room and slammed the door. "I knew I couldn't trust that Lee, I knew she would take my Dad away!" All week long I thought about how my Dad had been too busy to see me . . .*

I do not think it is my personal investment alone which makes me feel that Kira's story has more voice and significance than the stories we saw earlier in this chapter. I am not saying that children's stories need to be about divorce, death, or traumatic moments. Nor must they be realistic. Although Kira wrote from the real details of her life, she could have conveyed her feeling through a fantasy tale about a family of squirrels. What I *am* saying is that if I had the opportunity now to teach children about fiction writing, I would want them to see the important topics that already exist in their lives. Since Roberto often writes about his dog, Duke, and the fear of someday losing him, I might suggest that he consider writing a fictional piece representing—and perhaps even resolving—this fear. Morat writes a poem about how he wishes for a best friend, and so I might suggest that he could write a story on that topic. Our children do not need to make up topics, but rather, to recognize those which already exist for them. "You cannot worry a poem into existence," Robert Frost has said, "but you can work upon it once it exists." I think this is true also for a story.

In some ways, what I am saying about fiction is similar to what Georgia said about poetry. "Write from a topic that burns. Choose a topic that is so important that you can feel it in your body." When I have the chance to teach fiction again, I will say the same thing to children. "Write from a topic that burns," I'll say, and I will also say, "Make a picture in your mind."

It seems to me that there is a huge difference between encouraging students to add descriptive passages to their writing and telling them, "Make a picture in your mind." When Mrs. Cohen demonstrated the power of fine descriptive passages by reading aloud sentences from literature selections, she inadvertently encouraged Sarah to insert a few "descriptive" sentences in her piece of writing. Sarah's readers learn, therefore, that Nancy has brown hair and green eyes, but we do not come into the story and see the world through Nancy's eyes. Mrs. Cohen and Sarah have missed the point. The goal is not for writers to "add description" but rather for writers to see the drama unfolding as they write it, and to write in such a way that readers can also see that drama unfolding. Gardner (1984) suggests that it is when fiction writers enter into their stories, viewing the world through their characters' eyes, that the writers can create rich, vivid, continuous dreams in their readers' minds. Gardner describes reading in terms of this dream:

> *We read a few words at the beginning of the book or the particular story, and suddenly we find ourselves seeing not words on a page but a train moving through Russia, an old Italian crying, or a farmhouse battered by rain. We read on—dream on—not passively but actively, worrying about the choices the characters have to make, listening in panic for some sound behind the fictional door. . . . In great fiction, the dream engages us heart and soul (31).*

With small, concrete details, the writer of fiction makes his or her dream vivid. The separate components of good writing (setting, point of view, dialogue, and the like) are all woven together into the fabric of the dream. Each of these elements is important only in conjunction with the others. Because the writer fills his or her mind with a dream, readers are able to re-create that dream for themselves.

In her work with poetry, Georgia told the children that she almost never *explains* in a poem, she just presents images. Fiction is similar. It is no wonder that Grace Paley says, "Poetry is the school I went to in order to learn to write short stories." In fiction, as in poetry, there is no room for explanations. Fiction is built with images. The story is not told, but lived. Most fiction writers say that in order to write, they must become their characters, living in a particular place at a particular moment. "Writing is acting on paper," Richard Price says. "I don't try to transcend my people but rather, to become them. If I can trance myself into becoming a character, I can load every gesture and interaction with enough information for a book in itself. It is a simple matter of show and tell. There is a way to "show" every "tell." There is a physical action, a mannerism, a tone of voice, a phrase that will nail down every conceivable experience."

Price is not telling us to describe our characters: he is telling us to become them, all of them. The reader will be drawn into our stories if we are drawn into our characters. In his chapter on "Power in Writing," Peter Elbow (1981) reminds us that if a blind person focuses attention on where the cane bumps against the street instead of where the cane connects with the blind person's hand, the cane becomes an extension of the person's arm and the tip of the cane has the life force of fingertips. In a similar way, if a writer's focus is not on the character him/herself, but rather, on what the character is seeing and feeling, then the characters take on a life force. Instead of thinking about old Mr. Smith, the writer stands in Mr. Smith's dusty, well-worn shoes, seeing the old battered barn through his eyes. In this way, the writer *lives* the fictional dream, and allows readers to do the same.

If I were to work with children now on writing fiction, my first priority would be to help them write from feelings and insights that matter to them; my second priority would be to help them create and attend closely to their own fictional dreams. I would teach the components of fiction—plot, character development, mood, setting, etc.—only as parts of this dream. Rather than discussing character development one day and plot another, I would try to show children that each of these elements is woven into the fabric of fiction. I would want children to understand that fiction means creating a motion picture of one's own, and that we create this motion picture by standing in our characters' shoes, and by feeling with their hearts.

I could only convey this idea to children if they had plenty of time for rehearsal. This rehearsal would not involve plot outlines, brainstorming lists, or character descriptions so much as living with a sense of one's story. Philippa Pearce (1977) says that a story must take root and grow:

A book that is worth writing, that you really care about, is only partly made. You may be able to make all the parts hold neatly and strongly together, as a carpenter does a good job on a box; but from the beginning—perhaps even before you think of writing a story at all—the story must grow. An idea grows in your mind as a tree grows from a seed. . . . It grows with the slowness of growth . . . gaining in strength and in size and in its branching out (182, 183).

If I wanted the entire class to write fiction, I might talk about the new genre for a month in advance. While the children worked on other pieces, they could also brood, plan, talk, avoid, dream and brood some more about their upcoming stories. "The important thing is to wait," Pearce says, "to think about your story only when you want to and even then not to think hard, not to reason, but to let your mind rove freely, almost lazily" (185). Children could swap ideas with friends, and perhaps they would meet regularly in response groups to talk through their ideas. Meanwhile, they could read fiction from the perspective of insiders, sharing ideas generated by their reading.

Throughout all of this, in share meetings and in conferences, we can be helping children with their still embryonic stories. The problems they will encounter are predictable. Some children will choose topics that are not important to them. If Jerome tells me he plans to write about falling into the sewer, I will ask him to consider whether the topic is truly an important one for him. Some children will have the germ of a story, but they will still need to develop it into a story line. If Sarah told me she wanted to write about Nancy's messy drawer, and Carmella told me she wanted to write, "Once upon a time I won the lottery," I would help both youngsters see that, although they might have the nucleus of a story, they needed to make it more concrete, a picture or an image, and to let those images or mental pictures drift about in their imaginations. Nancy Hale found the seed-image to her story, "A Summer's Long Dream," as she stood in her stone summer house, washing dishes and gazing out the window. Each day she watched two old ladies "crawling down the road like black beetles." Those two old ladies were cared for by their niece, a brilliant, tense young woman, and as Hale imagined how oppressed that young women must feel by her bondage to the pitiful old ladies, the story began to form in her mind's eye. Hale describes the slow, incremental growth of the story this way:

The story continued to rise, as stories do, in my mind as I woke up in the morning, each day with some new addition, as though it were a log of driftwood that I kept pushing down into the sea only to have it rise again with more seaweed, more barnacles encrusted on it (Hale 1961, 123–24).

It is by climbing inside the mental scene that a plot begins to form. When Hale knew the feelings and motives of that brilliant young woman who was caring for the beetlelike old ladies, Hale could live in her shoes and discover the crisis around which the story would center. Usually the crisis in a short story centers on the individual's problems, fears, sorrows, and above all, decisions. The crisis *is* the character, the character's existence is a continuous dream, and it is all interwoven into a single fabric.

In time, Carmella's story-idea could become embedded in particular true-to-life people, and those people could lead Carmella to see a crucial predicament. Perhaps her main character wins the lottery on a number she and a friend chose together. This predicament would give Carmella the makings of a story. Will the heroine give over half the money? Does the heroine's friend realize what happened? Into this story line, Carmella could weave drama, conflict, and a series of setbacks. It has the makings of a story—and children who read a great deal will be able to recognize this.

We can predict that children will have a hard time putting their fictional dreams on paper because of logistical problems. The stories will get so long no one will want to read them. The writers' hands will begin to hurt and their energy to wane. Some of these problems can be avoided by assigning children to ongoing response groups. Members of a response group meet together daily, they become familiar with each other's pieces, and it isn't necessary for writers to go back and read their entire piece over for each new conference partner. Then, too, we can suggest that writers break their stories into chapters so that the experience of reading and of writing the texts is punctuated by beginnings and endings. We can also show children examples of short fictional pieces, perhaps from magazines, and help them see some of the techniques writers use to limit the length of their stories: telling an entire sequence of events through a focus on one incident only, moving forward in time quickly, limiting the number of characters, leaving a great deal to the reader's imagination, and so forth.

But more than all of this, we can predict that in learning to write fiction, children will encounter unpredictable problems and they will make unpredictable discoveries. The most important thing we can do in teaching fiction is to take our cues from students. We need to hear their changing ideas on what it means to write fiction. We need to observe their developing strategies. We need to know if Carmella feels fiction doesn't matter because it's not real, and if Jerome just makes up a weird story to go with a crazy title. We need to be learners as well as teachers.

In the end, perhaps the most important reason why we need to encourage our children to try new modes is that when *we* move on to new frontiers, we, as teachers, discover the essentials of our craft.

29

beginnings

My ideas on fiction writing are embryonic. When a reviewer responded to an early draft of this book, saying, "The chapter on fiction seems not ready to have been written yet," I knew she was right. My first instinct was to rush the ideas into real classrooms, quickly documenting the results so that my tentative notions would seem fully developed. My second instinct was to delete the chapter entirely, or to move it to a less prominent position. It seemed all wrong to end the book with an unfinished chapter, with a chapter which was not ready to have been written.

I have come to believe that it is exactly right to end the book with an unfinished chapter. Throughout the book I have tried to show the pathways of my learning: to suggest ways one idea spawned another, to show the dead ends which led to surprising beginnings, to share the answers which were always there, waiting to be seen. As the book comes to an end, I want to show that the pathway does not culminate in answers but in new questions, my own and yours. I hope that for all of us, the ending of this book is the beginning of a journey. That is the joy of it.

works cited

Applebee, A.; F. Lehr; and A. Auten. 1981. Learning to write in the secondary school: How and where. *English Journal* 70: 78–82.

Applebee, Arthur N. 1981. *Writing in the secondary school, english and the content areas.* Urbana, IL: National Council of Teachers of English.

Atwell, Nancie M. 1984. Writing and reading literature from the inside out. *Language Arts* 61: 240–52.

———. Forthcoming. *In the middle.* Upper Montclair, NJ: Boynton/Cook Publishers.

Barnes, Douglas. 1976. *From communication to curriculum.* Stamford, NY: Boynton/Cook Publishers.

Barzun, Jacques, and Henry G. Graff. 1957. *The modern researcher.* New York: Harcourt Brace Jovanovich.

Bellack, Arno A. 1963. *Theory and research in teaching.* New York: Teachers College Press.

Bereiter, Carl. 1982. From conversation to composition: The role of instruction in a developmental process. In *Advances in instructional psychology,* ed. R. Glasser, vol. 2. New Jersey: Lawrence Erlbaum Associates.

———. 1980. Development in Writing. In *Cognitive processes in writing,* eds. Lee W. Gregg and Erwin R. Steinberg. Hillsdale, NJ: Lawrence Erlbaum Associates.

Bleich, David. 1975. *Readings and feelings: An introduction to subjective criticism.* Urbana, IL: NCTE.

Braddock, Richard; Lloyd-Jones; and Schoer. 1963. *Research in written composition.* Champaign, IL: National Council of Teachers of English.

Brown, Roger. 1968. Introduction. In *Teaching the universe of discourse* by James Moffett, xi. Boston: Houghton Mifflin Company.

Bruner, Jerome S. 1966. *Toward a theory of instruction.* Cambridge, MA: The Belknap Press of Harvard University Press.

———. 1982. The formats of language acquisition. *Semiotics,* 3: 1–6.

Bussis, Anne M., and Edward Chittenden. 1970. *Analysis of an approach to open education.* Princeton, NJ: Educational Testing Service.

Calkins, Lucy McCormick. 1980a. Punctuate, punctuate? Punctuate! *Learning magazine* (February): 86–89.

———. 1980b. Research update: When children want to punctuate. *Language Arts* (May).

———. 1983. *Lessons from a child*. Portsmouth, NH: Heinemann Educational Books.

Cazden, Courtney. 1972. *Child language and education*. New York: Holt, Rinehart & Winston.

Cullinan, Bernice. 1981. *Literature and the child*. New York: Harcourt, Brace, Jovanovich.

Donaldson, M. 1978. *Children's minds*. New York: W. W. Norton and Company.

Elbow, Peter. 1981. *Writing with power: Techniques for mastering the writing process*. New York: Oxford University Press.

Emig, Janet. 1982. Non-Magical thinking: Presenting writing developmentally in schools. In *Writing: The nature, development and teaching of written communication* (Vol. II). Hillsdale, NJ: Lawrence Erlbaum Associates.

Erikson, Erik H. 1964. *Insight and responsibility*. New York: W. W. Norton and Company.

Ferreiro, E., and A. Teberosky. 1982. *Literacy before schooling*. Portsmouth, NH: Heinemann Educational Books.

Fish, Stanley E. 1982. *Is there a text in this class? The authority of interpretive communities*. Cambridge, MA: Harvard University Press.

Flower, Linda, and John R. Hayes. 1980. The dynamics of composing: Making plans and juggling constraints. In *Cognitive processes in writing,* eds. Lee W. Gregg and Erwin R. Steinberg. Hillsdale, NJ: Lawrence Erlbaum Associates.

Friere, Paolo. 1970. *Pedagogy of the oppressed*. New York: Seabury Press.

Frost, Robert. 1964. It bids pretty fair. In *Complete poems by Frost*. New York: Holt, Rinehart & Winston, 555.

Fulwiler, Toby. 1982. Writing: An act of cognition. In *Teaching writing in all disciplines,* Eds. Kenneth Erle and John Noonan. San Francisco, CA: Jossey Bass.

Gardner, Howard. 1980. *Artful scribbles: The significance of children's drawings*. New York: Basic Books.

———. 1982. *Art, mind and brain: A cognitive approach to creativity*. New York: Basic Books.

Gardner, John. 1984. *The art of fiction*. New York: Alfred A. Knopf.

Goodlad, John I. 1984. *A place called school.* New York: McGraw-Hill Book Company.

Graves, Donald H. 1983. *Writing: Teachers and children at work.* Portsmouth, NH: Heinemann Educational Books.

Hale, Nancy. 1961. *The realities of fiction.* Boston: Little, Brown and Company.

Hall, Donald, and Clayton Hudnall. 1982. *Writing well.* 4th ed. Boston, MA: Little, Brown and Company.

Halliday, M. A. K. 1973. *Explorations in the functions of language.* London: Edward Arnold.

Hansen, Jane, and Donald Graves. 1983. The author's chair. *Language Arts* 60: 176–83.

Harste, Jerome; Virginia Woodward; and Carolyn Burke. 1984. *Language stories and literacy lessons.* Portsmouth, NH: Heinemann Educational Books.

Hawkins, David. 1974. *The informed vision.* New York: Agathon Press.

Heath, Shirley Brice. 1983. *Ways with words: Language, life and work in communities and classrooms.* Cambridge: Cambridge University Press.

Hoetker, James. 1982. A theory of talking about theories of reading. *College English* 44, 2 (February): 175–81.

Holdaway, Don. 1979. *The foundations of literacy.* New York: Ashton Scholastic.

Jensen, Julie M., ed. 1984. *Composing and comprehending.* Urbana, IL: ERIC Clearinghouse on Reading and Communication Skills, and NCRE.

Lynch, Priscilla. 1984. Presentation in District 15. Brooklyn, NY (May).

Macrorie, Kenneth. 1976. *Telling writing.* Rochelle Park, NJ: Hayden Book Company.

MacLeish, Archibald. 1959. The teaching of writing. *Harper's magazine* (October).

Martin, Nancy. 1983. *Mostly about writing.* Montclair, NJ: Boynton/Cook Publishers.

Moffett, James. 1968. *Teaching the universe of discourse.* Boston: Houghton Mifflin Company.

Morrison, Philip. 1964. The curricular triangle and its style. *ESI Quarterly Report* 3,2: 63–70.

Murray, Donald M. 1968. *A writer teaches writing.* Boston: Houghton Mifflin Company.

———. 1982a. The listening eye. In *Learning by teaching.* Upper Montclair, NJ: Boynton/Cook Publishers.

———. 1982b. Teaching the other self: The writer's first reader. In *Learning by teaching*. Upper Montclair, NJ: Boynton/Cook Publishers.

———. 1984. *Write to learn*. New York: Holt, Rinehart & Winston.

———. 1985. *A writer teaches writing*. 2nd ed. Boston: Houghton Mifflin Company.

National Assessment of Educational Progress. 1981. Reading, thinking and writing: Results from the 1979–80 National Assessment of Reading and Literature. Report no. 11-L-01. Denver, CO: National Assessment of Educational Progress.

National Family Options, Inc. 1984. *Education week* (April 4, 1984).

Newkirk, Thomas. 1982. Young writers as critical readers. *Language arts* 59: 451–57.

Pearce, Philippa. 1977. Writing a book. In *The cool web*. Eds. Margaret Meek, Aidan Warlow, and Griselda Barton. London: The Bodley Head.

Perl, Sondra. 1979. The composing processes of unskilled college writers. *The teaching of english* 13: 317–36.

Piaget, Jean. 1962. *Play, dreams and imitation in childhood*. New York: W. W. Norton and Company.

Rogers, Carl R. 1961. *On becoming a person*. Boston: Houghton Mifflin Company.

Rosenblatt, Louise. 1978. *The reader, the text, the poem*. Carbondale, IL: Southern Illinois University Press.

Sartre, Jean-Paul. 1975. Sartre at seventy: An interview. With Michael Contat. *New York review of books* (7 August).

Shapiro, Laura. 1985. A woman of principle. Interview with Grace Paley. *Newsweek* (April 15), 91.

Shaughnessy, Mina P. 1977. *Errors and expectations*. New York: Oxford University Press.

Silberman, Charles E. 1970. *Crisis in the classroom*. New York: Random House.

Smith, Frank. 1983. Reading like a writer. *Language arts* 60: 558–67.

———. 1978. *Reading without nonsense*. New York: Teachers College Press.

———. 1982. *Writing and the writer*. New York: Holt, Rinehart and Winston.

Sowers, Susan. 1979. Young Writers' preference for non-narrative modes of composition. The Fourth Annual Boston University Conference on Language Development (September).

Squire, James R. 1984. Composing and comprehending: Two sides of the same basic process. In *Composing and comprehending,* ed. Julie M. Jensen. Urbana, IL: ERIC Clearinghouse on Reading and Communication Skills, and NCRE.

Temple, Charles A.; Ruth Nathan; and Nancy Burris. 1982. *The beginnings of early writing.* Boston: Allyn and Bacon.
Tompkins, Jane P. (ed.) 1981. *Reader-response criticism: from formalism to post-structuralism.* Baltimore, MD: Johns Hopkins University Press.

Vygotsky, Lev Semenovich. 1962. *Thought and language.* Cambridge, MA: The MIT Press.

Welty, Eudora. 1984. *One writer's beginnings.* Cambridge, MA: Harvard University Press.
Whitman, Walt. 1949. Song of myself. In *Leaves of grass and selected poems.* New York: Holt, Rinehart & Winston.

Zindel, Paul, quoted in Audrey Eaglen. 1978. Of life, love, death, kids and inhalation therapy: An interview with Paul Zindel. *Top of the news* 34, 2 (Winter). 182.
Zinsser, William K. 1980. *On writing well.* 2nd ed. New York: Harper & Row, Publishers.

recommended readings

Bissex, Glenda. GNYS AT WRK: A Child Learns to Write and Read. Cambridge, MA: Harvard University Press, 1980.

In this unusual book, Bissex provides a detailed documentation of her son's independent growth as a reader and a writer. The book is beautifully written and solidly grounded in theory. It is particularly helpful as a statement on invented spelling and on purposes for writing.

Britton, James. *Language and Learning.* Middlesex, England: Penguin Books, 1970.

This book about language acquisition provides an important foundation to current work on the teaching of writing. Chapters include "Language and Experience," "Learning to Speak," and "Participant and Spectator."

Calkins, Lucy McCormick. *Lessons from a Child: On the Teaching and Learning of Writing.* Portsmouth, NH: Heinemann Educational Books, 1983.

Through a story of one child's growth in writing, Calkins has conveyed the essentials in teaching writing. The dramatic tale of one student, Susie, is part of a larger story encompassing 150 children, their teachers, and their classrooms. The book invites teachers to become observers of children, watching and extending their development in writing.

Elbow, Peter. *Writing with Power: Techniques for Mastering the Writing Process.* New York: Oxford University Press, 1981.

Elbow's book is a smorgasbord of ideas and metaphors on teaching writing. In a style which is recursive and full of voice, Elbow portrays writers and their ways of working. He suggests an array of composing strategies, and these will be invaluable to teachers of writing.

Gardner, Howard. *Artful Scribbles: The Significance of Children's Drawings.* New York: Basic Books, 1980.

Readers will learn from Gardner not only about children's development in art, but also about artistic development in general. Gardner speaks about the artistic flowering of the six-year-old, and about the dogged realism which inhibits the drawings of many older children and adolescents. This is only one of Gardner's many books on development, and each is important.

Graves, Donald H. *Writing: Teachers and Children at Work.* Portsmouth, NH: Heinemann Educational Books, 1983.

This concrete, practical book is an invaluable guide for teachers of grades K–6 who are new to the idea of the writing process. With chapters entitled "Survive Day One," "Help Children Choose Topics," and "Publish Writing in the Classroom," the book is helping teachers who want something to hold onto as they begin turning their classrooms into writing workshops. The book is already a best-seller.

Hale, Nancy. *The Realities of Fiction.* Boston, MA: Little, Brown and Company, 1961.

This is not a new book, but it is one which deserves to be taken down from the shelves. Hale's insights provide a fresh perspective on fiction writing. The book will be particularly helpful to teachers of upper elementary and secondary school grades.

Harste, Jerome; Virginia A. Woodward; and Carolyn L. Burke. *Language Stories & Literacy Lessons.* Portsmouth, NH: Heinemann Educational Books, 1984.

This book has been heralded as providing a major breakthrough in our understanding of developmental issues in writing. Although the book focuses on young children, it's an important book for anyone interested in the teaching of writing.

Jaggar, Angela, and M. Trika Smith-Burke, eds. *Observing the Language Learner.* Newark, Delaware: International Reading Association; Urbana, IL: National Council of Teachers of English, 1985.

This book will be particularly important to teachers who are interested in the theoretical underpinnings of an integrated approach to the language arts. Although each of the articles in the anthology is written in simple, clean language and filled with anecdotes, the articles are far from lightweight. Each is written by a leading researcher and grounded in theoretical ideas on language learning.

Jensen, Julie M., ed. *Composing and Comprehending.* Urbana, IL: ERIC Clearinghouse on Reading and Communication Skills, and NCRE, 1984.

This volume provides an excellent collection of articles on the interrelationships between reading and writing. Readers will find many favorite articles from *Language Arts,* as well as new articles by authors such as Squire, Smith, Tierney, Moffett, Dyson, Applebee, and Chall.

Moffett, James. *Teaching the Universe of Discourse*. Boston: Houghton Mifflin, 1968.

This book presents a comprehensive theory on how one learns discourse. Moffett suggests a curriculum based on his hierarchy of abstraction. Students move from personal towards abstract writing, from an audience which is intimate, towards one which is distant. The book is densely written and theoretical.

Murray, Donald M. *Learning by Teaching*. Upper Montclair, NJ: Boynton/Cook Publishers, 1982.

————. *Write to Learn*. New York: Holt, Rinehart and Winston, 1984.

————. *A Writer Teaches Writing*. 2nd ed. Boston: Houghton Mifflin, 1985.

Pulitzer Prize–winning writer Donald M. Murray is a leading mentor for teachers of writing. Each of these books is beautifully written. On every page readers will find lines which they want to pin onto their bulletin boards and excerpts which they want to share with colleagues and students. Murray's trust in his students and his involvement in his craft are infectious. *Learning by Teaching* is an anthology of his articles; *Write to Learn* is a guide for people wanting to begin their own writing; *A Writer Teaches Writing* is an overview of his current ideas on teaching writing in secondary schools and colleges. All three books are invaluable.

Temple, Charles A.; Ruth G. Nathan; and Nancy A. Burris. *The Beginnings of Writing*. Boston: Allyn and Bacon, 1982.

This is a comprehensive theoretical book on early writing. The authors focus on the evolution of invented spellings and on the application of Britton's work to the primary school classroom. The book is filled with samples of students' writing.

Zinsser, William. *On Writing Well*. 3rd ed. New York: Harper and Row, 1985.

Zinsser's book, a classic in the field of writing, is an essential text for anyone interested in simple, clear writing. Zinsser writes with the warmth, humor, and simplicity that he advocates.

index